THE 5TH SISTER

THE 5TH SISTER

ESCAPING THE DARKNESS OF DOMESTIC VIOLENCE

PATRICIA MCRAE DONALDSON

EMBASSY ONE PUBLISHERS • HOUSTON, TEXAS

COPYRIGHT

Your comments about this book are encouraged and welcomed. Please post online at your favorite book retailer and on your favorite book review and social media sites. You may also post comments on our website below or write to us at the email address. Thank you for your love.

Copyright © 2024 by Patricia McRae Donaldson

ISBN 978-1-944539-10-8 (Paperback)
ISBN 978-1-944539-09-2 (Hardcover)
ISBN 978-1-944539-11-5 (EPUB)

All rights reserved. No part of this book may be reproduced, distributed, or transmitted in any form or by any means without prior permission in writing from the author, except in the case of brief quotations embodied in critical articles or reviews and certain other noncommercial uses permitted by copyright law. For permission requests, email the publisher at info@BibleThreads.net.

All Scripture quotations, unless otherwise indicated, are taken from the Holy Bible, New International Version®, NIV®. Copyright ©1973, 1978, 1984, 2011 by Biblica, Inc.™ Used by permission of Zondervan. All rights reserved worldwide (www.zondervan.com). The "NIV" and "New International Version" are trademarks registered in the United States Patent and Trademark Office by Biblica, Inc.™

This memoir depicts actual events of the author's lived experience (with domestic violence) as truthfully as recollection permits, which may not capture every detail or perspective. It is written solely for the purpose of sharing insights, fostering understanding, and promoting healing. All persons mentioned are actual individuals. Names have been changed to protect the privacy and identities of those involved.

Publisher's website: www.BibleThreads.net

I dedicate this book to all the women who have suffered at the hands of the men who said, "I love you," especially to the women who lost their lives before they could break free of the distress that dominated their lives.

This one is for you, my sister.

ACKNOWLEDGMENTS

First and foremost, I thank my Lord and Savior, Jesus Christ, because He has covered me through the years. I am in this present time to take the bad times in my life and allow Jesus to use them for good.

To my parents, Mr. James Grady Sr. and Mrs. Easter Alberta Lloyd McRae,

thank you for how you loved me, raised me, and gave me a Christian foundation upon which I continue to build my life.

To my brother, Arlington McRae,

author of "The Bible for Beginners and the Rest of Us: A Guide to Making Basic Bible Sense," and his latest book, "Born Dead: Genesis 2:16-17," in the series, *BIBLE THREADS: Keys to Understanding the Bible*, I thank you for your help when I needed it and for being an inspiration.

To my sister, Carrie McRae Doneghy,

who encouraged me years ago to write a book about my life. I told her and myself that I could not write a book. But since then, the Holy Spirit has said to me, "You are a writer." Thank you.

To my friend, Dr. Miyoshi Umeki Gordon,

author of *Broken But Still a Masterpiece*, for igniting the spark that inspired me to tell my story.

CONTENTS

Introduction	11
1. The Beginning	15
2. Adulthood	41
3. And So, It Begins	51
4. Decisions, Decisions, Decisions	65
5. The Beat Goes On	73
6. Simply Lost	85
7. The Winds of Change	99
8. Caught Off Guard	115
9. Moving On	145
10. Back to the World	169
11. Out of Control	181
12. Never a Dull Moment	193
13. God's Doing a New Thing	201
14. Court	223
15. No Restraint	237
16. The Beginning of the End	247
17. Better Days	261
Conclusion	273
My Testimony	279
Resources	281

INTRODUCTION

A female takes on a lot of different roles in her lifetime. First, she is a baby daughter. She learns what love feels like when her parents hold her in their arms as they feed her, play with her, and when they rock her to sleep. All that becomes a part of her. Her parents protect her and teach her right from wrong, what's good and what's bad. She learns there are consequences when she decides to do something wrong. She is taught how to care about someone other than herself and how to share with others. If her parents are Christians, they teach her about Jesus and how much He loves her. They tell her that the love of Jesus is so deep that He took on the sins of the world and died on the cross to save us all from sin and death. No matter where she goes, Jesus will always be with her, and she can cry out to Him in her time of need; they teach her how to pray. Her mother and father take care of her until she is capable of taking care of herself. If they decide to have another child, she becomes a sister. She learns to share with her sibling the love that her parents have shared with her. She learns to look out for her or him. They both share in common the love they feel for their parents.

Then, she goes to school and becomes a student. She learns about other cultures and that people are different all over the world—the way they live, how they treat each other, their belief system, and the importance of family. She learns how to take instructions from someone other than her parents. Along the way, she becomes a friend. She learns to trust her secrets with a best friend that she does not share with her parents.

Pretty soon, the opposite sex catches her eye. She watches them and feels an attraction that she doesn't yet understand. She puts herself in awkward situations to investigate why she feels the way she does when she is near them. Before long, she learns about the romantic relationship between a male and female by dating. At a certain age, she becomes a girlfriend to a male she has chosen. As she dates, she continues her scholastic and romantic relationship education. In time, she becomes a high school graduate.

Into The World

Now, it is time for her to go out into the world and put to use what she has learned to create a life for herself. Whether she continues her education or gets a job, she feels she is well-equipped to use what she knows to make difficult life decisions. She meets a man. They date for a while. They fall in love. But she doesn't know that she needs to recognize the red flags of a dysfunctional relationship when they present themselves. She never saw this kind of relationship growing up. Her parents did not educate her about the possibility of being in this type of dangerous courtship. She is not prepared to deal with an abusive man. *So, she tells herself that she can fix him.* Women like to think that they can correct things, that they can change a man, not knowing that his ability to abuse her is deeply rooted in his formative years. Perhaps he grew up in a home where his mother was abused and came to believe that it was customary to hit a woman. Along her journey from being a baby to an adult, she was not taught how to live as a physically or mentally abused woman. Because, in our society, it is unacceptable for the stronger being of our species to hit or emotionally abuse the weaker being. Therefore, she knows no protocol for when she finds herself in a violent relationship. When this evil comes into her life, she is not equipped with what she needs to confront it, deal with it, or escape it. She has gotten involved with a man who is an expert at hiding who he is underneath. He makes her feel so special and convinces her that she doesn't need anyone but him. Before she knows it, she is seeing her family less and less and Her friends have somehow disappeared out of her life. Now, he has her fully dependent upon him. She is right where he wants her.

Red Flags

When I found myself in a physically and mentally abusive relationship, I already had feelings for him. I did not take the red flags as seriously as I should have. I had no education in domestic violence. I had never been exposed to it. I did not realize that the person I was in a relationship with, who told me he loved me, was capable of the things that he put me through. I trusted him; that was my first mistake. I underestimated the red flags, my second mistake. Then, I didn't know how to seek help from anyone, my third mistake. To tell you the truth, I didn't suspect that he was as dangerous as he was. By the time I was aware of his determination to control me and my life, I was so deep in the abuse that my rational thinking had suffered a significant loss. I had been through so much it started to feel normal. I did not know that there were organizations that could help a woman or man escape the traumatic devastation of being abused. It took such an enormous toll on me that I thought I would have to live like that for the rest of my life. Because I no longer had the strength or the ability to free myself.

The stress of being an abused woman morphed into mental and physical side effects that affected my quality of life. It took me a long time to realize that I deserved a better life than the one I was living. One day, I just changed my mind about the oppression being inflicted on me. This couldn't be why I was created, not to live like this! When I let go, that is when Jesus stepped in, and things started to change. I believe Jesus took my wrong and used it for my good. There is no other way to explain what happened to me once I changed my mind. Jesus can use anything and anybody to bless you. I didn't know that I was about to witness the glory of the Lord in my life and my situation. Never give up on Jesus, for He is always right on time. "Arise, shine, for the light has come, and the glory of the Lord has risen upon you" (Isaiah 60:1).

CHAPTER 1
THE BEGINNING

Wiping the sleep from my eyes, I could hear a phone ringing in the background. Then I heard my fiancé speaking to his mother on the phone. She wanted him to come and show her where the Civic Center was located; she had gotten lost. She needed to start decorating to get everything prepared for our wedding reception. After the sleep fog lifted from my brain, suddenly, it dawned on me what day it was. It was December twenty-fourth, Christmas Eve, my wedding day. My heart started pounding. I was about to say "I do" to another man. If anyone had asked me two years ago if I would get married a second time, I would have definitely said no. But there I was, preparing to do it again.

Family Matters

I am the youngest of twelve children and the only one born in a hospital. All my other siblings were born at home. That one thing sets me apart from the rest; this is an observation for you to keep in mind. I'm not saying that I am better than any of my sisters and brothers, just different. My parents also raised my nephew, Thomas, like one of their children. We were born two years apart. He was treated the same way as the rest of us. We used to argue over my mama like siblings. We both wanted to be her baby. We sometimes fought over who would sit in her lap. We were jealous of each other when it came to her. My daddy was a sharecropper on a farm owned by someone else. All I remember is my parents called her Ms. Mary. We lived in an old wooden shack with no running water or bathroom facilities. When we needed water, we got it from a hand pump located outside, and we used what is called an outhouse for our bathroom. I was afraid of insects and spiders that were known to make their home inside of it. I believe that's where my fear of spiders originated. I am still not a big fan today. When we had no toilet paper, old newspapers and the previous year's edition of the Sears and Roebuck catalog would suffice. Not very comfortable, but we used what we had. Also, I have a fear of snakes. There were many tall weeds around our yard, and we had to be careful where we stepped. One day, Thomas and I were in the backyard, playing and chasing each other. I remember looking down and seeing something colorful on the ground. I bent down to pick it up. But before my hand reached it, I realized that it was a snake. I bet I jumped ten feet into the air and started running towards the house, yelling for my mama, saying, "Snake, snake." My mama was the snake killer at our house. She would grab a hoe and put it to death. To us, she seemed so brave. I was too afraid even to attempt to kill a snake. The thought of getting close enough to slay a snake with a hoe sent chills up my spine.

My daddy was a hard-working man. He and my mama provided for us so well that we weren't even aware of how poor we were. I had nothing to compare our lifestyle. All the people I knew were living just like us. We had farm animals like chickens, pigs, a mule, and a cow. Being the youngest of the family, many of my older sisters and brothers had already grown up and left the farm to pursue their dreams by the time I was old enough to understand who they were. The only way that I knew some of them was that my parents told me, "This is your brother, or this is your sister." Those of us still living on the farm worked hard from sunup to sundown. After all my brothers left the farm, my sister Samantha helped my daddy by plowing with our mule. She was as good at it as any of my brothers. It was not an easy job, but she nailed it. We all did what was required of us, no matter what it was. In retrospect, it was a real blessing that we grew most of our food. We could not afford to buy everything from the grocery store. My daddy planted butter (Lima) beans, corn, tomatoes, cucumbers, cabbage, sweet potatoes, white potatoes, green beans, sweet peas, field peas, sugar cane, strawberries, cantaloupe, watermelon, and much more. He also grew wheat, cotton, soybeans, and tobacco. Eventually, Ms. Mary provided my daddy with an old tractor that helped take a lot of the work off of him by not having to plow the fields with our mule. I'm sure that it made Samantha very happy.

Super Woman

As you can see, our farm kept us very busy daily. We ate well, though. Until this very day, I love vegetables. They were always on our plates. My mama rose early every morning to make breakfast for us. Everything she cooked was from scratch on a wood-burning stove, no less, including homemade biscuits. We were sent to the woodpile to chop wood for the stove my mama prepared all our meals on. We gathered it up in our arms, took it into the house, and placed it in the wood box beside the stove. This continued until the box was full. She cooked three meals a day, every day except Sunday. She was also a master at baking cakes in that wood stove. All the mixing was done by hand, and she was great at it. My mama did not own an electric mixer until later on in her life. I don't understand how she knew what the stovetop and oven temperature was when she prepared a meal. Somehow, all her dishes came out great. She was an excellent cook, and she kept all her recipes in her memory. During the summer, she would tell us if we went to pick wild blackberries, she would make us a cobbler from them. We grabbed whatever container would hold the berries and began our search. Most of the time, we could find them growing wild alongside the road. When we thought we had enough, we would rush home, wash them, and give them to Mama. Her cobbler was always deliciously worth waiting for. We didn't know how good we had it until later in our lives. I would go into the kitchen as a little girl and watch Mama when I wasn't working on the farm or outside playing with Thomas. I learned a lot about cooking by watching her do it. She made a Peach Cobbler and Banana Pudding that was out of this world delectable. I could not duplicate her Peach Cobbler, no matter how hard I tried. As I said, my mama did not write down her recipes. My sisters and I have often discussed how we wish she had. We could use them to write a cookbook or make them for our families to enjoy. When I became grown, I decided to teach myself how to make a Banana Pudding that tasted as great as my mama's did. I searched out different recipes and used the knowledge I had gleaned from her, and one day, I did it. But let me tell you, I wrote my recipe down so that I could make it the same way every single time. My memory is not as good as my mama's.

Mama did a lot of, as they used to say, "canning food for the winter." In mason jars, she canned peaches, tomatoes, pears, sweet pickles, and apples. She made apple jelly from apple peels and grape jelly from muscadine grapes. The vegetables were blanched, put in plastic bags, and then frozen. At slaughter time, she made pork sausage, liver pudding, crackling, and hog head cheese. She did not waste anything. Mama used our worn-out clothes to make quilts to keep us warm during the winter.

She put patches over the holes in our clothes by hand and later on with a sewing machine. She also made some of our dresses on the sewing machine from the McCall and Butterick patterns she used to cut fabric for a dress. She made lye soap in a large cast-iron pot outside over the top of a wood-burning fire. She used the soap to wash our clothes, and we sometimes used it for bathing. She learned to recycle before it was a thing. When you have twelve children, you learn to find a use for everything; nothing goes in the trash.

Paid Worker

Occasionally, we worked for Ms. Mary's son, who owned farmland near us. I remember getting up early in the morning, getting a mason jar or a mayonnaise jar off the kitchen table, putting in ice, and filling it with water. Then we made our lunch and placed it in an old brown paper bag. We got dressed in old, worn-out clothes and headed to one of his cotton fields to chop cotton (remove all the weeds that grew amongst the cotton). We put our food and the ice water under a shade tree and went to work. We worked hard on rows of cotton that were so long that we could not see where the row ended. The sizzling hot sun bore down on our heads, and sweat rolled down our faces like a facet as we worked. At midday, we went to sit on the ground under a large shade tree to relax and cool off while we ate our lunch and quenched our thirst. After our lunch break, we went back to chopping cotton, only taking breaks to drink water to keep ourselves hydrated or to take a bathroom break in the nearby woods. The workday came to an end when the sun commenced going down.

We were paid three dollars a day for our work. It was the way we did things to survive. My mama used the money to help take care of us. On some occasions, she gave us maybe fifty cents, and my daddy took us to the store to buy whatever we wanted. I sometimes purchased cookies where I got three for one cent, a honeybun for ten cents, and a bottled drink for maybe twenty-five cents. Those were some happy days during my childhood. The work was hard, but it was sprinkled with some fun times. As I think of those times, I am transported back to a time some call "the good ole days." They are treasured memories that are close to my heart. A not-so-pleasant memory is when Thomas and I went for a walk with my daddy one day to visit his brother. We did not live far from my mama's parents and my daddy's brother. Between our house and his brother's house, there was a bridge that we had to cross to reach our destination. We talked as we were walking. Sometimes, we found plum trees growing wild beside the road. We picked and devoured the ripe ones. Thomas and I played, chasing each other along the way. When we got to the bridge, we could hear someone crying out for help. To our surprise, there was a car sitting in the water with several people inside. If they had been traveling at a high rate of speed in the curve right before the bridge, the driver would have found it difficult to miss hitting the side of the bridge. And would have ended up in the amber-colored water. As my daddy talked to the people inside, he realized that one of the passengers was my mama's youngest brother. My daddy told Thomas to run back home and tell my mama to call the police. I had never seen an accident before. The man who was driving was killed. He was dead before we arrived. We were told later by the police that when the car hit the bridge, his chest hit the steering wheel and busted his heart. No one in the vehicle was wearing a seatbelt. But that was not unusual because it was not required by law at that time. It was upsetting as I watched the tow truck pull the car out of the branch (my parents called it that). My uncle was intoxicated, as were all the people in the car, but otherwise, he was okay. Subsequently, after dealing with all that, we went back home. We stopped by my grandparent's house to let them know what had happened and that my uncle was okay.

Lessons Learned

On some Saturdays, my father loaded his truck with a lot of the vegetables we grew. He had a scale to weigh them and brown paper bags to put them in for his customers. He headed to the City of Raeford, NC (my hometown) to different homes all over the city, selling the vegetables. Sometimes, I went with him and enjoyed seeing the houses we went to. It was an adventure because that was the only time I saw such beautiful homes up close and the white people living there. My daddy exhibited a particular posture whenever he talked with them. It was always, "Yes ma'am, no ma'am, thank you, ma'am," as he conducted business with them. Whether they were older or younger than him, it did not matter. He approached them with a specific degree of humbleness. I did not know it at the time, but this type of behavior was expected from him, being that he was a black person. I did not know anything about racism as a child. It was customary for me to see my parents conduct themselves in this way. I'm sure my daddy had experienced it throughout his life. But I never saw him act as though it degraded him or made him feel less than the man he was; I am very proud of that. I remember one instance where flagrant racism was exhibited. Whenever we needed to go to a doctor, we went to see Dr. Wallace in Wagram, NC. Sometimes, he made house calls, too. But, when we went to his office, there was a waiting room for black people and one for white people. I was so young I did not understand why things were this way. It all seemed normal to me. Everyone was polite, and I didn't feel less of an individual by being separated from the white people. My daddy took everything in stride and treated everyone with the same respect. I never saw him mistreated by anyone because of the color of his skin. Perhaps I had been protected from it so successfully that I did not notice it. His customers appeared friendly as he interacted with them while picking out the vegetables they wanted to purchase. He weighed them and put them in a bag. Being exposed to two very different worlds did not affect the way I saw my life. I did not feel the way we lived was beneath anyone else. The Lord provided us with everything we needed to have a good life. By the end of the day, everything was gone. The money he earned helped supplement our income. I learned a work ethic and good manners from my dad, and that has followed me into my adult life. He did not put up with laziness or disobedience; I am very grateful for the lessons he taught me because they have served me well and helped to make me who I am.

Farm Life

Living on a farm has its perks. We had plenty of room to play in our bare feet. Whenever a thunderstorm came up, and the wind started to blow, I would stand still and smell the rain in the air before it started coming down. It is an unmistakable smell. Once you smell it, you cannot forget it. In the distance, I would hear the thunder roll and, soon after, the lightning flash. It was a warning sign to take cover. A downpour was on its way. I would run to get to the front porch of our house to keep from getting soaked. The sound of rain coming down on a tin roof was soothing, and at night, it was a lullaby that rocked me to sleep.

In the mornings, we got out of bed before dawn to go to the field to sucker (prune) tobacco, pull corn, pick cucumbers, pick tomatoes, or whatever job we were required to do that day, with everything still covered in the morning dew. After the sun came up, we went home soaking wet to eat the breakfast my mama had prepared for us while we worked in the field. I could smell fresh pork sausage frying on the wood stove in the kitchen as we reached the house. We stopped at the hand pump outside and washed up before going in for breakfast. These types of days were common when we were harvesting our crops. My daddy took them to the market to be sold. The work was not easy, and I wouldn't say I liked it, but I made it through and learned a lot along the way.

The Sabbath Day

On Sundays, no work. Saturday nights, we took a bath in a number ten tin tub. Mama heated the water on the wood stove and then poured it into the tub. Afterward, she poured in enough cold water to reduce the hot water to bathwater temperature. While we bathed, mama would be in the kitchen preparing portions of our Sunday dinner. We got up early the next morning, had family prayer, washed up, ate breakfast, and dressed for Church. When I got ready for church, my outfit consisted of a can-can slip, a flared-tail dress, black patent leather ballerina shoes, and white lace-trimmed Bobbie socks. My hair was braided, and sometimes, on special occasions, I was allowed to wear ponytails or wear my hair loose. Sometimes, we girls got to get our hair pressed and curled by one of our neighbors, Mrs. Shirley Mae. Mama would shampoo and braid our hair at home. Mrs. Mary Lizza pressed our hair with a hot comb heated on a wood stove. I had to sit still to keep from being burned by the hot comb. Once my hair was pressed, she used hot curlers placed on the stove as she parted sections of my hair and curled it. It was very rare for me to have curls, but I felt so special when it happened. When we returned home, I tied a scarf on my head before going to bed to preserve my hair duo. The next morning, after I was dressed, my mama would comb out the curls and style them. That was considered to be my Sunday best. I strutted like a peacock in full plumage. You couldn't tell me anything. My parents took us to church every Sunday morning. On the first and third Sundays of the month, we attended only Sunday School. On the second and fourth Sundays, we attended Sunday school and Morning Worship Service. We went to church like this because our church, Walls Chapel United Methodist Church in Raeford, NC, had a sister Church, Mt. Zion UMC, located in Maxton, NC, that was pastored by the same pastor as far back as I can remember. As was expected of the families of the church, my mama sometimes prepared Sunday dinner for our Pastor; it was a church tradition. The Saturday before, we girls were instructed to clean the front yard. This consisted of picking up and burning all trash. Then, we used brooms made from the branches of a sturdy bush, tied them together with twine, and swept the yard. We walked backward as we swept so as not to make footsteps in our artwork. It was, in reality, quite beautiful when we finished. We did this because we did not have grass growing in our yard. The design that the brooms made in the sand was like a Zen Garden. The next step was to clean the house. This included sweeping and mopping all the floors, especially the ones that would be seen by our guests. After Sunday morning worship service, my mama would be in the kitchen finishing the dishes she had not completed the night before. A typical Sunday dinner consisted of Fried Chicken, Potato Salad, Rice and Gravy, Field Peas, Collard Greens, Fried Okra, Cornbread, Biscuits, Cake, and Sweet Potato or Coconut Custard Pie. Before dinner, we girls set the table with my mama's special-occasion white lace tablecloth. We retrieved from the china cabinet our best china and placed it on the table. In the draw of the china cabinet, we took out our best silver flatware and put a knife, fork, and spoon on top of a freshly pressed white linen napkin beside each plate. And lastly, we brought out our most delicate glassware and put them on the table. Now, the table was ready to receive our guests. Our Pastor and his family would come to our home after Worship

Service and join us for dinner. My mama put the food in serving bowls with a large serving spoon and placed them on the table. When everyone was seated at the table, grace was said, and the food was served. The children would either eat in the kitchen or wait until the adults finished eating and then they would eat at the dining room table. After dinner was over, we were sent outside to play after changing out of our Sunday clothes, of course. The adults sat around and talked for a while, a conversation the children were not allowed to join. The members of both churches took turns preparing dinner for the Pastor every Pastoral Sunday, which was twice a month at each church.

Rules and Regulations

My parents were devout Christians and brought all their children up in the church. They were very strict, too. They believed in "spare the rod, spoil the child." One Sunday, during morning worship service, my cousin (who was also my very best friend) and I were sitting together near the front of the church. I was very young at the time, maybe around five years old. My daddy was sitting across from us where all of the deacons sat, on the right side of the pulpit. We were giggling and talking while the Pastor was preaching. I happened to look towards him and saw that "I'm going to whoop your butt" look on his face. I knew right then I had better shut my mouth and pay attention to the sermon. When church service was over, my parents conversed with some of our family and church members for a spell as the children played. Afterward, we all got into the car and started home. I was so nervous because I had done what I had been warned not to do. All the way home, he never said a word. When we got home, we all went inside the house. Then I was told to change out of my church clothes, go outside, retrieve a switch from a bush, and bring it to him. I started crying right then. My daddy disciplined me for disrespecting God and His

House, and he warned me never to do it again. "Train up a child in the way he should go, and even when he is old he will not depart from it" (Proverbs 22:6). At the time, it was a very painful and complex lesson, and I never acted up in church again. That incident taught me that there is always a consequence for the choices we make. This was done out of love for me; as a grown woman, I am grateful for the discipline I received as a child. It guided me to who I am today.

My sisters told this story to me: I don't remember this, but they said I had disobeyed my mama. To discipline me for it, she told me to get a switch, and I did. Right before she started to whoop me, I took off running, and she was dead in behind me, trying to catch me. My sisters all said they were cheering for my mama to catch me. They were saying, "Get her, mama, get her." We have laughed about that many times at family get-togethers. It is a funny memory now, but it wasn't funny when it was happening. I can assume that she did catch me, and I got what I deserved. It may seem to you like their way of punishment for the things we did wrong was harsh. But I thank God today for my parents because they loved us enough to teach us right from wrong and the consequences thereof. Some parents today do not teach their kids to know the difference. I am grateful for the lessons my parents taught me. I don't believe that I would be the woman I am today if they had not disciplined me the way they did. It was out of their love for me, not what some would see as child abuse. No, there is a difference between the two.

There is another memory I have of my mama that was not funny. It was almost a tragedy. My daddy had an old light blue Chevrolet pickup truck at the time. The passenger side door would not close entirely. My mama was sick and needed to go to the doctor. To get to the doctor's office, my daddy needed to make a sharp left turn a few yards from my grandparent's house. When he made that turn, the truck door swung open, and Mama fell out. He stopped the vehicle as quickly as he could and got out to see about her. She had a gash on her forehead that was bleeding. Since they were already going to the doctor's office, my dad helped her back into the truck and continued to the doctor. We didn't learn about it until they returned home. My daddy told us what had happened. Thank God she did not break any bones. She had a big bandage on her forehead, but otherwise, she was okay. It was scary for me because I was so young, and I was afraid for my mama. It all turned out to be okay, but it could have been worse. I don't recollect if my daddy got the door repaired or not. I want to think that he did after that terrifying incident. She did not let that event stop her from doing her daily chores. I believe she saw her accident of no consequence; she had to take care of her family. She was a very strong and determined woman.

Family Christmas

Christmas was my daddy's favorite time of the year, and mine too. He made it as unique as he could. My dad, Thomas, and I would go into the woods surrounding our home to search for a Christmas tree. It felt as though we would walk for miles. It was so exciting for me to explore the woods. We never saw it as dangerous, but as I think about that memory today, there were possibly hunters in those woods, and we could have been mistaken for wild game. Praise the Lord that did not happen. I would not ramble through the woods these days. But anyway, once we found the right tree, he'd cut it down with a hand saw, drag it back to the house, put it in a tree stand, and place it in our living room. That night, we decorated it with colorful lights, ornaments, and silver and gold tinsel. It gave our house a wonderful smell, the smell of Christmas. Thomas and I talked about what we wanted Santa Claus to bring us. We would pull out the Sears and Roebuck Christmas Wish Book catalog, sit on the floor, and pick out all the toys we wanted. There were so many wonderful toys to choose from; it was so overwhelming we thought our heads would explode. We enjoyed looking at all the toys in the catalog and dreaming of having them to play with. That Christmas list of ours got incredibly long at times. But it was fun hoping for all the things we thought Santa was going to bring down the chimney on Christmas Eve, not knowing that our parents were Santa. They could not afford to buy everything we wanted for Christmas, but we never went one Christmas without something under the tree. We were happy to get whatever our parents had placed there. The excitement of the gifts we did receive made us forget that extremely long list of the toys we wished for.

My mama would bake a chocolate cake, pineapple cake, coconut cake, apple jelly layered cake, fruitcake, sweet potato pies, cherry cobbler, and coconut custard pies that we could not touch until Christmas Day. She wrapped the fruitcake in aluminum foil to keep it fresh. Occasionally, after inserting holes in the top of the cake, she warmed wine and poured it on top of it. Come Christmas Day, it was moist and delicious. My dad slow-roasted a turkey, and Mama made turkey dressing with gravy, baked a picnic ham, cooked macaroni and cheese, mashed potatoes, green beans, field peas, hot fresh biscuits, and all the different fixings of a great Christmas dinner. A week or two before Christmas, my dad went to the farmer's market and bought a box of apples and a box of navel oranges. He placed them in the closet of the guest bedroom. The aroma from the apples and oranges filled the entire house; it was intoxicating. Our home smelled like Christmas morning. He gave Olivia, Thomas, and me one of each to help us endure our exuberant excitement leading up to the big day. On Christmas Eve, we placed shoeboxes under the tree so that Santa had somewhere to put our goodies. We went to bed early, so excited about what the next day would bring; we had an awful time trying to sleep. The tree lights were left on so Santa could find our house. Before daybreak one Christmas morning, I woke up, and from my bed, I could see a beautiful babydoll standing up against the wall in our living room where I had placed my shoebox under the tree. The anticipation of playing with her was almost maddening. When the sun came up, we rushed into the living room to see what we had gotten for Christmas. There were dolls and tea sets. In the shoebox, I had all kinds of Christmas candy, pecans, Brazil nuts, almonds, walnuts, firecrackers, sparklers, and, of course, an apple, orange, and sometimes a tangerine. After we played with our gifts for a while and enjoyed some of our treats, my father took us outside to show us Santa's sleigh tracks imprinted in the sand when he landed in the front yard to put our gifts under the Christmas tree. Oh, what joyous days we had. We played until it was time to have dinner. I have such fond memories of all the Christmas days I spent on the farm. My mama and daddy made Christmas so special. It helped us forget for a little while that we did not have some of the things that other families had. But we had what we needed: each other and parents who loved us and sacrificed to make Christmas memorable for us. I am so grateful for all those unforgettable memories.

Going Visiting

Sometimes, we would visit some of our family and friends on the days we were not working on the farm, usually the weekend. All the children would enjoy playing in the yard together. When we visited my mama's cousin, Ted, we played with his daughters. Then his wife, cousin Lois, would slice a piece of her pound cake for each of us. I can taste it now. It was bursting with the flavor of fresh butter; It was so delicious that I tried to make it last as long as I could—what a treasured memory. We played until my parents were ready to leave for home.

Before we left the farm, my mama cared for her parents in our house when they were so sick that they could no longer take care of themselves. I have one vivid memory of them. When I visited my grandparent's home, I remember the aroma of fresh-brewed coffee in the air as I walked through their house to the kitchen, where they were seated at the kitchen table. Grandpa would pour his coffee into a cup that was sitting on a saucer. Then he poured a little of the piping hot coffee into the saucer, blew on it, and slurped it from the dish. I can see him doing that like it just happened yesterday. To this day, I love the smell of freshly brewed coffee, and I like drinking it, too. But as children, we were not allowed to drink coffee. My mama's parents passed away before we left the farm and moved to Clay Hill in Raeford, NC. First, she took care of Grandma until she passed, and later on, Grandpa. During each wake, which was held at our home, the funeral home director brought their bodies to our house and put them in our living room for viewing the day before the funeral. They spent the night at our home, and the next day, the funeral director placed their bodies in a hearse and took them to the church for the funeral. I was so young that I don't have many memories of my maternal grandparents. I never met my fraternal grandparents because they had both passed away before I was born.

New World

Both Samantha and Alice drove a school bus. I got the chance to familiarize myself with what it felt like to sit on a bus before starting school. Their buses did not go to my school, which was disappointing. After parking the bus in a field next to our home, they were responsible for removing all the trash and sweeping the floor so it would be clean and ready to roll the following day. My first day of school was at West Hoke Elementary in Raeford, NC. Before catching the school bus, one of our daily chores was to slop (feed) the hogs. If I were not careful, some of the mud from their pin would get on my clothes; it had a disgusting, smelly odor, and I would have to carry that smell with me all day because I did not have time to change my clothes before leaving for school. It would be humiliating, so I did my best to avoid getting mud on myself. I remember my first day of school as if it was yesterday. I was scared and cried all day long, suffering from separation anxiety issues because I had never been away from my mama and family before, surrounded by strangers. It took a few days to accept that I had to be on my own at school. Learning that I had a chance to play with my classmates at recess didn't hurt matters because I loved to play. At that time, all my classmates were black. My early school years were during the period of segregation in our country. I'll never forget April 4, 1968, the day that Rev. Dr. Martin Luther King Jr. lost his life to an assassin. All of my teachers were crying. I did not understand the significance of that horrible day, but I did learn as I got older that he fought peaceably for my people and all people to have the same equal rights as other people. I spent the rest of my elementary years at West Hoke, except the eighth grade. Because of desegregation, I attended Upchurch Junior High in Raeford, NC, that year. When I was promoted to the ninth grade, I attended Hoke High School until I graduated.

During this transition, my family finally left the farm and moved into the first home purchased by my dad in Clay Hill (a small community in Raeford). It was the first home I had ever lived in that had indoor bathroom facilities. I was so very grateful for that amenity. Our neighbors lived right next door to us. On the farm, our nearest neighbors were at least half a mile or more away because of all the farmland that separated us. That was an experience I had never known before. My daddy got a job at Scotland County Memorial Hospital located in Laurinburg, NC. My mama continued to be a housewife. We all did chores around the house to help keep things clean and moving smoothly.

Attending high school was a vast difference from elementary school. I enjoyed being more independent and responsible for myself. It gave me a chance to experience life without the watchful supervision of my parents. In my junior year, my school created a Gospel Choir. My cousin and I tried out and were accepted. She and I loved singing but had never had the chance to do it on that scale; it was an excellent opportunity to learn more about singing and journey to different events to sing. The Gospel Choir traveled quite a bit. I was surprisingly selected to be one of the lead singers in the choir. I believe the choir director saw something in me that I had not yet seen in myself. After we had sung at several engagements, the coordinators of the choir planned a school concert, and I was picked to lead one of the songs that we sang. My parents were in attendance, and afterward, on the way back home, my dad expressed to me that he did not know I could sing like that. Pride rose in me because I was pleased that my dad was proud of me. Years later, after I was grown, I ran into Tony, one of the directors/musicians of the choir, in a retail store. I had not seen him since high school. He startled me. Because he had grown up so much, I did not recognize him. He knew exactly who I was. He asked me if I had been training my lead singer voice. With an embarrassed smile, I replied, "No." He encouraged me to work on it because he felt that I had talent and I should use it. I have never forgotten what he told me; it has inspired me through the years to improve my voice by singing in the church choir when I could. I often think of him when I sing or practice a new song. I remind myself to try harder because he believed in me; I do it in honor of his memory because he is no longer with us.

After moving to Clay Hill, I started dating a neighbor's son. His name was Wayne. Don't get me wrong; this did not come about easily. I had to be sixteen years of age before I had permission to keep company with a boy. My parents were strict, and the only dating I did was sitting on the couch in my parent's living room. I did not go out on dates away from their supervision. Wayne and I got to know each other better when he visited me and when I saw him at school. Before long, we fell in love and made plans to be married after we both had finished high school. He was my very first boyfriend and my first love. Wayne would walk me to class while we held hands. We would meet before and after school; we searched for a spot with some privacy to make out. This went on until he graduated a year ahead of me. I believed that I had met the person I was supposed to marry. Of course, I did not share these plans with my parents. There was no need to because I had to reach the age of eighteen before legally getting married. It wasn't something I was ready to share with them. They would have squashed that idea right off the bat by telling me I was too young to be thinking about marriage. I didn't want to hear about their reasons for my not getting married, so I kept our plans secret.

Family Reunion

My Aunt Teresa and one of my cousins were talking one day and came up with the idea to start an annual family reunion. They chose the Fourth of July for all our family members to get better acquainted and enjoy each other while partaking in some good homemade dishes. Every Sibling of my father and their family members were responsible for bringing food. Our first reunion was held at my two aunts, Teresa and Bessie's, home in a small community called Queenmore in Raeford, NC. My step-grandmother on my daddy's side lived with them. I did not know I was related to so many people. I met cousins that I had never seen before. The older people would sit around and reminisce about the days in which they grew up, laughing and talking about what they used to do. The young people would listen to their stories and get an insight into what they lived through growing up. It was a fun time. Later in the afternoon, some of my aunts, who were ministers, would hold church services in the backyard. I was a teenager, and I did not appreciate what they were doing. I felt like religion was being forced on me. I did not understand they were trying to share Jesus with the members of the family who did not have a personal relationship with Him. If I consider why they did it, I believe I would conclude it was because of their love for us that they did what they did, but I was not feeling it and was ready to go home. As an adult, I am grateful for that special love they had for our family. We have continued the tradition of having an annual reunion to this day. It is not like it used to be, but we come together every year to celebrate our family. I have missed quite a few reunions through the years, but I am thankful for my entire family.

My Mama's Illness

Daddy started to notice my mama was not acting like herself. Her daily household duties were seemingly getting to be too much for her to handle. Later, my mama got very, very ill. After seeing her doctor, we found out that she had advanced diabetes (a very high A1C)

According to https://medlineplus.gov/a1c.html, A1C is a blood test for type 2 diabetes and pre-diabetes. It measures your average blood glucose, or blood sugar, level over the past three months. Doctors may use the A1C alone or in combination with other diabetes tests to make a diagnosis. They also use the A1C to see how well you are managing your diabetes.

I don't know if she knew how long she had it. Her mother had the same disease and had been in the hospital, where they amputated both her legs before she eventually passed away.

Diabetes is a chronic (long-lasting) health condition that affects how your body turns food into energy. Most of the food you eat is broken down into sugar (also called glucose) and released into your bloodstream. When your blood sugar goes up, it signals your pancreas to release insulin. Insulin acts like a key to let the blood sugar into your body's cells for use as energy (www.cdc.gov).

I didn't know anything about this disease, and it ravaged her body quickly. She got to the point that she could no longer walk. I could see her condition worsening, and I lived in fear of something happening to her. My sister, Olivia and I helped her do the things she could no longer do for herself. One afternoon, we were helping her into the car to go for a ride to give her a change of scenery. All of a sudden, her body got stiff, and her eyes rolled back in her head. It scared me so bad that I started to scream. My dad directed us to get her back into the house and then to bed. We did it as rapidly as possible while trying unsuccessfully to keep our emotions in check. My dad called 911. While we waited for them, I sat by the bed, holding her hand. As I sat there with tears rolling down my face, I watched and listened in horror to hear what is called death rattles coming from her seemingly lifeless body. As I watched over her, praying that the ambulance would soon be there, I looked at her hands. I could see all the hard work that they had performed over the years for my siblings and me, all the sacrifices she made to ensure we had what we needed. If her hands could tell the story of her life, it would be full of love for her family. There was not one selfish bone in her body, and I did not want to lose her. As I gazed at her face with my heart beating like a drum, I witnessed her take her last breath. All I could do was cry. I could not believe that my mama was gone. It was the worst day of my young life, March 10, 1972. I had never known that kind of pain in my life. Her death crushed me. Grief took over and consumed me. I loved and adored my mama. I could not have asked for a better one. She worked tirelessly day in and day out without one complaint. She sacrificed everything for us. You know what they now call "me-time" nowadays; she never had that. She birthed and raised twelve children, and along with my dad, we were her top priority. I used to tell her about all the things that I was going to do for her once I was grown and got a job. I wanted to show her my love and appreciation. I was going to shower her with all the beautiful things she deserved to have but did not get. Now, that could never happen; she was gone.

Back then, when people lost a loved one, their family, neighbors, and friends came to their homes to bring food to help take away the worry of having to cook. They would "sit up" (visit most of the night with the family) to help keep their minds from over-thinking the loss of their loved one by telling stories, laughing, talking, and eating. The grieving process continued nightly until the day of the funeral. After the funeral was over, the family was left to work through their grief in private, with an occasional check-in or two from family. The night before Mama's funeral, her wake was held at Buies Funeral Home of Raeford for family and friends to view her body, visit our family, and share their condolences. Many people were at our home when it was time to go to the funeral home that evening. I did not want to see my mama lying in a casket, so I hid until everyone was gone, thinking no one would notice my absence. I was so hurt that she was gone that I didn't think I could survive looking at her that way. My daddy found out what I had done and sent one of my brothers back to the house to get me. He took me to the funeral home. I had to witness my mama lying still in a casket. The very image I tried to avoid so that I could hold on to remembering her as she was when she was alive. It was a terrible sight that I could not unsee.

The Funeral

I'll never forget the day we laid Mama to rest. After we were all seated in the Church and the service began, a terrible thunderstorm arose. It was almost dark outside, and the rain poured down in buckets. The lightning flashed, and the thunder roared so loud that it shook my whole body. I was in such distress that I cried during the entire service. I have no memory of what the Pastor preached about that day. By the time we were preparing to exit the Church, the storm had subsided, and there was a light rain still falling. The Funeral Home directors moved my mama's casket to the door of the Church to open it one last time for viewing. I tried to pull myself together as I readied myself to walk by to look at my mama's face one last time. I lost all my strength and could no longer stand on my own. Two of my brothers caught hold of my arms to support me. As I got closer to her, I watched my brother-in-law lean over to kiss her goodbye on her cheek. It was one of the most heart-wrenching and extraordinarily heartening things I had ever seen. When I reached that point, knowing that it would be the last time I would have the opportunity to look upon her beautiful face on this planet, I lost it. I wanted to touch her one last time, but I was not allowed to because I was so hysterical. My brothers let me stand there for a few moments to look at her, and then they helped me down the church's steps and put me in the family car. As I sat in the car with Olivia, I remembered an old saying that goes something like, if rain touches a person's casket before burial, they are going to Heaven or something like that. I knew what kind of woman my mama was. She was a God-fearing Christian woman, and I knew she had gone to Heaven, which was very comforting. We buried her at Piney Grove Church in Clio, SC. My dad was originally from South Carolina before he met my mama. That is where he had purchased burial plots for him and Mama. When they lowered her casket into the ground, the tears of inconceivable loss fell from my face. I could not see how my life would go on without her. Someone put their arms around my shoulders and guided me back to the family car, where I waited to return home. I didn't want to think of her in the ground all alone. I felt that she might be cold in that environment, but I had to remember that she was no longer in her body. She was gone to be with Jesus. That thought helped me not to feel guilty for leaving her there.

After her funeral, we had to find a way to get on with our lives. That was a complicated task. Olivia, Thomas, and I returned to school, but nothing would ever be the same again. Olivia and I took over all the duties of taking care of our home and doing the cooking. I don't know if she ever noticed it because we never talked about it, but I would wake up in the middle of the night, and I could hear my daddy crying. It broke my heart because I knew he loved my mama with all his heart and was missing her so much. Listening to him made me start to cry because I missed her too. I buried my face into my pillow and sobbed until I fell back to sleep. It was going to take some passage of time to accept that she was no longer physically with us, but the memories we carried in our hearts would never let us forget her.

The Prom

In my Junior year, Wayne asked me to attend his senior prom. I was very happy and honored to go with him. It was exciting because I had never dressed formally before. My dad was a little uncomfortable about letting me go. He no longer had his partner's help in making decisions like that. But he finally agreed to let me go. My older sister Ellen made my prom dress. I was so excited because it would be my first date without supervision and leaving the house with my boyfriend. I put on the beautiful dress Ellen had made for me. The bodice was a lovely solid blue with see-through long sleeves, and the bottom had a blue background with an assortment of colorful flowers. I put on a paltry amount of makeup and pearl earrings and topped it off with a pair of white pumps. I felt like a princess. Wayne came to the door and knocked. My daddy let him in. He had a beautiful corsage for me to pin onto my dress. Then we were given "the talk," and afterward, Wayne walked me to the car and opened the door as a gentleman should. I got in, pulling my gown in behind me to ensure it did not get caught in the door when it was closed. He got in, and we were on our way. When we arrived at our high school gymnasium, we found a table to sit down at. It wasn't long before Wayne asked me to dance. We had never had the chance to do that before this event. We danced fast, and we danced slow. I don't remember how I learned to dance, but I sure did it that night. We enjoyed the food, laughed and talked with our friends. We posed for our prom picture under a garden lattice decorated with flowers to remember our momentous occasion. This country girl had the time of her life that night. Wayne had to have me back home by midnight, according to my dad. I did not want him worried about me, so I intentionally made sure we left the prom early enough to arrive home on time. We had a magical night, but it was time to go.

Days before we went to the prom, I had been trying to decide whether or not to have my first sexual experience with the guy I planned to marry. Of course, I considered the teachings of my faith concerning fornication. I was encouraged to protect my virginity by my parents and what I believed. I convinced myself that it would be alright. After all, we were going to be married. He would be the only man I would ever be with. I wanted so badly to prove to him just how much I loved him. I decided to give him my virginity, not realizing that having sex with him was not the way to prove my love. After the prom was over, we went to a private spot to make out before going home, and one thing led to another until it was over. I couldn't decide how I felt about what I had done. It was not at all how I had envisioned it would be. Was what I had given away more valuable than I thought? I knew I had let God and my daddy down, and I would realize later how much I had let myself down. My mama would have been very disappointed in me. After thinking about it, I regretted what I had done, but there was no undoing this life-changing development. I got back home on time, but not the same as I was before I left. Something was missing that I could never get back. This was the very thing my dad was afraid would happen and had warned me about, but I did not listen. I took off my beautiful dress with a sad heart, put on my nightgown, said my prayers, and climbed into bed, forever changed.

CHAPTER 2
ADULTHOOD

Wayne and I were closer than ever. We couldn't seem to stay away from each other. He enrolled in a community college after graduating from high school. Without the knowledge of my dad, I skipped school to go with him sometimes. I would wait for him in the student lounge while he attended his classes. Afterward, he would drop me off at home before my daddy got home from work. I acted as though I had been in school all day. When I got home, I cooked dinner as usual and went to my room. This went on until I graduated from high school in 1973. I had big dreams of going to college or getting a great job. My dad could not afford to send me to college, so I wanted to leave Raeford and pursue my dreams elsewhere. I asked my dad if I could go to Charlotte, NC, to live with one of my older sisters. I had two sisters who lived there. Reluctantly, He decided to let me go. I was thrilled to be starting a brand-new chapter in my life. I believed that Wayne and I could continue a close relationship, only it would now be a long-distance one. We agreed that I would see him when I came home for a visit, and we could also talk on the phone sometimes.

I lived with my sister, Alice, for a while, and then I moved in with my other sister, Samantha. Alice helped me to get a job where she worked. I trained in the mailroom on how to sort mail with the young lady who had previously held that position. She had been promoted to the billing department. She showed me how to open, sort, and deliver the mail to all the different offices. I also picked up the outgoing mail and got it prepared to be picked up by a coworker to take to the US Post Office near the end of the day. I enjoyed using the typing skills I had learned in high school in my new job; they came in handy. In my job, I also received mail that needed to be addressed, folded, placed in envelopes, sealed, weighed, stamped with the correct postage, and put with the outgoing mail. My work area was in a large room with several architects who became my close friends. They were some of the nicest people I had ever met. We talked, laughed, and joked a lot as we got to know each other better. I told them all about Wayne and our plan to be married. They were happy for me but warned me not to rush things, that I was still young and had plenty of time to get married.

In the absence of my daddy's supervision, I picked up a smoking habit. It wasn't a brilliant thing to do. I thought I was so grown up. I was making decisions for myself; I had a great job and a wonderful fiancé. My life was unfolding as planned. I thought about how much I loved Wayne and sometimes wondered if I had made the right decision to leave him. The longer I was away from him, the more I missed him. After I had saved enough money for a down payment on a car, I went home one weekend, and my dad co-signed for me to buy my very first vehicle. He made sure all his children could get their driver's licenses by the age of sixteen. He helped me learn to drive, plus I took driver's education in high school. Now that I had transportation, after work on Fridays, I packed a bag and went to visit my family quite often and to see Wayne. Everything was going well. I was enjoying my new life in Charlotte, and Wayne was finishing up Community College. We had not set a specific date or year to be married, but I was confident that it would happen. I guess everything wasn't going as well as I thought because disaster struck. Unfortunately for me, I found out from friends that Wayne had been dating someone else, and that wasn't all; she was pregnant with his child. I was utterly heartbroken. I went home to confront him about it. He admitted it. I was so destroyed that I didn't know what I was going to do. I trusted him because he had never given me a reason not to. I couldn't be with him anymore; I couldn't bear to look at him. He was not the man I thought he was. We broke up because I could no longer trust him. If he could cheat on me before we got married, more than likely, he would do the same thing after we were married. I gave him the most treasured gift I possessed because I thought we would be married someday. I rushed something that should have waited for our wedding night. I felt so betrayed. That was the first time a man had broken my heart, but it would not be my last. My life was no longer what I thought it was, and all my plans went up in smoke.

I continued my new life in a new city. It wasn't easy moving on because now all my plans had changed. I had to find a way to keep moving forward. After a while, I started going out to clubs by myself. One night, I met this nice-looking guy. His nickname was Slim. We did a lot of dancing that night. We laughed and talked; we hit it off quickly. Before the night was over, he asked if I would go out on a date with him. I felt comfortable with him, so I said yes. We loved going out to nightclubs and dancing. We even got to dance on a TV Show similar to Soul Train. We dated casually for a while, but then our relationship moved on to a more intimate one. Even though I had broken up with Wayne, I still had a semi-intimate relationship with him whenever I would go home to visit. I could not completely let go of

Wayne; one minute, I was with him, and the next, I wasn't. I was all over the place emotionally. I also really cared for Slim. It wasn't fair to either of them. I only thought about what I wanted, not comprehending I was doing the same thing to them that Wayne had done to me.

Oh No, Not Me

One morning, when I got out of bed, I felt sick to my stomach, which made me vomit. I wasn't concerned until it started to happen more often. I felt nauseated all the time. I noticed my period was a few days late. I suspected what was wrong because I had all the symptoms, but I prayed it wasn't true, even though I was not on birth control. I called and made an appointment with my doctor. He asked me questions, examined me, and gave me a test. After that, he informed me that I was pregnant. I was disappointed in myself for allowing this to happen to me. I should have taken better care and used protection to prevent this from happening. I don't know why we always say to ourselves, "It will never happen to me." The things of life are going to happen whether we prepare for them or not. Don't give yourself a false sense of security by thinking you are exempt from certain things. If you do the things that adults do, you must take the responsibility of being one and everything that comes with it.

I had to muster the courage to tell my sister Samantha about it. After telling her, I had a decision to make. Assessing my ability to take care of a child at that stage in my life and considering the advice of others, I felt that I was not ready to be a mother. I discussed my dilemma with my friends at work, and they suggested that I do what was right for me. I thanked them for their input, but the decision was ultimately mine to make. I couldn't sleep worrying about what I was going to do. It took some time, but I finally concluded what I thought was best for me. Reluctantly and with careful thought, I decided to have an abortion. This decision is the greatest mistake of my life. I can't tell you how many times I have regretted what I did. This action went against my faith. Being so young, I did not consider my child in my decision-making. My child could have grown up and done something that could have changed the world, but I destroyed that possibility. I made a colossal mistake, one that I have grieved over my entire life. I worried more about what others would think of me. I thought about how my dad would feel about what I let happen, let alone what that would announce to him: I was no longer a virgin. I didn't want to face his disappointment in me. And I did not want him blaming either of my sisters for something I let happen. I was responsible for my careless behavior, no one else. I was promiscuous in my conduct, and now I had to pay the consequence of it. Before I acted on my difficult decision, I reevaluated my situation and still came to the same conclusion. I was not ready to be a mother. So, without my dad's knowledge, to avoid his disappointment and judgment, to stop what I thought was not right for me that would alter my life forever, I made my decision.

I also felt responsible for telling Slim that I was pregnant for someone else. He was such a wonderful and loving man that after I told him, he asked me to marry him; he wanted to help raise my child. He did not care who the father was. I considered Slim's offer. I respected him greatly, but I didn't feel that would be fair. This was a situation that I had created, so I turned him down. It was enough that I had messed up my life; I did not want to mess his up, too. We had not known each other long enough to become husband and wife. I sometimes wonder if I made two mistakes. I was so young and naive that I did not realize how not giving birth to my child would affect me for the rest of my life. I also contacted Wayne and told him that I was pregnant. I wanted to believe that Wayne was the father, but I was not one hundred percent convinced about that, but it didn't make any difference now. Wayne didn't fight against my decision and sent me the money to pay for the procedure. I called my doctor and made an appointment. I went to the hospital alone because Samantha had to work. The anesthesiologist put me under, and when I awoke, I was no longer pregnant. I had to stay at the hospital for a while to make sure there were no complications. I was released after a few hours and went home. Once I had healed and regained my strength, I decided to quit my job and move back home, hoping to resurrect my relationship with Wayne. I believed that I could get past the betrayal, past the judgment I made not to carry my child to term; can you believe it? I don't know why I was so determined about that. So, I told Slim that I was going to move back home. He was very unhappy that our relationship was ending, and I was too. Slim had always treated me with love and respect. It was not easy saying goodbye to him, but I felt I needed to return home and try and rekindle my relationship with Wayne. I couldn't let go despite all that had happened. He was my first, and I wanted him to be my husband, as I initially believed he would be. I told myself that we still had a chance, but I would need to move back home to revive our relationship.

I moved back home to live with my dad. I did not divulge to him anything about the abortion. I knew it would upset him, and I couldn't bear to see the disappointment and ridicule in his eyes. Plus, talking about it would just degrade my self-esteem even more. I not only let him down, but I also did an excellent job of letting myself down. I had to let go of my past, or I could not move forward with my life. I told myself that I would have another chance to have a child, and hopefully, the next time, I would have a husband. Wayne and I dated for a while, even though he had become a new father. I resented him for being the father of another woman's child. It should not have happened, but it did. I harbored some deep-seated anger in my heart. I believe it blocked my feelings for him from becoming as they were before all the changes in our lives took place. After giving it a go, we were unsuccessful at rekindling our relationship. We dated occasionally, but the closeness we once shared did not come back to life. Our relationship faded into the abyss, and we went our separate ways. Everything in my life was scrambled. It seemed as though every decision I was making was the wrong one. My confidence was low, and I thought about the advice my former coworkers had given me. They were so right; I had the body of an adult but the mind of a child. I should not have been so eager to be grown. I should have waited for my brain to catch up with my flesh. I was so confused that I didn't know what to do next. Nothing had turned out the way I had planned.

Starting Over

I needed to change my environment, and eventually, I dreamed about getting a place of my own to live, but first, I had to find a job. I had heard about a manufacturing plant located in the city limits of Raeford that was hiring. So, I got up early one morning and went to apply at a company called TexElastic Yarns and got a job as a doffer. The lady in Human Resources took all the people hired that morning inside the plant for a tour to give us an idea of what type of work we would be doing. We were all issued earplugs to protect our hearing because the running machines were loud enough to damage our hearing. It looked like nothing I had ever seen before. I began to wonder if I could learn how to do what I saw other employees doing. The giant machines had tubes of rubber at the bottom on rollers so that when the engine started, the rollers would begin to turn. The rubber came off the tube, went behind a wire, and up through a spool of nylon and then another spool as they both were spinning around to cover the rubber. And then, it made its way up to the top of the machine, where an empty tube was receiving the finished product. After the machine ran so many hours, the tubes on the top would fill up, and a group of women would come along, stop the machine, and do what they called a doff. They took the tubes of what was now called yarn, put them on a rack on wheels, put new tubes on the machine, and restarted it again. Most of the machines ran two doffs before the spools ran out of nylon and needed to be changed. TexElastic sold the yarn to manufacturing plants that used it to make socks and pantyhose, and some would be sent to the Scragg Department in C-Plant to be rewound onto new tubes before shipping. I needed a job to take care of myself. So, I came back at the appointed time and began my training. I was placed with a trainer to learn my new job. She showed me how to change the spools of nylon and then how to thread the machine. Once it had been completely threaded, the engine would start. When the yarn reached the tube, the doffer would pick up the tube running on the top of the machine, pull the waste off the tube, and restart it. If the rubber or nylon broke down during startup, the doffer was responsible for rethreading it with a specially designed needle. All this was done while the machine was running. It could not be stopped once it started. It took a while, but I learned how to do the job.

It became like second nature to me because I did the same thing over and over again. I made new friends and ran into friends I already knew. I found out a while later that Wayne also worked there on the first shift in the maintenance department. His department repaired the machines when they had a malfunction. He was shocked to see me because we had not seen each other for weeks. We got along as coworkers, but our intimate relationship no longer existed. I was so in love with him at the beginning. So many things could have contributed to the loss of the love we felt for each other, or at least the love I felt for him. Our trust in each other was shattered beyond repair. I could forgive but not forget. I knew I would always be suspicious. I would probably find myself wondering where he was and what he was doing behind my back, and maybe he would think the same about me. That was not the sought of life I wanted for myself. I put my past behind me and made an effort to press on. I lived with my family, saved my money, and planned for my future.

CHAPTER 3
AND SO, IT BEGINS

I worked on first shift for a while to complete my training. After 90 days, I was labeled as fully trained and could now be transferred to third shift. My shift hours were from 11:00 pm to 7:00 am. It was a big adjustment to learn to sleep during the day. As time went on, after a hard night's work, I had no problem falling asleep during daylight hours. I slept about 4 hours and got up to do my chores around the house, go out to the grocery store, shop, or pay bills. I cooked dinner for my family before I laid back down later in the evening. They worked during the day. I was the only one at home, so I was the obvious choice to prepare the evening meal. I slept until time to get up around 10:00 pm, showered, got dressed, and headed out for another night's work.

One morning after work, I stopped at a convenience store to buy gas and a pack of cigarettes. I pumped the gas and went inside to pay and to get the cigarettes. I was on my way back out of the store when I met this lady coming in. I backed up out of her way, smiled, and said, "Excuse me." She stopped me as I attempted to walk past her and said, "You have such a bright light around you." When I looked at her, all I remember seeing was a dark-skinned beautiful woman with a brilliant smile on her face. I thanked her, puzzled by what she said, and went back to my car. I did not have a clue what she was saying to me. I never forgot her proclamation. I have carried it with me all of my life. I believe I looked into the face of an Angel that day, sent by God. I didn't know why she said what she did, but I would understand years later.

TexElastic had three shifts with a seven-day operation. We were issued schedules that notified us of what days we would have off each week. Usually, we got one weekend a month. When we were scheduled off, it would be for four days, two for the current week and two for the upcoming week. I really looked forward to those four days off to finally get some well-deserved rest and get a chance to socialize with some of my friends. During one of my days off, I went to visit Virginia, a girlfriend from work. She lived a few miles from me in a Mobile Home Park. She and her sister were sharing a mobile home. I complimented her on her home and mentioned that I was interested in getting my own place. She informed me that a mobile home across the street from her was up for rent. I had been saving my money so that I would be prepared when the opportunity presented itself. As long as I lived with my dad, I needed to abide by his rules. I felt I was grown up enough to move out on my own and take care of myself. I was almost twenty years old, and I believed I knew what I was doing. I felt this was my chance to be independent.

When my dad came home from work that day, I talked to him about moving out on my own and told him about the mobile home that was up for rent. He flat-out said, "No," and that was the end of that conversation. I was very disappointed that he disapproved of my wanting to move out and that he wouldn't even entertain the idea. But I was a very stubborn and determined person also. I was a grown woman, and I could decide for myself. I did not need his permission. The next day, I went to the mobile home park manager's office and asked about the mobile home across from my girlfriend, Virginia. She took me over to have a look at it. I was pleased when I walked through it. It was small, but I was ok with that because I would be the only one living there. It was not fancy, but it was clean and in good shape. When we returned to her office, I decided to rent the mobile home. I filled out all the papers, paid the deposit, paid the first month's rent, and she gave me the keys. I went back to my dad's house, packed my things, and moved to my new home. After my dad got off work that afternoon, I called from Virginia's house and told him that I had rented a mobile home and moved out. It almost seemed like he was not surprised. He said, "I guess if that's the way it has to be, then that's the way it has to be." I was a little shocked that he didn't get angry. But I was relieved that I had not ruined my relationship with him by moving out.

I settled into my new place. I went out and bought some of the things I needed, like sheets for my bed, dishes, cookware, flatware, and drinking glasses. I decorated as best I could on my budget. It felt good to finally be able to make all my decisions for myself. I was thrilled. I continued to work on third shift, but now I had someone to share the ride with. Virginia and I went to work together every night. Her sister worked on second shift. Everything was going well. Virginia and I hung out at each other's homes and had fun laughing, talking, and listening to music. I didn't cook much, but I always kept a pitcher of cherry cool-aid in my refrigerator. She would come over sometimes just to get some. She always told me that I made the best cool-aid. One day, I went over to her home, and the guy she was dating had come by to visit. She introduced him as Brad. Then she said the guy sitting on the steps at the end of her walkway was Brad's older brother, Ricky. She took me out to meet him. She knew I wasn't dating anyone at the time and thought it was a good idea to introduce us. She went back inside and left me alone with him. He seemed to be very shy as he sat there smoking a cigarette. When I tried to hold a conversation with him, he would answer the question I asked, and that was it. That piqued my curiosity, and I wondered what it was about him that made him act the way he did. He was cute, dark-skinned, and tall like his brother. Now that I was no longer dating anyone, I decided to take him on as a challenge to see if I could draw him out of his shyness and get to know him. Sometimes, we women get too curious. I should have taken his quiet demeanor as a sign. I have always heard that it is the quiet ones that you need to watch out for. Remember what happened to the curious cat? After he and his brother left, Virginia and I acted like little schoolgirls comparing notes about the two brothers as we giggled and laughed. Eventually, I had to leave because we had to work that night, and we both needed to get some sleep. I went back home, got my clothes together that I would be wearing, and laid down to get some rest. As I slowly started to fall asleep, I recalled the day's events and questioned if I wanted to get involved with anyone. I had been through a lot in the past few months. Did I want to complicate things by inviting another man into my life? Before I knew it, I had fallen asleep, and my alarm loudly reminded me that it was time to get up for work.

Days went by until one day, I heard a knock at my door. I went to answer, and it was Ricky. He asked if he could come in, and I said of course. We sat down at the kitchen table and got to know each other a little better. I was surprised to see him. I thought he was too shy to initiate a visit with me. I told him about my family, and he told me about his. He had lots of sisters and brothers, as I did. He, too, worked in a manufacturing plant. While we were talking, he asked if I got high. I told him no. He said that he smoked a little marijuana on occasion. I didn't know anything about marijuana because I had only heard about it. I brushed it off because I didn't think it was a big deal. He went on to explain that his schedule was different from mine. He worked for twelve hours three days a week and was off for four days, and the following week, he worked twelve hours a day for four days and was off for three. I knew that probably took some getting used to, but he seemed to like the convenience of it. He had enough time off to get his business taken care of or maybe take a trip if he wanted. It started to get late, so I told him I needed to rest because I had to go to work that night. We said our goodbyes, but before he left, he asked if it would be alright if he came back to see me again, and I said sure. I told him the best time of day to come by because of my sleeping schedule. After he left, I was kind of excited because I liked him. I realized that there was a possibility that I may have found someone that interested me enough to date.

Ricky and I started seeing each other quite often. Before I knew it, we were classifying ourselves as boyfriend and girlfriend. We went out on dates, and he would drop by to see me sometimes after work. I was enjoying keeping company with him. He seemed to be a very nice guy. Virginia was also happy with Brad, and we both thought it was great for us to be dating brothers. I suggested to Ricky that we go to a Hoke High School football game one evening to watch my nephew, Thomas, play. We parked and were on our way to the stadium when this group of girls came up behind us saying some things about Ricky. I looked back and did not recognize them. Ricky held my hand as we continued to walk towards the stadium. It appeared that one of the girls was or had previously dated him and was upset to see him with me. He never told me that he was dating anyone. When I looked to him for answers, he didn't want to talk about it. He said, "Don't pay any attention to her." So, I did what he asked. Soon, they went away, and we found somewhere to sit that was not near them. I did not press him on why the girl was so upset. It was obvious that she cared for him. That's why she and her friends were making such a ruckus about him being with me. He was with me because that was where he wanted to be. We watched the game, and I cheered for Thomas. When it was over, he took me back home. Ricky and I had been dating for a while; I confess that even though we had a close relationship, my thoughts sometimes still drifted back to daydreaming about what could have been with Wayne. I literally gave my all to him, and I resented him for cheating on me, but I had to admit that I was not completely true to him by dating Slim before our relationship had resolved itself. I still felt something for him; he was my first love, and sometimes, you can't easily shake that off, whether you want to or not. Whether you are seeing someone else or not. It takes time to get over a failed first love. I had to make peace with my past to move into my future. I tried not to think about him and remain in the present. I knew rehashing the past would not help me at all. It would continue to cloud the life I was living now.

Girls Night Out

Virginia and I went to our supervisor's office one night to ask him if he could schedule us off on the same days because we came to work together. He didn't seem to have a problem with our request. He had to consider that he could not afford for either of us to not report for work. That would put more work on everyone else, so he agreed to give us the same days off every week. When we were off work, it gave us a chance to hang out together and see our boyfriends. We were very delighted about that. It was almost time for us to have our four days off. We decided that we would go out on Saturday night. It was just going to be us girls. We went to a dance club and drive-in. There was a jukebox outside and a concrete platform, surrounded by pine trees, for people to dance on. There were also a few picnic tables for sitting down. When we got there, I ran into Thomas, who was also having a fun night out. We spoke, then he went his way, I went mine, and continued with my evening. I loved dancing, and it was a sultry, warm, breezy late summer night. One of my old classmates from high school asked me to dance, and I accepted. We were having a good time dancing and showing off our moves. After we danced, he said thanks, and he went on about his way.

I stood on the sideline watching Virginia and other people dancing and having fun when, all of a sudden, Ricky walked up and told me he needed to talk to me. I was surprised and happy to see him because we didn't have anything planned for that night. He grabbed me by the arm, and we walked away from the loud music to talk. When we could hear each other better, he asked me, "Who is the guy I saw you dancing with?" I started to explain who he was and how I knew him, not anticipating that he was about to punch me in the stomach with all his might. I felt like I had been hit by a Mack truck. I was doubled over in pain as he was cursing me for making a fool of him.

While this was going on, someone ran and told Thomas that a guy was beating up his sister. Thomas started running towards us, and when Ricky saw him coming, he took off running. Thomas was a well-built football player; he was a very muscular guy, making him quite scary, especially if he was angry with you. He stopped long enough to see if I was alright, and then he started after Ricky. Ricky was so scared of Thomas that he didn't even try to get to his car. He just ran into the nearby woods in the pitch-black dark of night. Men who hit women are cowards when it comes to facing another man. Thomas was so angry that I was afraid that he was going to do something crazy.

We grew up together, so he was more like a brother than a nephew.

Virginia found out what was going on with me from someone and came to get me and helped me back to the car so she could take me home. This was not the night out that we had planned or expected. I just wanted to have a little bit of fun. It was not my plan to look for another man to date. Somehow, Ricky got things all twisted. I had never seen this side of him before. I would never have suspected he could do anything like this to me. I was heartbroken, in excruciating pain, and crying in disbelief. Who does this kind of thing to a woman just for dancing with someone? I was so embarrassed and ashamed of what he had done to me in front of my friends and the people at the club. It made me feel like I had done something wrong, but I hadn't. Before Virginia and I left the club, Thomas returned and told me he could not find Ricky, that he had disappeared into the woods. Maybe that was for the best. I don't know what Thomas would have done to him had he been able to catch him. (That event was my first red flag.)

When I got home, I just wanted to go to bed and forget that horrible night. Growing up, I had never been exposed to domestic violence. I didn't even realize that was what it was called. I took a long hot bath, put on my nightgown, and headed towards my bed. Virginia came over to check to make sure I was OK. I told her I was a little sore but otherwise okay. I just wanted to go to bed. She explained that she had no idea Ricky was like that. I didn't blame her; I wasn't aware either. After she left, I took a couple of aspirin and I got into bed. I couldn't sleep, wondering what was wrong with Ricky. How could he hurt me like that after being so sweet and gentle with me? I spent most of the night awake just thinking. I finally fell asleep around daybreak.

Later that morning, I heard a knock at my door, which startled me and woke me up. I put on my house coat and went to answer it. It was Ricky, all dirty and sweaty, begging me to please let him in. He had traveled through the woods for miles from the drive-in on foot. I was scared of what he might do now that I knew what he was capable of, but he kept pleading with me until I cautiously let him come in; that was my second mistake. The apologizing began. He was so sorry, and he didn't know what he was doing. He said he loved me so much he could not stand to see me with another man, even if I was only dancing with him. He promised me over and over again that he would never do that to me again and begged me to please forgive him. He looked and acted like he was sincere about what he was saying. He probably did mean it when he was saying it. Against my better judgment, I forgave him, not knowing at the time that he was displaying classic abuser behavior. They always say they are sorry and will never do it again. That is a total lie. If he hits you once, he will hit you again. Unfortunately for me, I did not know that at the time.

Ricky and I continued to see each other after that. I always had this feeling that I needed to be careful what I did when I was around him. I adjusted my life and my behavior to accommodate his insecurities. That was something I should never have done. I was changing myself for him. Thomas respected my decision to continue to see Ricky. I did not tell my dad or my family what had happened to me. I didn't want to get my dad upset and insist that I move back home. Thomas did not tell him either, at my request. Ricky seemed to be trying to convince me that what he had done at the nightclub was a one-time thing. Weeks passed, and it appeared that we were getting along just fine. Still, it could have been because I now knew what he would do to me if he thought I was not being faithful to him, and I adjusted my personality to what I thought he expected from me. I hoped the monster I had been introduced to at the nightclub was gone. I found myself clearing everything with him to make sure he didn't feel threatened by anyone. Somehow, I knew deep down inside that I had witnessed the true Ricky, but I didn't want to see him as that violent person who threatened me. I came up with all kinds of excuses to continue my relationship with him. Neither did I know that I was being assimilated into a less confident woman; I was becoming a victim.

Lay-offs

One night, when Virginia and I went to work, our supervisor had everyone come to the break room for a meeting. We were told that Spanco's customer orders had declined and that some people would need to be laid off. But first, he wanted to know if there was anyone that would volunteer to be laid off. Virginia and I looked at each other, and we both raised our hands. He told us we could start that night; we collected our things and went back home. We were so happy to not have to go into work anymore. We had no idea what we had just done. We would get unemployment checks for a while, but they would eventually run out, and then where would we be? We may have had enough seniority to keep our jobs during the slow business of the plant. Being young and immature prevented us from thinking seriously about our future. We still had to pay our bills in order to live on our own. We were living in the moment and didn't really care much about the future. It wasn't long before I realized that my small unemployment check wasn't gonna cut it. I had rent, a car payment, car insurance, an electric bill, a water bill, and a food bill. I recognized it would not be long before I would have to move back home. Virginia was in a better position than I was because her sister was still working, and they split their bills in half. I gave it some thought, considered my financial situation, and concluded that I would have to move back home to keep a roof over my head. I talked to Ricky about my plans. I had never introduced him to my dad or my sister, Olivia. Thomas was the only one who knew I was dating him. I don't know; maybe I already knew in my heart that my dad would disapprove of our relationship, especially if he knew that I was sleeping with Ricky and that he had abused me in a jealous rage.

During one of Ricky's visits, I told him that I would be moving back home soon when he blurted out, "Marry me, I can't live without you." That blew me away and completely caught me off guard. I asked if he knew what he was saying. He replied, "Yes, I do. I can take care of you. I want us to be together always. I don't want to be away from you." I was so shocked that I told him that I would have to think about it. Marriage was not one of the things I thought about when it came to Ricky. I didn't know what else to say. We had only known each other a few months, and there was that incident of him being so jealous that he punched me in my stomach to consider. We talked a bit longer, and he left. My mind was exploding with what-ifs. I knew that he chose to hit me when he felt that he was being made a fool of. I knew that I didn't know very much about him, and I knew that I was too young to be considering getting married, especially after what happened with Wayne, but what if? When I was growing up, girls were conditioned to be wives and mothers, but I had decided that I was not ready for that yet. I had not been introduced to his family. Brad was the only one I had met. Always meet the family and get a clear picture of who you are dating. Their parents and siblings play a huge part in the man they have become. Take your time and observe and listen to them. They will tell you, without being aware, who they are. I wholeheartedly recommend you do this before becoming deeply involved with someone. It could save you a lot of heartache and pain and maybe your life.

The next day, I was up early, still thinking about what to do about Ricky's proposal. I started cleaning to keep myself busy while mulling over what to do. I had thought of reasons not to accept his proposal, and they were valid ones. The only positive reason I could come up with was to remain free from having to move back home; sad but true. That afternoon, someone knocked on my door. I opened it, and a lady was standing there I had never seen before. She introduced herself as Shirley, one of Ricky's older sisters. I didn't know how she knew who I was. Ricky had never allowed me to meet his family. He did take me down the road that his family lived on one day while we were out for a drive and showed me where they lived. He wasn't interested in stopping to let me meet them. I didn't understand it then, but I didn't make a big fuss over it. She said that Brad had told her that Ricky had asked me to marry him. She said she knew it might sound strange coming from her, being that she was Ricky's sister, but she had to warn me about the kind of man he was. Ricky hadn't had any successful relationships with women. He would always do something that would end up with the women not wanting to have anything to do with him. She told me that he was, in her words, "Abusive towards women" and that she couldn't, in good conscience, let me marry him without letting me know who he was. I listened to what she had to say. But I prided myself on being an independent-thinking woman. I would not let someone, especially someone I had never seen before, tell me that it was not a good idea to marry Ricky. Her visit made me even more confused than I already was. We finished speaking, and she left. I found out later that she had been in an abusive relationship and had finally broken free. That was why she felt so compelled to warn me about her own brother. When you have been an abused woman, you don't want to see another woman go through what you have been through. She had to leave her abuser to protect herself and her children. Her motives were genuine, being that she made it her business to come to talk to me, but should I listen to her? I believe that her visit may have had the opposite effect of what she set out to do. My rebellious nature pitted me against what she told me. It may have tilted me toward Ricky instead of away. Take the time to meditate on a warning you have received about someone before making a final decision. Use your head, not your emotions, to make that decision. You could be getting ready to make a colossal mistake. Investigate what you have been told. Do it on the down-low because you don't want him to find out you are researching him. It may cause an adverse effect that you don't want to see. Take it seriously; this is your life we are talking about. (Second Red Flag).

CHAPTER 4
DECISIONS, DECISIONS, DECISIONS

Ricky and I continued to see each other while I considered all that had happened. It struck me that his sister made it her business to come to see me and warn me about him. I suspect that he did not know she had visited me. I didn't think it would be a good idea to tell him, knowing he probably would have lost it. I don't believe she wanted him to know because she had Brad bring her to see me while Ricky was working. The day came when I had to make some decisions. I had to move out of my home and go home to live with my dad or marry Ricky. I had enjoyed my freedom, and I knew that if I went back home, it would be the end of that. Then, I had to consider the fact that if I married Ricky, I would also be giving up my freedom to him. You know, when you are young, you make bad decisions, decisions that you regret later in life. You always think you know what you are doing. When in reality, you don't have a clue. I didn't see things as they were or the consequences of them. It was like I was, as they say, "blinded by love," or was it love? My desire not to move back home outweighed my common sense. I decided to marry Ricky even though his sister had warned me about him. He had been so sweet since the incident, and I believed that everything would be ok. Thinking back on my decision to marry Ricky, I may have been doing it for selfish reasons. I wouldn't have to move back home, proving I had been a failure at living on my own to my dad. Also, I hadn't come to terms with what Wayne had done to me, and this would be a way of getting back at him for breaking my heart and ruining our future together. The door would close to Wayne and me getting back together or getting married. Foolish thinking, right? I know it sounds crazy, but we all do crazy things when it comes to matters of the heart. I told myself that it would all turn out ok. I wasn't aware how this misguided decision would change my life forever.

I told Ricky that I would marry him, even though I knew I still cared for Wayne. He moved in with me before we were married. I convinced myself that I would learn to love Ricky as a wife should, in time; I already had feelings for him. I had to admit that what I felt for Ricky was not like what I felt for Wayne. Ricky and I went on to make plans to be married. We didn't have the money for a Church wedding. We didn't have very much money at all. So, we decided to go to South Carolina to a Justice of the Peace to get married. Before we left, Ricky took me to meet his family. As we passed the house where he had shown me his family lived, I said, "Wait a minute, didn't we pass by your home?" He said, "No, my family lives just up the road." There I was, staring at him with my mouth hanging open, realizing he had lied to me. I should have shut things down right then, now that I knew that he was a big liar, too. He made me think that the lovely home he had shown me was where he grew up instead of the less prominent house's driveway that he turned into. I was stunned by this, but I had no judgments on where he grew up. I had grown up in an old wooden shack. So I just let it go, but there was no need to lie to me. It is incredible how we can talk ourselves into things to justify our actions. He had just proven to me that he was a liar, and I dismissed it without taking it seriously. Take their ability to lie to you with a straight face as a sign that it won't be the last one because he is comfortable doing it. If a man loves you and respects you, he will not lie to you about anything, no matter how small. (Third Red Flag.)

I met his parents and some of his sisters and brothers. I also met his older sister, Shirley, who had come to see me and warned me about him. She acted as though it was our first time meeting, so I went along with pretending I didn't know her. She lived next door to her parents. His home was ok, but I felt that he was ashamed of where he grew up. There was no need for him to be ashamed of his home. I was just disappointed that he felt the need to lie to me about it. He explained to his parents that we were on our way to get married. They had no objections, not in my presence anyway. I found that strange since it was their first time laying eyes on me. Maybe they knew what would happen if they disagreed with Ricky. Perhaps they knew all about my relationship with Ricky and were not shocked by his announcement. So, we left his parent's house, but before we went to South Carolina to be married, we stopped by TexElastic so I could ask Wayne for money to help pay the justice of the peace. Yeah, I did that. I had told Ricky all about my rocky relationship with Wayne, so he was not surprised by my suggestion to talk to him. I believe I did it just to hurt him. After giving him the rundown on why I needed the money, I was surprised that he reached into his back pocket, pulled out his wallet, and gave me some money. I know it was very brazen of me to go to him, but he was the only person I knew would help me. He told me later on that he did not believe that I was going to get married. That's why he gave me the money. I would never have gotten it had he known that I was for real. I thanked him, got back into the car with Ricky, and we drove away.

We got married in late October. On our way back from getting married, we stopped by my dad's house to tell him. That was not a conversation that I was looking forward to having. He was deeply agitated with me because he didn't even know I was dating, much less to hear that I had married someone he had never met. He refused to believe me. I had to show him my marriage license to prove it. I believe I hurt my daddy that day. I gave him news that I knew he did not expect to hear from his baby girl. I will never forget the hurt look on his face when he realized I was telling him the truth. He accepted my announcement once I proved that I was married, but he was not happy with me. I thought what I had done was the right thing for me. It seemed like it was in the moment. I was relieved that my dad and Ricky's parents knew about us. It was now public knowledge that we were a married couple. Everything was nice and legal. Growing up, I never saw myself as a problem child. Still, it is reasonable to think that my independence, stubbornness, and determination put me in situations that caused my dad to worry about me. I have always seen myself as what is called "the black sheep of the family." I did things that my siblings would see as unconscionable. I don't know why I was so different from them. We had the same parents and grew up in the same house, doing the same things. As I think about it now, I believe that I was set apart for a particular purpose. And everything that happened to me was for a reason. Eventually, Ricky met my sisters and brothers. They were kind to him because he was married to me, which made him family.

After a few weeks, Ricky came home from work and told me that he had been laid off from his job. I wasn't surprised because the economy was not doing well, and many people were losing their jobs or their work hours were being cut. When Virginia's sister was laid off, they moved to another city to get jobs doing work similar to what we did at TexElastic. So now we had to figure out what to do next. I knew it was not a good idea to ask my dad if we could move in with him. He was still processing the fact that his soon-to-be 20-year-old daughter was married. So, Ricky talked to his parents about our situation, and they told him that it would be okay for us to move in with them for a while. We left our first home together and moved in with his family. It was a little crowded because he had younger siblings, plus his parents, and now us, all living in one house. They all welcomed me into the family and treated me like family. I got to know his sister Shirley a lot better. As a matter of fact, we became good friends. When I got overwhelmed by living in a home with so many people, I walked over to her house, and we'd sit and talk. I learned that she was also a smoker like me and smoked marijuana like Ricky. I had never tried it, and I didn't like the smell of it burning. I did not feel I knew enough about it to judge the ones who did smoke it. She was a grown woman and was capable of making her own decisions. As I interacted with Ricky and his family, I observed that they differed from any family I knew. I hadn't made up my mind if it was a good thing or a bad thing. As time went on, I met more and more of Ricky's family, friends, and neighbors. It gave me a sense of how he had grown up and how different his childhood was from mine.

His family was not devout Christians as my family was. They did go to church sometimes, but it was not on a regular basis like my family. Through all of what I had already been through and the things I had done, I lost touch with my relationship with God. In those days, I didn't even think about God very much anymore. I am so grateful that He did not forget about me. I still had that solid foundation lying dormant inside me. The one my parents laid out for me when they raised me. In the time to come, I would need it and appreciate it.

Anger

Ricky and I started looking for work. It was not an easy thing to do, but we had to try in order to receive our unemployment checks. Life was hard, and Ricky and I started to have some predictable problems. He seemed to be getting angry over everything. I wasn't in control of what was happening in our lives, but his anger was misdirected at me as though I was. One day, we left his parent's home, and he took me for a ride on an out-of-the-way back road that I had never been on before. He started to argue with me over something I knew nothing of. He was so mad that I started to get very afraid of what he might do. Even though he had promised me, he would never display the type of violent behavior that he had exposed me to that night at the club. I started to feel anxious. Then he told me what he was planning to do. He said that there was a lake nearby and that he was going to take me there and drown me. I started to cry because I didn't understand what was happening or what I had done to him to make him even think about doing something so horrible to me.

That day, I was reintroduced to the "Real Ricky." A Ricky that I had only met once. I forgave him for punching me in my stomach and believed him when he said he would never do it again. The one who declared his undying love for me and declared he could not live without me was now threatening to kill me. I was so upset and afraid that I felt I needed to take him at his word. I believed that he was capable of doing exactly as he said he would because I had experienced that anger before. I was trying to decide what I should do as I tried to get him to tell me why he wanted to do this terrible thing to me. He just kept right on saying he was going to drown me. I didn't understand where this madness was coming from. I just made up my mind that I had to do something extreme to save my life. I felt that there was only one thing I could do. I was so desperate and frightened that I opened the car door while he was driving down the road and jumped out. I don't know what speed he was driving at the time. All I knew was that I had to escape him to save my life. I know that it was the "Grace of God" that took care of me that day. I'm telling you that I should not be here right now.

When Ricky realized that I had jumped out of the car, he stopped quickly and came running to see if I was ok. I was screaming and crying at the top of my lungs. No one could see or hear me. We were in an area where there was no one around. I had never been so afraid in my life; knowing that my husband had made me so scared that, out of desperation, I had jumped out of a moving car was too much to bear. I had bumps and bruises and a big gash on the back of my head. It was a miracle that I didn't break bones or lose my life from the ill-advised action I took by jumping out of a moving vehicle.

He apologized and said that he loved me while promising that he would not threaten or hurt me again, as he was fumbling trying to pick me up off the ground. I couldn't comprehend the reasoning behind why he was threatening my life in the first place. I no longer believed him because I had heard that same song before. For here I was in fear for my life, banged up because I thought he was capable of killing me. His actions were very troubling to me, and it would take a lot on his part to convince me not to leave him. We had only been married for a couple of months, and he was acting a fool over who knows what. In my head, I reviewed the teachings of God, my faith, and my vows, "For better or worse." This was most definitely the worst. I felt those vows were binding, and I had to adhere to them no matter what.

It took some doing, but I managed to find it in my heart to forgive him again. I have never been the type of woman who gives up easily. I found out later that he was so jealous that all it would take to set him off was a man to look at me or speak to me. But I was the one who had to deal with his anger as though it was my fault that a man decided to look at me. I know you may be saying to yourself that what Ricky did to me would have been enough for you to leave, but that is not always an easy thing to do. Circumstances can stop you from doing what you know is right. I was trying to be the one who took the high road by forgiving him. I searched for a way to help my husband see that he had no reason to worry. I wanted him to know that I was devoted to him and I was not looking for another man. One man in my life was plenty. We went back home, and he continuously doted on me to regain my confidence and trust in him again. His family was not aware of what he had put me through. I kept my mouth shut because of humiliation.

He knew what he had done was wrong, and he kept on apologizing until he got me back to where he wanted me. My mind was filled with doubt and fear, and asking myself if I was taking this thing as seriously as I should. He had already proven to me that he could hurt me. Did I want to spend my life with a man that I could not trust to keep me safe, not even from himself? I did not know what to do, but I was now thinking more about my faith in God and what I was taught to believe. Marriage has its ups and downs, but was being abused one of the downs? I could not answer that question. I did not know enough about the Bible to make sense of making and keeping a lifelong vow to someone no matter what they did to me. I didn't know what chapter in the Bible could explain how to survive whatever came my way. I didn't believe that God's Word sanctioned a husband beating his wife. There must be something in the Bible that could help me with this dilemma, but I sure didn't know what it was and where to find it.

CHAPTER 5
THE BEAT GOES ON

It took a while for us to find new jobs. Everywhere we went, no one was hiring. But we had to keep trying because Ricky's unemployment money was about to run out. We went to a meat processing plant, The House of Raeford, in our community. Just so happened that they were hiring, and we both got hired that day. We had to get physical exams before starting work because they produced food. After completing all of their requirements to be employed, they issued the equipment we would need for our jobs. We were told what day and time to report to work. I got a job working on the meat cutting line. It was always very cold in that department because the meat had to stay at a certain temperature. I loathed being cold, but I had to endure it. My job required me to work quickly and correctly to keep the line moving even though I was freezing. Ricky and I were trying to save enough money so that we could purchase our own mobile home. He got a job transferring finished products with a hand jack to and from the freezer. I don't remember exactly how it happened, but after a couple of weeks of working on the cutting line, I was transferred to the box department. There, my job was putting together boxes for the finished product to be placed in for shipment. It was great that I was now working in a warm place. I remember some envious talk amongst my coworkers about my being transferred to the box department after only working there for a few weeks. I didn't let it get me down because I was so happy not to be working in the cold anymore; I didn't care what they thought.

Ricky and I were progressing in saving our money to move out of his parent's home. I was looking forward to having a place of our own again and the privacy and freedom it would afford us. We thought our finances were stable enough to start looking for our new home, but we did not have the credit to buy a house. After a few months, we finally had enough money to make the down payment on a new mobile home. His parents offered to help us by co-signing with us so we could buy our very first home together. We went to a Mobile Home Dealer located in my hometown. We found a two-bedroom that we liked. So, we started the process of purchasing our new home. His parents co-signed, and we finally had it. The next thing on our agenda was to find a mobile home park to live in because we did not own land to put it on. Just so happened we found a lot available about three miles from his parent's home, so we rented it. It was a small lot, only a few feet of yard, front and back, but it gave us everything we needed to have electricity and water hooked up to our home. Satisfied with where we would be living in the foreseeable future, we notified the mobile home dealer where to deliver our home.

Moving day came. The Dealer brought our home to our lot and set it up. We were delighted to be moving out of his parent's house at long last. I set out to put our past behind us and start anew. Months went by as we settled into a new life, but I always kept how jealous Ricky was in the back of my mind, and I carried myself accordingly to keep peace in my home. We were happy together as long as Ricky didn't feel threatened by anyone, but I lost myself in his world of insecurities. I was starting to give up little pieces of myself to feed them. Trying to keep him satisfied was at the top of my list of things to do. But it should not have been that way. My quality of life was important, too. But to reassure him of the resilience of our relationship, I put my wants and needs on the back burner and put his first. It seemed to work because he behaved as a husband should: loving, caring, and attentive. I should never have been made to feel that there was something wrong with me, having to change who I was to please him to keep from being hit. I was not the cause of why he allowed himself to become so indignant that he would ultimately lose all self-control. I was the woman he fell in love with. But because of his low self-esteem, I had to acclimate myself to who he needed me to be for him to feel validated as a man.

Don't ever decrease yourself to increase others. God fearfully and wonderfully made you, and He does not make mistakes. He intended for you to be who he created you to be, for His purpose, not man's. Some people will try to force a metamorphosis of who you are for their gratification. Violent, dysfunctional people are very needy and will do whatever it takes to feel what they consider to be normal (or what they think is normal), including raking you over hot coals, if that is what it takes.

Work was work. We sometimes worked long hours. But I was very appreciative that we could pay our bills and take care of ourselves. At work one day, someone from Human Resources came to the box department and told me that I needed to go to the office upfront. When I got there, I saw a familiar face. It was Linda, a distant cousin and friend of my family. She told me to take a seat and began talking to me about her job. She worked in Quality Control, and she recommended me for a vacant position in her department. She told me that she would train me in everything I needed to know. She described all the things I would be responsible for. It sounded like a job I could do. It was better than working in the box department. When she asked me if I wanted the job, of course, I said yes. It was a job that put me into a leadership position and a higher pay grade. When I got off work that day, I told Ricky what had happened, and he was happy for me because it meant a much-needed infusion of money into our finances. I finished out the week in the box department. I did not say anything about my new position to anyone because I remembered how upset some of my coworkers got over my transfer to the box department. As I think of it now, Linda may have had something to do with that, too. She held a high-ranking position, and she might have used her influence to get me transferred to the box department.

New Job, New Problems

Monday came, and I reported to Quality Control to begin my training. Linda gave me a clipboard with some papers attached and a white coat to wear that said "Quality Control" on it. When we walked out into the plant, I got some not-so-nice looks and comments. But I expected that because normally, it would take employees months to be in the position that I now held. I was determined to do my best to learn everything I needed to know to show Linda that I appreciated the confidence she had shown in me. She took me to all the different departments we were responsible for ensuring that all the quality control (USDA) standards were being followed. She introduced me to the supervisors and leaders I would be closely working with. Part of my job was to check the quality of the products being produced and correct it if the standard was not being met by informing the supervisor of what I had found. I learned all I could until one day, Linda sent me out on my own. As I walked out to the plant floor, I got a lot of ugly looks, eyes being rolled, tongues wagging. But I had a job to do. And I did not want to let Linda down.

In my new job, I had to talk to people, male and female. I did not forget that Ricky got upset when he would see me talking with a man because of his unrelenting jealousy. We didn't see each other much because I was constantly on the go and worked in several different departments. I was enjoying my new position and the freedom I had in performing my duties. My days were happy ones. Ricky and I were not only enjoying our new home and each other, we were blessed enough to be working in the same place at the same time. I thought that was a wonderful thing because we only had one car. My automobile had been repossessed. I could not make the payments. Working in separate places would have caused a transportation problem.

One afternoon, I was on my way to the freezer, and a guy came up alongside me. We innocently started to talk as we walked down to the freezer. He was not saying anything out of the way to me. It was a normal conversation between two human beings. On my way, I passed Ricky in the hallway just as I was laughing at a silly joke the guy had just told me. His facial expression made me recognize that it was about to be on again. I felt safe for the moment because I didn't believe he would attack me while we were at work and in front of witnesses. I continued to the freezer to do my quality checks. I was nervous and afraid, but I tried not to show it. When I returned to the main floor, Ricky came over to me and leaned over to whisper, "I need to talk to you." I knew that I was once again in trouble. We were next to one of the shipping docks, so we walked outside where there were no eyes on us. He demanded to know what I was saying to the guy he saw me speaking to. I told him that it was nothing specific. The guy made a joke, and I laughed at what he said. Before I could get the words out of my mouth, I felt the first blow. The pain weakened me in the knees while he repeatedly hit me. Finally, he stopped. I think someone had walked outside, and he didn't want anyone to see him hurting me, so he quickly walked off and left me reeling in pain. I couldn't believe that he would do this to me again. And, making matters worse, he was doing it at our job site. I straightened up, attempted to pull myself together as best I could, and went back to the office, trying not to show my tears. Linda saw me and asked me what was wrong and what had happened to me. I began to cry even more and admitted that my husband had seen me laughing and talking with a guy I didn't even know, and he beat me up for it. She got so upset that she went and found the floor manager and told him what had happened. The manager then went and found Ricky and fired him on the spot, and told him to vacate the premises. Linda told me what the manager had done. This left me with no transportation to get home. At the end of my shift, the manager found me to tell me that he would have to lay me off. He couldn't fire me for doing something against company policy because I had done nothing wrong. He wanted to get rid of me because of what Ricky had done. So he used his ability to lay me off to get rid of me. I was being punished for being a victim of domestic violence, which was so unfair. Not only did I get humiliated at my workplace, but I also lost my job on top of it. I went and got my belongings and walked out to the parking lot, not knowing how I would get home. Suddenly, Ricky drove up beside me and asked me to get in the car. I was so hurt and embarrassed by what he had done to me that I couldn't stop crying. Plus, I was afraid that he might hurt me again. Yeah, you guessed it. He started telling me how sorry he was for hurting me the way that he did. But he couldn't stand to see me talking to another man. I didn't want to hear any more of his empty apologies. I already knew that they were only temporary; what he said meant nothing. The credibility of his apologies was preposterous. They only lasted until the next time he got angry. I had no other choice but to get into the car with him so I could go home, hoping I would be safe. After we got home, he proceeded to beg and plead for my forgiveness, promising that he wouldn't do it again. Shaking my head, I told him, "You are not the only one who lost a job today. The plant manager laid me off because of what you did to me." One minute, we both had jobs, the next minute, we were both unemployed again because of his insane jealousy. We had only been in our new home for a few months, and now we were in danger of losing it. He couldn't sign up for unemployment because he had gotten fired. And I couldn't sign up because I had not worked long enough to qualify for unemployment again. Not only did I have to worry about what would set him off next, but now, I also had to worry about how we were going to pay our bills and feed and clothe ourselves.

Food Insecurity

The area that we lived in was surrounded by farmland, and corn was growing nearby. I don't like admitting this, but things got so bad that Ricky would go out late at night and help himself to some of the corn growing near us so that we could have something to eat. This happened quite often, I'm ashamed to say. His parents helped out whenever they could. They still had their younger children to feed. Ricky would work odd jobs now and then when he could get them. Sometimes, his older siblings helped us out by giving us some of their food stamps. It was hardly enough to get us by. I know you are probably asking yourself, "What about her family? Where are they?" Well, my dad did not know anything about what we were going through. I very seldom saw or talked to my family anymore. I was ashamed and embarrassed by what I allowed Ricky to do to me. I didn't want my daddy to know that my marriage was disintegrating; it would prove to him that I was a failure. I was living in a way that I did not grow up in, and with everything else that was going on in my life, I didn't want to deal with the disappointment my dad would have in me because I married an abusive man that I barely knew, no less. It would be thoroughly frustrating to him to know these things were happening to me; at least, that's what I thought. I could have been wrong in my assessment of him. Maybe I wasn't protecting him but watching out for myself. I did not need another source of pressure.

Trauma Drama

We were holding on by the Grace of God. Every day was a difficult challenge. So, when Ricky came home and told me his young nieces wanted to come over and spend the night with us, I took it as a welcomed distraction from our complicated life. They had come to visit his parents and wanted to spend some time with him. I didn't have a problem with it. His family had done so much for us that I couldn't say no. He went to pick them up and brought them over. I had only heard Ricky's stories about them while he spent some time at their home in another state. I was introduced to them; then we chatted for a while. After a time, he left me alone with them to take care of something I could only assume he thought was important. I had the task of entertaining people I had just met. I suggested to them that we go for a walk through the mobile home park. It was a nice sunny day outside. The park we lived in was set up like a horseshoe. A person could ride through the entire park and come back out to the highway on the other side. The park manager lived in the first space on the same side that we lived on. There was also a swimming pool for the residents and a phone booth located at the front of the park. I thought it would be a pleasant walk if we went up to the highway and back. We chatted about the park and their lives where they lived. We even started to joke with each other as if we were old friends. As we walked by a man working on his car in his yard, I made a frivolous joke by suggesting to the oldest teenager that he was the kind of man she needed to be looking for. We all had a good laugh about it. When we got to the highway, we turned around and headed back to my house. Upon returning home, I asked them to excuse me for a few minutes, and I would be right back. I left them alone in the living room. The next thing I knew, Ricky came busting into our bedroom out of his mind with anger. I wasn't aware that he had returned home. He grabbed me and threw me on our bed. Neither did I know that his oldest niece had lied to him and told him that we had taken a walk up the street and that I had been flirting with the man that we had joked about. I never even said a word to the man. I didn't know him. But Ricky believed what his niece said. I still don't understand why she lied about me to him. He put his knees on my arms to pin me down, sat on my stomach, and began to punch me in my face with both his fists over and over again as though he was working out on a punching bag. I was so traumatized by what was happening to me that I just prayed for the pain to stop. I struggled to get him off me. I screamed and cried so much that my face started to burn from the salt in my tears running down into the bruises on my face. Finally, he came to his senses and let me up, but not before he had struck me so many times that the pain from the punches sent me into hysterics. I was screaming and hollering, trying desperately to understand why he had committed this horrendous act. That's when he told me what that child had said about me. I couldn't believe that she had told such an appalling lie. I knew how crazy my husband got when he even thought that a man was looking at me. I would not have done such a foolish thing like that in the first place. He should have realized that, especially with witnesses to tell him what I had done. I did not enjoy getting beat up. He never even stopped to think. He just acted on what she said and never doubted her. He didn't even bother to ask me about it; he just acted on what she said. I was faithful to him even though he did not trust me. I had never given him a reason not to trust me, but that didn't stop anything. I don't know if another woman had been unfaithful to him and I was being judged by what she had done to him or not. I couldn't make sense of it in my head. Of course, when he stopped and realized what he had done to me, he started trying to hug me, saying he was so sorry that he had let himself get so out of control. Once again, I didn't want to hear it. He acted as though he could not control himself, as though someone else made him do those awful things. I was disgraced and humiliated knowing that those girls had heard the whole confrontation between Ricky and me while sitting quietly in my living room. I told him to get them out of my house right now, still crying while my face felt like it was on fire. I had only tried to be a good hostess to them. That's what I get for being kind to strangers. After he left with the girls, I lightly touched my face and realized it was badly swollen, so I walked to the bathroom to look in the mirror. I could not believe what I was seeing. I was stunned that I did not recognize myself at all. My face was bruised, red, and swollen so much that I didn't even know who that person was in the mirror staring back at me. I lost it again, even though my tears caused me intense pain. To think that the man who claimed that he loved me had beat me to a pulp for something I had not done. I was so hurt and felt so low that I had to admit that I was married to an undeniable sociopathic psychotic abuser. I didn't have a phone to call anyone for help. The only phone I could use was the one located at the front of the park. That was out of the question. I was too mortified to let anyone see me like that. I couldn't stand looking at myself. I'm sure I needed medical attention. But all I could do was get in bed, ball up into the fetal position, and sob uncontrollably. After I sat up in bed, the pain in my face was so excruciating, like it was on fire, that I could hardly bear it. To cool it off, I went back to the bathroom, got a washcloth, and put cold water on it, gently pressing it to my face to try and put out the burning flames that consumed it. The relief was only temporary. I had to continue the process to ease the pain.

This was the worst beating Ricky had ever given me. I no longer thought or even hoped that this would ever end. I believed that there was no help for me. I put myself in this situation when I didn't take heed to that very first red flag that went up and the ones that followed. I ignored it and trusted him when he told me he would never hit me again. He was untrustworthy, along with all the empty words that came out of his mouth. This man had no understanding of how to love a woman or what the word love even meant in the first place. Inflicting pain was his way of showing love. I cannot account for his understanding of what a loving relationship consists of. Somewhere along the way, he learned this behavior from someone, and he emulated it without examination of what he was doing or empathy for the person he inflicted that behavior upon, which was me.

In the days and weeks ahead, I began to drift into depression. I was so paranoid about anyone seeing me that I would run to my bedroom and close the door when someone would knock on my front door. I was at home alone a few days after the incident when Ricky's mother came by. She had found out what he had done to me somehow. Perhaps his nieces had told her when he took them back to his parent's house. She wanted to see for herself and to make sure I was alright. I peeped through the curtain and saw it was her. I was humiliated but reluctantly opened the door out of respect for her being my mother-in-law and let her in. The look on her face was unmistakable how shocked she was when she looked at me. I couldn't help it; I started to weep. No one had seen me for days except Ricky. She told me she didn't understand what in the world was wrong with him and that she was sorry for what he had done to me. She spent some time with me, just talking to take my mind off my situation for a little while. Then she left, and my mind returned to thinking about what my life had become. What my pure existence had become. Is this what our marriage would be like for the rest of our lives? Will Ricky continue to abuse me? Will I be able to withstand it? I had no answers to any of those questions. My mind was flooded with unanswerable questions about my future. Did I even have a decent future ahead of me, one that did not include violence? Judging from Ricky's past behavior, things did not look optimistic. The road of domestic violence is littered with fear and questions about what will happen if I tell someone. Should I give up and allow myself to be molded into this spineless, self-loathing human being with no control over the violence being perpetrated against me? Can I escape without retaliation, or can I live in this world, hoping it will change one day? My mental stability was suffering, and I could not see any way of doing anything about it; I was paralyzed.

CHAPTER 6
SIMPLY LOST

Something changed in me after that last beating. I felt like less than a human being who no longer had the right to choose what happened to her. For it to be my husband doing the hitting grieved me to the point that all I was concerned about was getting through the punches, the chokeholds, being slammed up against the wall, and being abused verbally. It kept happening over and over again without any hesitancy from him. I became someone I didn't even know anymore. What happened to that wise, intelligent, independent, beautiful woman I used to be? I lost her somewhere along the way. She retreated to the background because she couldn't deal with the departure of her self-esteem and self-worth, with the right to live her life without being threatened with pain. She could no longer demand respect as a living being, which fed her diminishing capacity for self-confidence. This new person that emerged just wanted to keep her head down, watch what she said, and stay as far away from the opposite sex as possible to keep her husband happy. I could no longer contemplate my happiness. That was a word that had lost all meaning to me. My pursuit of happiness was to stay alive from day to day.

According to a Google search, www.MedicalNewsToday.com, battered woman syndrome, or battered person syndrome, is a psychological condition that can develop when a person experiences abuse, usually at the hands of an intimate partner. People who find themselves in an abusive relationship often do not feel safe or happy. However, they may feel unable to leave for many reasons. These include fear and a belief that they are the cause of the abuse.

Symptoms: according to the NCADV article, "Dynamics of Abuse," a person experiencing abuse may:

- Feel isolated, anxious, depressed, or helpless
- Be embarrassed or fear judgment and stigmatization
- Love the person who is abusing them and believe that they will change
- Be emotionally withdrawn
- Deny that anything is wrong or excuse the other person
- Be unaware of the type of help that is available
- Have perceived moral or religious reasons for staying in the relationship

The person may also behave in ways that can be difficult for people outside the relationship to understand.

These behaviors include:

- Refusing to leave the relationship
- Believing that the other person is powerful or knows everything
- When things are calm, idealizing the person who carried out the abuse believing that they deserve the abuse

I was a perfect example of battered woman syndrome. I had almost all of the symptoms. At the time I was living in the midst of what was being executed against me, I was emotionally unaware of the criminality of it all. I could have had him arrested if I was convinced that I would receive justice. Back then, the law did not take domestic violence seriously enough. I was so messed up that I felt that if I reached out for help, I would end up hurting him. And I cared so much for him that I could not bring myself to do it. It sounds so ridiculous right now. But there were times I could have picked up something and hit him hard enough to hurt him. But it was not in me to do that. I couldn't do to him what he was doing to me; my heart would not let me.

My immediate attention was on the problem of being unemployed. It was easier to combat than what was physically happening to me. Our bills continued to mount and got further and further behind. My mother-in-law mentioned that there was a position open where she worked if I was interested. It was a janitorial position at a nearby high school. It was a way to bring some financial support to my situation, so I went to apply and got the position. It wasn't a job that I would have picked for myself, but times were hard, and we needed the money. I reported to work after school was out each weekday. I cleaned classrooms and bathrooms and swept hallways. I worked with several of Ricky's family members, neighbors, and friends. They treated me very well and were so friendly that I felt welcomed. We joked and laughed as we did our work, which helped me feel at ease with them. I had come to enjoy and appreciate their friendship very much. It was nice to be around people who helped me forget, even for a little while, that I was an abused woman who was constantly in physical and mental pain.

I was working in one of the classrooms that I had been assigned to clean when suddenly, in walks Ricky. He was upset over something again. By this time in our relationship, there was always something he was angry about. I realized that Ricky wasn't always angry with me. He was mad and disappointed in himself. He took his anger out on me. It no longer mattered what he was upset about. It was hard to keep up with all the absurd excuses he came up with for hurting me.

He walked right up to me and punched me dead in the stomach so hard that I screamed. It scared him so much that it made him flee the premises. There was no conversation about why he was there or why he hit me. I was always the person he knew he could lash out at without retribution. Apparently, he decided it was not a good idea to hit me in the face anymore because it would be too visible. This way, no one would see my bruises. My coworkers came running to see what had happened. But when my mother-in-law heard me scream, she already knew what had happened because she had seen Ricky frantically searching for me. They consoled me as best they could as I wept. I was devastated and ashamed for them to see firsthand the terrible things my husband did to me. I'm sure they had heard about it but had never witnessed it for themselves. I sat down for a while to wait for the pain to subside because I still had work to do. Our bills still needed to be paid, and we needed to eat.

I don't even know why I was attacked at that time. But I remember the pain and the embarrassment I felt as though it happened yesterday. I felt totally defeated. No matter what I did or what I didn't do, I always got blamed for something. The expectations I had for my life seemed so far out of reach. My life seemed like a natural disaster, with no first responders coming to rescue me. It was difficult to manage, but I finished my workday and returned home. Another abusive event to add to the mounting list of beatings in my daily life. I had to bury it deep inside to hold on to my sheer sanity. After getting home, I did what I always did: I forgave him.

Bait and Switch

Ricky was still trying to find some work when he was visiting with some of his friends. They told him that they were gathering pine straw onto a truck and taking it to a nearby town to sell for use in landscaping. So he joined them. The money wasn't bad. It allowed us to get some of our financial responsibilities settled, and we could finally afford some decent food. Sometimes, we lived as an average married couple dealing with ordinary problems that did not provoke so much anger that it led to punches. It almost seemed as though the abuse was dormant at those times. I would enjoy the good times as best I could because I knew from experience that it would not be that way for long.

With the incredible amount of crushing disappointments that filled my life, you would think that I had enough going on not to have more added to the pile of problems I was trying to tackle. But when it rains, it pours. After work one day, Ricky sat me down and explained to me how he needed some space. Life was not what he had expected it to be, and he needed some time to "find himself." I didn't understand what was happening, and I still don't know why I agreed to his request. Maybe I wanted to get away from him. Perhaps I saw it as a reprieve from the prison I had been sentenced to. I had made so many bad choices; what's one more? He asked me to stay with his parents for a while until he could get himself together. Being that my mental stamina had been beaten to a pulp, I didn't even realize that there was a reason for his request. I didn't fight him because I hoped this would be a turning point in our marriage. With every new shift in our relationship, I would try to look at it as a possible change for the better. Maybe with a temporary separation from each other, he would realize that our relationship was important to him, and we could grow closer and live our lives without the violence. I kept looking for that door that would lead me to a solution that would solve my problems. At the very least, I could get a break from the violence.

Because his parents had co-signed for our home, he believed it belonged to him. He didn't even consider that we were married and that I paid part of the down payment and helped make the monthly payments. Stupidly, I did what he asked me. And I went to live with his parents for a while. Ricky had our car. So I needed transportation to and from work. So I rode with his mother. After I went to stay with his parents, days went by that I didn't see or hear from Ricky. It was a relief not to worry about the next time I would get punched. But it was also disturbing. He figured he didn't have to worry about me being unfaithful because I was always around his family. After a couple of weeks went by, my gut feeling told me something was wrong. Thinking about what could be happening in my home made me angry. My imagination planted all kinds of ideas about what he was up to in my head. I decided to find out for myself. I didn't have any transportation, so I walked to my house. When I got there, Ricky wasn't there. I walked through it, looking around. I went to the bedroom, searching for any sign of another woman being in my house. And then, for some reason, I opened my closet door. Lo and behold, dirty clothes were lying on the floor, and amongst the clothes was a bra that was not mine. My gut instinct was right; there was something wrong. He didn't need to find himself. He just wanted to move his girlfriend into our home while he put me on the back burner just in case things did not work out with her. I cannot express the anger that rose up in me. Here I am, trusting him and getting beat up every time he even thought a man was paying attention to me. I waited for a while, hoping he would come home, but no such luck. I don't know what I expected to do to him if he had come back while I was there. All I could think about was getting my hands on the woman who had the nerve to be sleeping with my husband in my bed in my house. But subconsciously, I knew it wasn't her fault. All the blame belonged to Ricky. Women often get things twisted and blame the wrong individual for their husband's or boyfriend's infidelity. She didn't do any more than he allowed her to do. He was the one who was supposed to be loyal to me, not her. I ended up walking back to his parent's house, furious. As I walked, I was wishing I had caught him there with that chick in my house. I went back several times trying to do just that until one day, I did catch Ricky at home. But the side piece wasn't there. That was a good thing, probably for me. More than likely, he would have beat me up in front of her for interfering in what he considered his business. I told Ricky that I was no longer paying for a home that I wasn't living in. He denied that he had been sleeping with another woman in our home. Telling lies was Ricky's way out of everything. The only proof I had was a dirty bra in my closet, but it was all the verification I needed.

By this time, most people would assume that I had enough sense to leave him. Mainly because of the abuse he put me through for just thinking I might be cheating on him. When, in reality, he was cheating on me. Yet, I still kept on trying to make my marriage work. Even when I considered it, I could not walk away. I couldn't do it. I felt like I didn't have a life without him.

After that occurrence, I knew that he had probably been cheating on me the whole time, even before I left to live with his family. That was why he would get so upset when he thought I was seeing someone else. He was afraid that he was going to reap what he had sown. I had to give my marriage the best chance I could because I made a vow to him, for better or worse. And I forgave him once again. There was something inside of me that would not allow me to stop trying. I wanted to believe that it could work between us and somehow, we would figure it out. I eventually moved back to my home and tried to get our relationship back on track.

There were more times that I suspected that Ricky was cheating, but I couldn't prove it. I don't know what I would have done if I had been able to prove it. I wanted so much for us to be a regular couple, but the chances of that happening in our foreseeable future were an illusion on my part. I don't know what kind of relationship Rickey thought he was in. If I went by his actions, I would have to conclude that he thought he was a single man "sowing his wild oats," as it has been said. If you think about it, what did he need me for? I was in the way of him doing whatever he pleased with whomever he pleased. Why put me through the hell I was going through? He could have been a free man without the excess baggage of having a wife. It was illogical for him to stay married, living his life as he did, unless he saw me as his possession, something that he owned, and not seeing me as a human being with feelings and emotions that he could destroy. I don't believe he gave that any thought. It was how things were, and that was that. He was not the one being hurt, so what did he care?

Just a Pawn in a Chess Game

Our daily life was predictably dysfunctional. There was no way to call the deteriorated state of our relationship a thriving marriage. We were so far past it that it was almost laughable. He proceeded to actively have adulterous affairs with other women despite the possible effect on me. I was not in control of anything, not even myself. I spent a sizable amount of time alone. Ricky always had somewhere he needed to be. I kept on being the wife he did not deserve. Shirley would come by sometimes, and we would go shopping or visit some of her neighbors and friends. I did not think that Ricky had a problem with me being with his sister, but upon returning home one day, he was in our backyard, burning all my clothes and make-up. I couldn't believe this man. His jealousy had gone to the extreme. I jumped out of the car and ran over to him to find out why he burned my clothes. I only had a few decent things to wear. The response I got from him was that I looked too good in them, and he did not want other men looking at me. Is that not the craziest thing you have ever heard? It was impossible to live my life without a man looking at me. I had no control over that. I might as well be locked in a prison, and even then, I could not avoid being looked at by someone. I tried to reassure him that I was not interested in being with other men. He was my husband, and no one could change that. Shaking her head, Shirley returned to her car and left to go home. Ricky apologized for what he had done, saying that he knew it was stupid, but he was afraid he would lose me to someone else, while in reality, simultaneously, he was sleeping around every chance he got. It boggles my mind because it was okay for him to cheat but not for me to do the same. You would think that if he wanted to be with me so badly, he would let go of his ridiculous behavior and be my husband. We could live together without all the drama he created in our life. He wanted it all, no matter who it hurt. It is easier to inflict pain than to be on the receiving end of it. We must all remember that "you reap what you sow." Sooner or later, it will all catch up with you. Some people live as though they believe that rule applies to everyone except them. I'm here to tell you that I am a living witness that it is true; you have been warned.

Oh No He Didn't!

Months later, I started having some minor pain in my lower abdomen. I didn't think much of it at first. As the days passed, the pain increased in intensity, but I still thought it was inconsequential. Soon, the pain became unbearable; I could hardly stand up straight or walk well. It got so bad that I ended up in the emergency room. The doctor examined me and ordered some tests. Sitting on the examining table, waiting in horrible pain for my results, I wondered what now? I was afraid of what the doctor would say. Was this so bad that I would have to be admitted to the hospital for something threatening my life? After a few moments of waiting in fear, the nurse walked in with the longest needle I had ever seen. She informed me that I had been exposed to chlamydia. I had no idea what she was talking about. She explained that it was a sexually transmitted disease that I had gotten from the person or persons I had been having sex with, and that was only Ricky. That person got it from a person that they had sex with. She asked me who I had been sexually active with. I told her my husband and only my husband. Being a woman herself, she wanted to make sure that I understood that it was because of my "husband" that I had chlamydia. Then she progressed to give me a shot in both my thighs. The pain was so bad that I had to clench my teeth as the tears rolled out the corner of my eyes. I hung my head in shame for having to admit to a total stranger that my husband was cheating on me and that he had passed on a venereal disease to me. She gave me some pills for him to get rid of the infection and warned me not to have sex with him until the infection had cleared up.

Of course, you know that I was livid by the time I got home. Cheating on me behind my back was bad enough, but not protecting himself and me while doing it was complete lunacy. He tried to deny it, but getting chlamydia was an undeniable consequence of his having sex with other women. I gave him the pills the nurse gave me, instructed him on how to take them, and told him what the nurse said about how I got the disease. There was nothing left to be said. The truth was that he cheated, and there was no way he could convince me otherwise. I knew that I had not been having sex with anyone but him. I withheld sex from him for a long time. I was frustrated by the position he put me in. His constant deceitful attitude was driving me up the wall.

Marriage is not supposed to be a battle. We were not on separate sides; we were part of the same team; we were one, but I was always left on the sideline waiting to get in the game. I felt like I was his second choice, possibly his third, fourth, or fifth. I was determined not to give him the forgiveness he always sought after he knowingly did wrong. It was like I didn't know that I had a choice. No matter how much he hurt me, in my weakness, I gave in to him; I hated myself for being so weak. I know: I was young, dumb, and stupid, trying to make something work that wasn't. I can't explain to you why I kept on forgiving him for all the terrible things he did to me. I loved him, and I believed that we could be successful if we worked concurrently. I could not find it in me to quit. I kept thinking that it was possible that things could change; he could change. I wanted it to happen so badly that I put aside all the bad and concentrated on the minuscule amount of good that existed between us, losing sight of his latest atrocious debacle. I confess that I didn't have a complete and clear understanding of what getting chlamydia could do to my body. This is what I found out later on.

According to Google search, if not treated, **chlamydia can lead to damage to the reproductive system. In women, chlamydial infection can spread to the uterus or fallopian tubes and cause pelvic inflammatory disease (PID), according to the CDC. PID can damage the fallopian tubes and uterus and cause chronic pain, infertility, and ectopic pregnancy.**

After the Pain

Summer came, and the school closed down for summer vacation. Unemployed once again. There were no jobs, and Ricky had run out of places to gather pine straw to sell. It was looking like we were going to lose our home. We both tried to find work, but the economy was in a free fall. Weeks later, I got concerned about my health again because my period had come on and had not stopped. I put off going to a doctor because I could not afford to see one without insurance. After weeks of continuous flow, I had no choice; I went to see a doctor. He examined me and told me that I had probably had a miscarriage and needed to have a D&C to rid my body of anything that may have remained in my uterus. I was shocked because I had no symptoms that indicated that I was pregnant. Maybe I wasn't pregnant for long, or I was so stressed out that I was oblivious to what my body was saying to me until I noticed that my flow was not stopping as it should. When it wouldn't stop, I knew I had to do something before I bled out.

According to Google search, (Dilatation and Curettage, D&C), a dilation and curettage procedure, also called a D&C, is a surgical procedure in which the cervix (the lower, narrow part of the uterus) is dilated (expanded) so that the uterine lining (endometrium) can be scraped with a curette (spoon-shaped instrument) to remove abnormal tissues.

I was directed to the hospital to have the procedure done. I hadn't even processed what the doctor said to me. I was pregnant and had lost it. I had no clue that I was pregnant; I felt guilty that I was not aware I was a mom again, if only for a little while. I remembered that after the abortion, I told myself that perhaps when I conceived again, I would be a married woman, but this was not what I expected to happen. I didn't know how to feel about that. I wasn't ready to be a single mom with my first pregnancy, and being married did not make a difference this time because of all the cheating and abuse. How do I know that Ricky didn't cause my miscarriage? I was hit so much that I could not determine if that was possible or not. Anyway, it was an outpatient procedure, and after a few hours, I was released to go home. I was sad, but I also knew in my heart that bringing a baby into our marriage would not be a suitable environment for a child, and we were at such a low point in our lives that we would not have been able to support him or her. We couldn't take care of ourselves. I don't think it mattered to Ricky that I was pregnant and had lost it. It did not seem to affect him at all. I can only believe that it was not meant to be. I may never know the reason I lost my baby. It could have been a blessing that I did not yet understand. God's will is God's will; there is no way of getting around that.

The Unexpected Announcement

Without my knowing what he was up to, Ricky went out alone one day. When he returned at the end of the day, he announced that he had enlisted in the US Army as a last resort to keep our home. It was already too late, though. We were more than three months behind in our payments, and later, our Mortgage Holder informed us that they were going to repossess our home for nonpayment of our loan. We held on as long as we could, but it was now time to let go. It was a bittersweet relief for me. All the bad memories I had of living in our home caused me to feel a little ambiguous. There were also a few happy times there too. Maybe we were entering a new season in our relationship. Maybe being apart would help to bring us closer together. You know that old saying, "Absence makes the heart grow fonder," but what they didn't say was that it takes two willing hearts to make that happen. I tried my best to hold on to sanguinity. I couldn't foresee that his absence would intensify the abuse.

Now, he would not be able to see what I was doing. I still hoped and prayed that things would get better for us with him joining the Army. I saw only what I so desperately wanted to see: a glimmer of hope. That hope kept a flickering light burning inside me that I refused to let go out.

CHAPTER 7
THE WINDS OF CHANGE

Ricky left for basic training, and I was left to deal with the repossessing of our home we had worked so hard for. After I took one last look at it, I went to live with his parents for a while. I no longer had a job, and they were so generous to share what they had with me. I spent a lot of time hanging out with his sister Shirley daily. I would ride with her whenever she needed to pay a bill or buy food. It was almost like she was a blood sister. When people saw her, more than likely, they also saw me too. The kids were outside playing as we were cooking one day. Looking at them having so much fun, giggling and laughing, I got up and decided to join in. They were jumping rope, so I jumped in, believing that I was as flexible as I used to be. As I was jumping rope, my foot landed sideways in a small hole in the ground, and I cracked my ankle. Everyone helped me back into the house to sit down. I didn't think it was anything serious until it started to swell. I was in the kitchen baking cookies when I noticed it. When Shirley saw how much my ankle had swollen, she insisted that she take me to the hospital, where they placed a cast on my foot and leg up to my knee. It took six weeks for my ankle to heal. Everyone was sympathetic to what had happened to me and took excellent care of me while

I recovered. I went back to the hospital as it was time for my cast to be removed. I was happy to get that thing off my leg. The itching was enough to drive someone crazy.

Weeks had gone by before I heard anything from Ricky. Despite all that had transpired between us, I still loved him, and I was getting worried about him. He called to let me know he was okay. He also let me know that after eight weeks of basic training, he would be coming home for a while before leaving to train for the job he had been assigned to in the Army. The day came when he returned home. He didn't look the same, but he still acted the same. During basic training, they pushed his mental stability to see just how much pressure he could take. He told me that they would say things like, "Jodie has got your girl and gone." They did not know that Ricky would take these types of statements literally. When he came home, he accused me of doing all kinds of things while he was away. The punching and hitting returned to my life. I was reliving a very familiar pattern that had plagued me for the past two years. I'm sad to say, but glad at the same time that I was looking forward to his leaving again. Getting beaten for things I did not do was brutal on me physically and mentally. It was a blessing when he left for his military training, and I got to go back to my life without the abuse.

I am an optimist; I wanted to believe it was possible that he could change. My faith had taught me that "With man this is impossible, but with God all things are possible" (Matthew 19:26). I knew it could happen, but would it happen? He contacted me to tell me that after his job training, he would be stationed in West Germany. The Army allowed him to come back home for a while before leaving the Country. When he returned, nothing in his attitude about me had changed. It was as though I had to be disciplined, like I was a little child, before he left for Germany. It was his way of threatening me for something I hadn't done yet. I was told I had better not do anything, or I would regret it. I didn't know how life would be after he went to his new duty station. At this point, all I wanted was freedom, and I didn't very much care how I got it. I was glad when he departed for Germany. I could now breathe a sigh of relief. I could let my guard down and not have to constantly be worried about what Ricky would confront me with next. I could finally return to being myself. It was an enormous life-changing moment for me. He was going somewhere he had never been, and I was being left behind, getting my freedom back for a few years. I was heartsick, if you can believe it, and excited at the same time. I needed this time away from him to recover from the chaos he caused in my life. When you have been abused, your thinking is flawed. I knew I needed therapy to help me process what had happened and realize that I did not have to accept the abuse in my life as though it was a regular part of a relationship. Back then, I could not ask for the kind of help I needed. People thought that you were crazy when you sought out mental help, but I must admit that I also thought I was crazy. I didn't want to feel the way that I did about him. I was embarrassed by my situation, so I put that "I'm okay" smile on my face and got on with the business of living my life as best I could. Interacting with family helped me feel a lot better. Somewhere along the way, I had lost my sense of feeling worthy of receiving love. Once I regained control of my life without Ricky, I felt like a dark cloud had been lifted off me. I was experiencing happiness that I had been missing out on for so long. I didn't fear being admired by a man who walked up to me and said hello anymore because I would not get beaten up for being an attractive woman. It felt wonderful to be seen as a sexy, beautiful, confident woman without the drama of an insecure, jealous husband threatening my life because of it. He must have forgotten that was what drew him to me in the first place, or maybe he didn't forget.

Separation

I didn't return to my job at school the following year. I thought it was time to be with my family. I asked my dad if I could move back home while Ricky was away. He welcomed me back. I was missing Ricky, but I also felt a sense of contentment. I was finally getting a well-deserved break from being beaten down and used as a punching bag. I did not confide in my dad or anyone in my family about my problems. I kept my dysfunctional life with Ricky a secret. I didn't want them to be upset or worried about me. And I surely did not want their judgment. My dad was getting on in age and had some health issues that he was dealing with. I couldn't add more to the full plate he already had before him. I did my part around the house, preparing meals and cleaning or whatever needed to be done.

Ricky was going to be gone for a long time, and I had every intention of remaining faithful to him. When he got to Germany, it was too expensive to make phone calls, so we wrote letters. I wrote to him, telling him how much I missed him. I would be over the moon when I received a letter from him. As time passed, I started to hear from him less and less until I stopped receiving communication from him altogether. I waited and waited, but nothing. I wrote to him but never received a response. I had no way of contacting him except through letters. I went into depression. I stopped eating and lost a lot of weight worrying about him when clearly he was not worried about me. It was like he had forgotten that I was alive. I didn't go anywhere or do anything except attend Church. After six months of waiting to hear from him, I got angry and made a decision. It was time to stop watching my life pass me by while I sat around, waiting to get any word from him I could. As far as I was concerned, I felt he was deliberately ignoring me. So, I took that as a sign that it was time for me to move on. There was something or someone in Germany occupying his time now. I wanted to get out and have some fun and enjoy life again. I had not been able to do that since I got married. Besides, I was young, black, and beautiful, and my life was at a standstill. I came to the resolution that Ricky had taken enough from me. I put on my glad rags and sought the nightlife again.

On the weekends, a girlfriend and I would hit the NCO Club on the post. I enjoyed music and dancing, having an occasional mixed drink or two, being around people, and not worrying about getting beat up for something I hadn't done. Moreover, as time passed, I started to feel and act like a single woman. Ricky had all but divorced me by not communicating with me at all; that's the way I saw it. Besides, he was going to be gone for years. I wasn't about to sit and wait to see what he would do when those years came to an end. There was absolutely nothing I could do about not receiving any correspondence from him. He was a world away, and he was living his life as he saw fit in Germany. I was here in the United States, not even aware that he could have taken me with him or at least sent for me later on. But neither of those things happened. I just couldn't see myself sitting home like the dutiful wife while he pretended that he didn't even have one. I am not trying to justify the things that followed my decision. I'm just telling you how it was and how it was about to be. It was wrong, and I knew that. But knowing it was wrong was not enough to stop me. I dated while Ricky was gone, and for a while there, I almost forgot that I was a married woman. It was pretty easy to do, especially not knowing anything about his life in Germany. All I knew was it didn't include me.

In The Streets Again

I put aside what I was taught growing up attending Church: how I was advised to take all my problems to the Lord in prayer. But I chose to lean on my understanding, which did not help me very much. I got further and further away from the teachings of Jesus and did whatever I felt like I was grown up enough to do. I did some things and went to some places that no one knew about but me. I even shocked myself at times. I had been pushed so far beyond the person that I used to be that I didn't care what others thought of me. I was out of control, and I didn't fear retaliation from Ricky. Maybe it was my way of getting back at him for forgetting about me. After all, he had put me through hell, as he would always say, "because I love you so much," he was now treating me as though I didn't exist, and I felt I deserved more than that.

I often spent time at my dad's house, and sometimes I spent time at my in-laws. It kept them both off balance as to what I was up to. No one knew for sure where I was. I went out a lot to get my mind off my life. I would call a girlfriend to accompany me, or I would go alone. I enjoyed the nightlife, and I should have been afraid of going by myself, but I wasn't. My favorite club was the NCO on the post. While out alone one night, a guy came over to my table and asked me to dance. I accepted and went onto the dance floor. Back then, the "Bump" was the dance everyone was doing. We danced several times back-to-back. I was starting to get hot and sweaty, so I told him I needed to sit down for a few moments. He asked if he could join me, and I said sure. He introduced himself as Tony, and I told him my name. We ordered a couple of drinks and talked for a while as we both cooled down. We ended up dancing with each other for the rest of the night. He walked me to my car when the club closed and asked me if I would be returning to the club again. I said, "Of course; I like to party." He wanted to know when, and I replied that I probably would be back the following weekend. He said, "Good, because I would like to see you again." We said goodnight, and I went home.

Several times after our first meeting, we would meet at the club to party together. He loved to dance, as did I. We always had a great time together, and our relationship bloomed. He became a part of my life. I saw him as often as I could. We did a lot of talking about our families and where each of us lived. He was from Maryland and had a mother that lived there. I told him that I was married, where my husband was stationed, and how I had not heard from him in months. I let him know about my decision to live my life and not wait at home for Ricky. I confided in him about how I bounced back and forth between my dad's house and my in-law's house. After seeing each other for a few months, he told me one day that he wanted me to meet his mother. I was shocked and reminded him, in case he had forgotten, that I was a married woman, and I was sure that she did not want to meet me. He convinced me to take a bus trip with him to meet his mother one weekend. I was uncomfortable with this because I knew I had nothing to offer him, but he was very determined. I went to my daddy's house, packed a bag, and left. My dad never asked me where I was going. I'm sure he assumed I was spending time with my in-laws. When I wasn't with them, I believe they thought I was at my dad's house. It allowed me to do whatever I wanted without questions from anyone. No one ever knew for sure where I was, but I have to say that I was not concerned if anyone was worried about me or wondering if something had happened to me. I lived my life without considering who I could be hurting. I had been denied a life for so long that I didn't care whether anyone was worried about me or not. It was all about me for a change. I think about it now and realize I was living a dangerous life, and some bad things could have happened to me, and no one would have known about it. I am told that hindsight is 20/20. The decisions I made were reckless and thoughtless. Without careful deliberation on my part, we caught a bus to Maryland for him to visit his mother and for me to be introduced to her. I don't know why he was so insistent on me meeting his mother. I didn't feel what was going on between us was serious enough to involve his mother.

We were enjoying our trip when we decided to go to the bathroom together. If you have ever been on a bus, you know how small the bathroom is. Have you ever heard of the "mile-high club"? Well, Tony and I joined the "sixty-mile-per-hour club," if you know what I mean. We arrived on a Saturday morning and caught a cab to his house, where he introduced me to his mother. She was a lovely lady and welcomed me to her home. She told Tony to put our bags in his room and come back down to the dining room for some breakfast. We sat down for breakfast and chatted for a while. Then Tony and I went upstairs to his room to shower and rest. That night, we got dressed up, and he took me out to a nightclub. We danced and had a great time. It got late, so we went back to his house to sleep because we had to leave the next day. We got some rest and then packed our bags for our return trip home. Before we left, I thanked his mother for her hospitality and for welcoming me into her home. Tony had to be back on post by Monday morning. It was a short trip but a fun one.

It wasn't long after we returned home that Tony rented us an apartment to live together. I know all this sounds ridiculous because I had a husband, but I acted as though I didn't. I did not care about anyone but me. Ricky was away doing his own thing, and I was doing the same. We moved in together. I would go home every once in a while to make an appearance to show I was okay. Then I went back to be with Tony. He made me feel loved and appreciated, and I was missing that in my life. My feelings for him were complicated. I could not make up my mind how I felt about him. I cared for him, but was it enough? Tony seemed to be looking for more than I could give. I tried to explain that even though I had problems with Ricky, I was still obligated to him; he was my husband. He ignored what I tried to convey to him. I didn't want to lie to him. I was upfront and honest about myself and my life because I didn't want to hurt him. He was so good to me; he was the perfect guy, and he made me feel cherished.

After a few months of being together, Tony received orders that his next assignment was going to be in Hawaii. I did not want to see our relationship end, but it was best for Tony to move on and forget about me. It was great sharing some of my life with him, but it was over. A friend of his took over the apartment after we left. The day he left was a sad one. We held each other; I kissed him and said goodbye, then I went home. Still, no one knew how I had been living my life. I returned as if nothing had ever happened. I stayed with my dad for a while, and then I visited Ricky's family for a time. I didn't go to the NCO club very much anymore. I found myself missing Tony something awful and was hoping he was doing fine and had a good life in Hawaii. I never heard a word from him; I didn't expect to. We made a clean break from each other. It was the right thing to do.

An Unexpected Surprise

Months had passed, and I heard nothing from Ricky. He did not take time out to let me know how he was, what was going on in Germany, or anything. I believe he called his parents now and then, but I cannot swear to that. I was left in the dark about his well-being and what was going on with him, like we were not husband and wife. Whenever I went to see his family, I spent most of my time hanging out with Shirley. We always had a great time together.

One day, I was visiting with her and heard someone knock at her door. I was not concerned because it was her house, and who would be coming to see me anyway? Someone answered the door. I was sitting at the bar. I turned around to see who was coming in, and my mouth hit the floor. I could not believe I was seeing who I was seeing. It was Tony. I almost fainted, then I was scared because he had managed to find me at my in-law's house, of all places. The adrenaline was flowing rapidly through my veins. Can you imagine how I felt? Here I was with my husband's family and my former lover, whom I thought I would never see again. Somehow, he managed to find me using the conversations we had about where I lived. What would have happened if I had been at my dad's house when he showed up at Shirley's? Would he have questioned them about my whereabouts, revealing our past relationship? What would have happened if Ricky had come home? I was stunned; I couldn't take it all in. All I could think about was trying to keep this debacle from exploding in my face. My heart was about to jump out of my chest. It beat so quickly that I could almost hear it. When we talked about where I lived, I didn't know that he had paid such close attention that he would be able to find me. He came in, grabbed me, and hugged me so tight I could hardly breathe. He knew what he was doing and was very bold about it, too. He was ready for whatever he had to deal with. I imagine at that moment, he did not care what people were thinking. He was on a mission. I was looking around to see the reaction on my sister-in-law's face. He took an enormous chance. I couldn't believe Tony had done this. When I was finally able to speak, I asked him what he was doing back. He was supposed to be in Hawaii? The most astounding thing came out of his mouth. He told me he had come back to get me. With a look of disbelief on my face, I could feel the tears welling up in my eyes. This man had traveled from Hawaii just for me. He didn't care that I was married. He wanted me to go back to Hawaii with him. I was floored that he cared so much for me that he returned to take me away with him.

I had a tough and immediate decision to make. There was no time for me to think about it. I had to shut this visit down as quickly as possible. Did I want to forget Ricky and leave with Tony, or did I want to be loyal to a man who had mistreated me for years? I was afraid to face ridicule from my family and his family. Could I abandon the life and dreams I had been praying for with Ricky? What would everyone think of me for doing something so outrageous? Do I love Tony enough to say to hell with everything and everybody and leave with him? All those questions flooded my mind until I had to make an unselfish decision. I had to tell Tony that I could not leave just like that. I had a husband and family to consider. I turned him down after all he had done to come and get me. I broke his heart, the very thing I never wanted to do. He was a wonderful man and deserved to be with someone who didn't have all the excess baggage that I had. I cared enough for him to let him walk out the door without me. The look on his face made tears roll down my cheeks. He turned and walked out of my life forever. I have often wondered if I shortchanged myself out of a great life with Tony. What if I had gone with him? After Tony left, I never heard anything from him again. And I couldn't blame him. I may have destroyed him more than I will ever know. Ricky's sister asked no questions. She was cool like that. She let it go as if it had never happened, and so did I. Talking about it would have caused a tremendous amount of unnecessary confusion. I chose Ricky over Tony, and that was that. It didn't make sense. I know many women in my position would have chosen Tony. I had to think about more than myself.

The Visit

When Ricky finally came home for a visit, I put that part of my life aside and became his wife again. I got no explanation as to why he didn't stay in contact with me. He pretended that everything was alright. Without saying it, I want it understood that he abused me while he was home for general purposes. He assumed that I must have been doing something while he was away from me for so long, but he could not prove it. What he didn't know was this time, I had done exactly what I was getting beat up for. What he did while he was away wasn't an issue, being the saint that he was. He said that he had not cheated on me while he was absent. So, what had he been doing all this time I wasn't hearing from him. I knew what he was telling me was a lie because Ricky had cheated on me practically right in my face. Let's not forget that he gave me chlamydia while I was the faithful wife. The whole time he was home, he kept trying to convince me to tell him how I had been spending my time and what I had been doing. It was as though he was looking for justification for what he had been doing. He did not seem to be so concerned about that while he was in Germany. He wanted to take the attention off his deceit and place it on my possible deceit. Even though he would hurt me, I refused to admit anything. It became a vicious cycle that he continued to put me through. To think that I gave up a chance to live in Hawaii with a great man for this. I must have been out of my mind. Finally, his leave was up, and he had to go back to Germany. We said our expected "I love you and goodbyes." And he was once again on his way back to the life he had created for himself that did not include me. I returned to the life I had mapped out for myself and had grown accustomed to.

Back to Life

When Ricky returned to Germany, I went back to live with my dad. The economy picked up. I started looking for a job because I did not want to be a burden or a source of worry to my dad any longer. I went to TexElastic to see if they were hiring again. That's when I found out that the plant had been sold, and it was now called Spano Yarns. Though it really didn't make a difference. They still produced the same product, so I applied for a job and got one. I returned to being a doffer, but later on, my supervisor asked me if I would like to become a Machine Operator. The position paid a little more than what a doffer made, so I accepted the job offer. I was then placed with a seasoned operator to train for a few weeks. Then, I was transferred to work on third shift. In my new job, I constantly checked a certain number of machines to see if any of the rubber (elastic) or nylon had broken down or run out so that I could make repairs and keep all the yarn on all my machines running. It was an okay job. Sometimes, it did get difficult when it was time for my assigned machines to be doffed. The yarn broke down like crazy, and I had the task of making sure no bad yarn was on the finished packages (tubes of yarn.) I worked independently. Sometimes, some of the machine operators would help another operator if her assigned machines were running out of nylon. Not all operators would help others. That is one of the main reasons why I took the job: to limit my interaction with coworkers who only looked out for themselves. It was difficult working in a group, especially a group of women. And women, you know what I mean.

When I was not at work, I kept myself busy with family and friends and tried to stay out of trouble. I didn't want to create more melodrama in my life. Coming to terms with how my relationship with Tony ended was problematic for me. My life could have disintegrated before my eyes, or it could have become splendiferous. But I did not want to be involved in anything like that again. A few months later, I received word that Ricky was coming home, and that word did not come from him. He always attempted to slip up on me to try and catch me doing wrong. The nerve of this man was unbelievable. As they say, "the pot calling the kettle black." There were always skeletons in his closet that he thought I would never find out about. It was almost like a game we played that no one could win. "For there is nothing hidden that will not be disclosed, and nothing concealed that will not be known or brought out into the open" (Luke 8:17). The things we do are never hidden from God; there is no escape from His watchful eye.

Reassignment

Ricky finished his stint in Germany and was assigned a new duty station at Fort Bliss in El Paso, Texas. This time, he decided to take me with him, to my surprise. I informed my dad and family that I was accompanying Ricky to his next duty station. I put in my two-week notice on my job and continued to work up to the appointed time to leave. I used the rest of the time to pack before our departure. I admit that I was very excited because I had never lived in any other state other than North Carolina. I had to let go of the life I had been living during the years Ricky and I were not together. It was arduous to do because Tony kept coming back to my mind. I couldn't help fantasizing about him and our life together had I not chosen Ricky. The time I had spent with him was dear to my heart, but I had to let it go and focus on the possibilities of life with Ricky. I wanted to have a good life with the man I had married. I believed it could happen. Leaving the past in the past was the best thing to do to accomplish that goal. I assumed he would be doing the same thing to get on with our marriage with a fresh start. Why else would he take me with him? Letting go of whatever had happened in Germany was what I expected him to do. He had about a month's worth of leave before he had to report to his next assignment. We went through the same old thing: "What did you do when I was not here?" You know, the threats, the beatings, and his behaving as though he had been an angel while he was in Germany. It was always about me, never about him. Possibly because I could not punish him by beating him up as he could me. I'm not making light of what he did to me. I'm saying that I anticipated it. For him to deviate from his past behavior would have been a remarkable change. A change could have created a brand new marriage between us. But a person is who they are. And for something like that to come to pass, that person would need to make the change for themselves. No one else could do it unless it was God doing the changing.

We caught our flight to El Paso. This was my very first time flying. I was scared of what it would feel like being so far up in the sky. At take-off, I felt a strange feeling, like I was losing control of my insides, but once the plane leveled off, it subsided, and I felt better. It was exciting looking out the window at the landscape below. Everything appeared to be in squares. It was so beautiful seeing all the magnificent colors that painted the ground like a canvas. After changing flights in Georgia, a few hours later, we were coming in for a landing in El Paso. It was like nothing I had ever seen before. The city looked as though it was nestled in a valley in the middle of the desert, surrounded by mountains. There was hardly any grass, flowers, or trees, for that matter. We landed, claimed our luggage, and caught a cab to the post, where we got a room until Ricky could find a place for us to live. I noticed that because of this new adventure, Ricky was treating me like the wife he cared for, and things were going well for us. He reported for duty while I spent my days in the hotel room waiting for him to return. Finally, he found an apartment, which delighted us both. It was a furnished apartment on the second floor, not far from the post. We didn't have a car, but another soldier from his unit lived in the same apartment complex, and Ricky rode with him to post every day. I did things around the apartment to keep myself busy. If I needed to go out, I could walk. Everything that I needed was within walking distance. Getting around was costly if we wanted to go beyond the community that we lived in.

A few weeks later, Ricky came home with a car he had bought. Now, we could explore the place neither of us had ever been. We went for drives around El Paso and beyond the boundary of the city sometimes. I remember one day we were out driving, and we were like out in the desert. We saw something slowly crossing the road. As we got closer, we could see that it was a large tarantula. I started screaming because I had a phobia of spiders, and what I saw was a giant spider. Ricky stopped so that it could cross the road. I was convinced that if we drove over it, it might somehow get into the car. He thought I was hilarious. He made fun of me while we drove around sightseeing and making jokes about my fear of spiders. We continued on our journey exploring until it got late. We decided that it was time to make our way back home.

CHAPTER 8
CAUGHT OFF GUARD

Our daily life was great. He went to work every day, and I cooked and kept the apartment clean. There was no fighting, no accusations of infidelity. I was enjoying our stay at Ft Bliss. It was getting close to Christmas, and we had started discussing plans to go home for the holidays. Ricky suggested that I go home about two weeks before Christmas to have more time to spend with my family. He would join me later as it got closer to Christmas. It seemed like a great idea, and I thought it was very sweet of him to do that for me. I had no reason to think that Ricky had an ulterior motive for our plans, but as I found out later, he was not thinking about doing something nice for me; he was thinking of himself. He knew how much I loved Christmas, and having the opportunity to be at home with my family would be divine. I had been away from my relatives for months, and I missed them a ton. We agreed that I would precede him in our plan to visit our families for the holidays. I was so looking forward to seeing everyone and sharing all I had experienced in Texas that I could hardly wait.

While Ricky was at work one day, I was doing my usual housework. I gathered all the dirty clothes, towels, and sheets so that

I could do the laundry. I was elated over how incredible our lives were going in El Paso. Perhaps the change in our environment was exactly what we needed to help our relationship flourish. The violence wasn't happening anymore, and I thought it was because we were a long way from home, and we were all each other had, so we appreciated each other more, or possibly he had decided not to abuse me anymore. As I was going through Ricky's fatigues to make sure there was nothing in his pockets before I put them into the washer, I came across a letter from this German chick addressed to Ricky. First, I got furious. Then I got even angrier when I read the already-opened letter. She talked about how much she loved and missed him and how much she was looking forward to coming to the USA to spend Christmas with him. Oh, my goodness, I got so mad when I realized that he wasn't sending me home early to enjoy spending more time with my family. He was getting rid of me so that his girlfriend could come to stay in our apartment with him for the Christmas holidays. I started crying because it felt like a knife had pierced my heart, and the life I thought I had with my husband was a complete fallacy. What kind of a person does this type of unscrupulous stuff? I couldn't do anything else that day. The arrogance of this man almost drove me to the edge. I could not wrap my brain around how he had manipulated me into thinking he was sending me home as a grand gesture of how much he loved me. Here I was thinking that my marriage was finally working out the way that it should when all the time he had another woman in his life and was about to bring her to Texas to sleep in my bed with him while I was back home, thinking that my husband had done something truly spectacular for me. I can only assume he had an excuse he planned to give me when he did not show up for Christmas. I was so hurt that I couldn't rest. Only a diabolical mind could set such a devious plot into motion. I paced back and forth, strategizing about what I would do once he returned home. I was about to explode, realizing the horrendous scheme he was planning for me. Where was his compassion and love for me? I don't believe that if the shoe was on the other foot, he could take what he was dishing out. I may not have been the perfect wife while he was out of the country, but when he came back, I gave him the respect he was due as my husband, put that life aside, and he became the only man in my life. I didn't believe that I deserved to be treated in this way. I left my past in the past and gave my complete and undivided attention and loyalty to him.

I couldn't wait for him to get home so that he could explain to me what was going on. So, this was why he did not have time to stay in contact with me. He was living his life like he didn't have a wife back in the States. When he walked in the door, it was on. I wanted to know why he was getting mail from a woman in Germany. How did she know where to write him if he had not been in touch with her? And what was she talking about when she said she was looking forward to spending Christmas with him? When I got angry, I cried and said some not-so-nice words I had learned from him. He couldn't explain it. He told me lie after lie. How could we get on with our life as husband and wife when he was holding on to his past? There could not be three people in a marriage. I chose him over everyone and everything in my life. I understood that he probably got lonely so far away from home and started a relationship with someone. I know this because I did it. But I broke off my misstep. I don't know what happened that day. I just felt so degraded. I was getting beat up by him for his thinking that I had done something, and him not knowing for sure if I did, and he was having a relationship with another woman while he was beating me up for what he thought. I stayed upset. I just couldn't let it go. I tossed and turned in bed that night. During the night, I decided that I wouldn't put up with this. If she was who he wanted, he could have her. Besides, he could have left me in North Carolina, and he wouldn't have had to put me through any of this. I had a life back there. I did not need this extra drama in it; my entire life with him was always drama, no matter what. I couldn't understand why he put me in such a hurtful situation. I made up my mind that the following day I was leaving to go back home, but I had a problem: I didn't have very much money.

After he left for work the following morning, I called my brother Preston, told him my situation, and asked him if he would send me enough money for a bus ticket back home. He had a ticket to North Carolina waiting for me at the Bus Station when I arrived. I was very thankful that I had someone I could call on in my time of need. I packed my things and everything I could take out of the apartment, called a cab, and went to the bus station. I left El Paso that afternoon on my way back home. I was crushed thinking about how my life was a hot mess. It took me three or four days to get home. So, I had time to think about what I would do. It was a long and miserable ride. The bus stopped in every small town between Texas and North Carolina. When my trip was almost over, while the bus made one of its usual stops, I called my dad to ask him to pick me up from the bus station when I arrived. I don't remember what excuse I gave him for the reason I was coming back home. I may have told him the original plan. I was coming home to spend Christmas with him. My brain was preoccupied with what was probably going on back in El Paso. It takes a certain type of man to try and live two lives at the same time. He had me fooled into believing that I was the only woman in his life and quite possibly had the German woman thinking the same thing.

When my dad picked me up from the bus station, I felt he knew what had happened. But he didn't ask any questions. Preston had probably called him before I got home and told him all about what was going on. I settled into Thomas' old room. He no longer lived with my family anymore. It had been a very long and tiresome journey, and I was exhausted. Falling asleep was difficult because I kept thinking about my predicament. I had put up with and taken so much from Ricky, and this is what he does to me. I finally fell asleep sometime during the early morning hours. I woke up to a noise that sounded like it was coming from the bathroom. We always left the bathroom window cracked a little to allow fresh air to circulate. I sat up in the bed and listened. I knew my dad, and Olivia had already left for work earlier. So, I quietly got out of bed, tiptoed down the hall, and peeped into the bathroom. I saw a man almost halfway into the small bathroom window. I let out a scream and said, "What are you doing?" He gave me a look of shock and alarm, then jumped down and ran off. My blood was pumping through my veins so fast that I thought my heart would leap out of my chest. My knees got weak. I was so scared I felt like I was going to pass out. I managed to get to a chair to sit down. I thought to myself, "What would have happened if he had gotten in?" I don't believe that he was betting on someone being home. I was supposed to be in Texas, and my family was at work. I didn't call the police; I guess perhaps I should have. Since nothing had happened, I thought it wasn't necessary. He looked familiar. I think he was one of the neighbors' kids from down the street. He had planned to rob my dad, but thank the Lord, I was there and foiled his plans. There could be no more sleeping for me after that. Upon my daddy's arrival back home, I informed him of what had happened that morning. He was so thankful that I didn't get hurt and that my presence had impeded a thief from robbing him.

Meanwhile, Back in Texas

Days went by, and all I could think about was Ricky. I kept wondering if his German girlfriend had come to Texas as she and Ricky had planned. Out of curiosity, I mustered up enough nerve to phone my apartment, and she answered. I was so shocked that she had the audacity to answer the phone that I quickly hung up. I didn't know her. And I surely did not want to talk to her. I sobbed, knowing that Ricky had gone through with his sinister plan to bring another woman into our home. It wasn't the first time Ricky had pulled this stunt. He had another woman living in our very first home that we had purchased together. I should not have been so surprised, but I was. I thought our relationship was progressing. I guess I was the only one having that thought. It always seemed to boil down to what he wanted. He wasn't showing any consideration on my behalf, or his girlfriend's either. He must have lied to her unless she did not care about being in another woman's home. No descent woman wants to knowingly share a man with another woman when she thinks he is hers.

I felt sorry for myself and struggled to make it through the days as best I could. I had not decided what I was going to do. I only knew I was missing my husband so much that I contemplated going back to Texas despite what he had done. I convinced myself that I wouldn't give my husband to another woman on a silver platter that easily without putting up a fight. I know it sounds so crazy, but that was the way that I felt. I couldn't sleep most nights thinking about what I should do. I was no longer being logical. What woman in her right mind would return to a man who had cheated on her in her home, especially since he had done it before?

In the meantime, to show my appreciation to my dad for allowing me to come back home, I cooked and cleaned, along with the occasional breakdown. I was so messed up. I was scarcely managing to make it from day to day. Then the phone rang. It was the operator asking, "Will you accept a collect call from Edith?" Once I understood what was happening, I realized that she was saying Ricky's German girlfriend's name, which I had seen in the letter she wrote to him. I'm thinking, "What in the world is this chick doing calling me?" Once I caught my breath from gasping in disbelief, I gave the operator an absolute no! She didn't give up, though. She kept on trying to call me. I refused to answer the phone anymore until she gave up. I was wondering how she knew my dad's home phone number and where she got it from. Ricky must have given it to her, or she found it somewhere in the apartment. I didn't understand why she felt the urgency to talk to me. Did she even know who I was? Until this very day, I don't understand why she seemed so desperate to speak to me. I refused to talk to her. And I wasn't about to pay for a call from Ricky's girlfriend. Maybe that wasn't a great idea. I could have found out some things that I did not know from her. But I did give some thought to the notion that during her little vacation, while visiting her supposed-to-be "boyfriend" in the USA, she may have found out about Ricky and me being married. It was believable that he may have been lying to her, too. I couldn't believe it. It was like something out of a movie. You know, I was so darn mad that I could have spit bullets. The nerve of this chick calling me after she had just spent Christmas with my husband in my house. Though I wanted to, I couldn't put all the blame on her. Ricky was the one who put this thing into action and created this whole mess that disrupted all our lives.

Then, days later, Ricky started calling me. I felt nothing but contempt for him and what he had done. I had no interest in speaking to him. The egotistical behavior he displayed was unconscionable. It took some time to come to grips with how he had manipulated me into doing what he wanted. I was free of him, and I could stay that way if I so chose. At first, I wouldn't talk to him, but my emotions outweighed my common sense. Eventually, I did talk to him. That happens when you make important decisions with your feelings instead of your brain. He started apologizing for what he had done to me. He was so sorry for hurting me. He assured me that he and Edith were done. He wouldn't have anything else to do with her. He had made a colossal mistake. He loved me, and he wanted me to come back to Texas. What a fool I was for falling for that farce again. Women are too quick to believe what they want to hear, whether true or not. Looking at it now, I was out of my mind to believe anything he said. We want to be loved by someone so badly that we will talk ourselves out of the truth of our situation. I must say, I was insane to even consider going back. But I did consider it and, ultimately, decided to do just that. I know it sounds wacko, but that was the nature of the relationship Ricky and I had, wacko.

He sent the money for my flight back to El Paso. I packed my things and returned. My dad was hurt and disappointed in the decisions I was making. But it was my life, and I had to live it the way I saw fit. I'm sure that he felt used by me always asking for help. But I did not set out to hurt anyone. I was a confused young woman who had no inkling of what she was doing to herself or her life. I know that my brother Preston was disappointed because he helped me out of a crisis, and I went right back into it, which often happens with abused women. I owe him an apology for crying wolf and for going back to the wolf after he saved me from him. I don't believe that I ever apologized to him. Still, I am sorry for putting him in the middle of my marital problems, especially since I went back into them fully aware of my turbulent and violent relationship with Ricky. I hope he has forgiven me for that.

I returned to Texas to be a wife to a man that had just humiliated me. It was really hard to feel close to him at first. After some time passed, our relationship slowly got better, at least, that's the way I saw it. We lived in Texas for a few more months until Ricky got his new orders that he would be going back to

Germany again. I was boiling mad. But he assured me that I had nothing to worry about. I knew that he was very deceitful. But I wanted so much to believe in him. I had to accept where he was ordered to go because he was in the Army, and they decided where he would be assigned next. Before we left Texas, Ricky bought another used car because we were going to drive home. We needed a reliable car. It would be a very long drive from El Paso to North Carolina, so we tried to avoid possible car trouble by purchasing a more dependable one. We set out on our long trip back home. It was like a cross-country adventure. We got to see some beautiful places as we drove. Ricky would drive while I slept, and then we would switch. It took us around two to three days to get home with continuous driving. Everyone was so happy to see us. The trip home was tiresome. But we arrived safe and sound.

We stayed with his family while he was home. I went to visit my dad to ask if, after Ricky went to his new duty station, I could come back to live with him. My dad never turned his back on me, no matter what I needed or what I had done. There were so many things left unsaid between us. He let me make my mistakes, and he caught me when I needed to return to the nest. I am so very grateful for that because I made a massive number of errors. The time came for Ricky to travel to his new duty station. Once again, I was on my own. I didn't trust Ricky. But I still loved him. I wondered if he would break his promise to me and restart his relationship with Edith. There was no way that I would ever know for sure what he was doing. I had to let it go and live my life. I learned that I could only control my actions. Trying to control his, especially when he was out of the country and beyond my reach, was pure idiocy.

Gone Again

I went to live with my dad and returned to work at Spanco Yarns. On the surface, everything appeared to be going okay with Ricky. Instead of worrying about it, I picked up my old habits. I went out to party, hung out with my friends, and dated as though I was single. It was the only way I could make it through the time we were not together. I suspected that Ricky was doing the same. Nothing had ever stopped him before. He never let being a married man get in the way of having relations with other women. His past spoke for itself. I just did whatever I wanted to do. After a while, I left my dad's house and moved in with my girlfriend, Tammy, from work. We got along great. We went to the NCO Club a lot. On my days off, I would go to the Liquor Store and buy a fifth of Vodka, pick up some orange juice, and have a few drinks before we hit the Club. Yelp, it was stupid and careless, and I can't explain why I put my life and Tammy's life at risk by driving impaired. I don't know if it was the after-effects of what Ricky had put me through or if I didn't care anymore. Living life on the edge had become my normal. It became so easy to forget that I was married. I suspect that my decision-making skills were flawed. Some of the things I did were outrageously foolish. So far, my life had been a total train wreck, and I don't believe that I was dealing with it very well. Time was passing on, and instead of sitting at home feeling sorry for myself and worrying about what was happening in Germany, I laid my marriage aside and proceeded to live my life.

Tammy and I sometimes socialized with her neighbor from across the street. I thought she was a nice person. I got the feeling that she might be gay, but I didn't have a problem with that because she seemed cool. Plus, she said she was living her life for the Lord. I was friendly with her because she was Tammy's friend before I decided to move in with her. Besides, I never had any reason to suspect that she was not who she claimed she was. It didn't cross my mind that she might be attracted to me, being that she was possibly gay. Now and then, she would come by for a visit. I was in my bedroom one day, and she supposedly wanted to talk. She sat down on my bed, and we started to talk. The next thing I knew, the chick had jumped me and proceeded to try and rape me. I know, unbelievable, right? I was as shocked as you are right now. Let me tell you, she was a tiny woman but as strong as a man. I fought her with all my might until I was exhausted. I was determined that this was not going to happen to me. She finally gave up. Thank God! I cussed her out and told her to get out and never come back again. Tammy could not believe what that chick had tried to do to me. The girl had led her to believe that she was living a life saved from sin. Jesus won't make you force yourself on someone. I did not understand why she felt I would have sex with her. Besides that, I could not comprehend that a woman almost raped me, can you? That was the last thing I expected. Shocking, isn't it? We never had any more contact with her. I have seen her once since that altercation, walking along the street of my hometown. I just looked at her as I drove by, still in disbelief that it happened, and to me, of all people. I never gave her the impression that I would be down with something like that. I was heterosexual, and she knew that.

A year passed, and Ricky came home for a visit. The vicious, violent cycle continued. I can't tell you why we even stayed married. Neither of us acted like it. I had to go through the accusations and the hits and punches as usual. He told me that he had not been cheating on me. But I knew in my heart that was a lie. I did it, and I knew he did it too. He disapproved of my living with a single woman. I'm sure he assumed that we went out a lot, and we did. I had no intention of moving out because he wanted me to. He stayed almost thirty days and returned to Germany. Although I loved Ricky, I was happy to see him leave. The impact of being abused damaged my mental health, and I believe it contributed to the morally questionable choices I made. Tammy and I went back to partying regularly. We would hit the club for "Ladies Night" on Wednesday. Then we also went out on Thursday, Friday, and Saturday nights. It did not matter if we were working or not. We went early and left in time to get back home, changed into our work clothes, and headed to work. Those were some crazy times, but we had a lot of fun. Later on, I decided to move out of Tammy's house and into a place of my own in a mobile home park not too far from where she lived. I had a 3-bedroom rental. It was nice to be living alone again. At that time, the plant had all the shifts working overtime. Sometimes, I worked six to seven days a week. I was so tired at times and disoriented that I would wake up and think that I had missed my shift, and it was the next morning. I did not mind so much about my work schedule. I needed the money to keep a roof over my head. I worked like that for quite a while. I had to let go of my extra-curricular activities. At the moment, I no longer had the time for it.

Phone Calls and Visits

My dad occasionally called me in the mornings after I got off work to talk. He had retired from the hospital and had lots of time on his hands. I did all I could to stay awake while I talked to him. He called so regularly that it got to the point that to keep him from disturbing my sleep, I had to unplug my phone. I meant no disrespect to him. Working so many hours drained me, and I had to get my rest, or I would not be able to make it through my shift without falling asleep, which was dangerous around machines. I knew he was lonely at home while Olivia was at work. I'd call him in the afternoon after I had gotten some sleep. He would tell me that he had tried to call me, but he did not get an answer. Neither did he know that I did not hear my phone ring because it was unplugged. One afternoon, unexpectedly, he came by for a visit. I had already slept for a while, so I was able to spend some time with him. We would speak for a long time; my dad loved to talk. Then he said something that piqued my interest. He explained the reason why he was near my neighborhood was because he had taken the family dog and dropped him off by the Church near the mobile home park that Tammy lived in to get rid of him. He was a yard dog, but he was still our pet. I disagreed with my daddy's perception of domesticated animals, but instead of voicing my opinion, I decided to rescue the dog. The fate he had given him was something that just hurt my heart because I love animals. And I thought that it was a cruel thing to do. All that animal knew about was my family. So, as he was talking, I made up my mind that I was not going to let this stand. After he left, I waited for a time, and then I got into my car, went to look for the dog, and I found him just where he said he had left him. The dog started wagging his tail vigorously because he was so glad to see a familiar face. I opened the car door, and he jumped in. I proceeded to take him back to my daddy's house. My dad lived off the main highway a short distance up a dirt road. I drove up the road almost to his house so as not to give myself away. I did not want him to know that I had brought the dog back home. And then I let the dog out, and he ran the rest of the way. I turned my car around and went back home with a smile on my face, knowing the dog was safe at home where he should be. I am a staunch believer that animals are not garbage that you drop off by the side of the road. They are living, breathing beings with the same emotions as humans and the same needs. I was very proud of what I had done, but I was very careful not to tell anyone about it though. I did not want how the dog made it back home to get back to my dad. During one of my visits with him, I remember hearing him bragging to someone he was speaking with on the phone about how the dog was so smart that he had found his way back home after he had dropped him off by the side of the road, miles from home. I just smiled and never said a word about it. I just recently disclosed to my family that it was me who brought the dog back home. They couldn't believe that I had never divulged to my dad that it was me who brought the dog back home. He had probably told them the story. The dog got to live out his life with the people he loved. I was pleased about that.

A New Duo

My job finally calmed down, and we were working 40 hours a week again. Virginia and her sister moved back to Raeford and had come back to work at Spanco. After working so much, I had become accustomed to doing no maintenance to my mane. I kept my hair in its natural state in braids because I was allowing my perm to grow out. When I went to work, I tied a bandana on my head. Virginia asked me one night why I wore a bandana on my head all the time. I told her that my hair was short and had broken off because, at one time, I was doing my hair myself, and I was not that good at it. I didn't want to deal with it, as I allowed the perm to grow out, so I covered it up. Then she informed me about a beauty salon where she went to get her hair done. She had a new hairstyle called the Jheri Curl. She told me how easy it was to maintain and that her hair had grown a lot since she had it. I thought how nice it would be not to wear the bandanas anymore. So the next time she went to her beautician, I made an appointment, and I went with her. The only thing I did not like was the hours we spent waiting to get our hair done; it was outrageous. We would have an early morning appointment, and sometimes, it would be dark before we left. After I got my new duo, all I had to do was keep a plastic cap on my head while I slept, and when I got ready to go to work or wherever I was going, I sprayed a small amount of conditioner on my hair, shook it out a little, and that was it. I was now worry-free when it came to my hair. After two weeks, I would go back for a shampoo. Come to think of it; I spent a lot of time and a lot of money at that hair salon. After three months, I needed to go back to get my new growth styled. Virginia and I had a morning appointment after working the night before. We hoped that we could get in and out as quickly as possible, but no luck. They had booked so many clients that we did not leave the hair salon until 1:00 am the next day. I kid you not. I know it sounds ridiculous, but it's the truth. Instead of going to work, we called in sick and went to a club called "The Twenty-Grand. We danced the rest of the night, or should I say morning. The humidity in the air activated the curls in my hair to look even better. The club closed around 5:00 am, and we went home and slept the rest of the day. Virginia and I didn't get to party often. She had a family by then, and they were her top priority.

A New Friend

I started to hang out with another one of my coworkers at Spanco. Her name was Paulette. I remembered her from High School. We became friends and found out we had some things in common, such as husbands. Our relationship was based on our joy of shopping, talking about our marital problems, and sometimes going out to a Club. She became my very best friend. We shared a lot. When we went shopping together, we made it our business to stop at Wendy's. That was our favorite burger place. It was a new restaurant during that time, and we loved it. We always ordered double cheeseburgers, fries, and a drink. They were so delicious that we practically inhaled them. We were as close as sisters, maybe even closer. I could trust her with anything. I went to her house to visit, and she would come to my house to visit me. She was dealing with a problem in her marriage, and so was I. We discussed everything. We liked the same type of music, and we both liked to clown around. Sometimes, when we were riding together, a song would come on the radio that we liked dancing to. I'd stop the car. We would open our doors, jump out, and dance in the street. It was so much fun being with her. We just clicked.

I found out that one of our favorite groups, Chic, would be giving a concert at Carowinds in Charlotte, NC. We just had to go even though we were not scheduled off work. On the day of the concert, we went home, showered, changed clothes, and hit the highway. I knew the way because I had lived in Charlotte at one time and often traveled that highway. I was a bit fuzzy on the directions after we passed Charlotte because Carowinds is located on the borderline of North and South Carolina, but we made it to the park on time, purchased our tickets, and went in. The only thing we were interested in was seeing Chic perform, so we walked around for a bit until it was finally time to attend the concert. When they came on stage, and the music started, we jumped to our feet to dance, forgetting and not feeling like we had worked all night long and were supposed to work the night ahead. We did not let that prevent us from enjoying ourselves. The concert was great, and we had a blast. It was late, and we had not slept a wink. We left the park, heading home. I drove for a while, and she slept. Then she drove for a while, and I slept. I woke up one time, and she had gotten lost. I took over, and we made it back home. Even though we were exhausted, we went to work anyway. After a few hours, we couldn't take it anymore. We pleaded with our supervisor to please let us go home. He got tired of us begging, and he let us go, and boy, we were so happy. We went to my house and went to bed. It was worth all we had gone through to get to see one of our favorite groups. This is the type of thing that we enjoyed doing. We put in our lives as much fun as we could. It helped us to get through the hard times that inevitably always came our way.

Here I Go Again

There was a guy named Johnathan at work that we both knew and joked around with a lot. After one of my machines had been doffed, he would come and push the yarn to a staging area. We laughed, talked, and played around, which, in turn, helped our work seem easier. He was a big flirt, funny, and cute. Slowly, we started to become more than friends. Before I knew it, we had developed a relationship. I liked him a lot, and he liked me. We went out on dates, and I very much enjoyed his company. He followed me home one morning, and I asked him to come in. I didn't plan on going as far as I did, but we ended up in my bed. From then on, we were involved in an affair. I discussed with him all about Ricky and how much he had hurt me. Johnathan could not understand why I was still married to him. To be truthful, I couldn't explain why. I was deeply rooted in my belief that when you get married, you stay married. It's funny that I wasn't so committed to my faith that I felt the same way about adultery. I cannot explain that either. He became very important to me, but we tried to keep our relationship private. I am sure some of the people we worked with figured it out, but we did not let that deter us from caring for and seeing each other. We didn't live together, but we spent lots of time together. He made me feel loved and wanted.

Homecoming

Ricky's time in Germany was up, and he was on his way home. I had to tell Johnathan that we had to stop seeing each other until Ricky left for his new assignment. He was very upset about that because he knew that Ricky was an abuser, and he did not want to stand by while he hurt me. I convinced him that I would be okay, but it was difficult getting him to agree to stay away. I hoped and prayed that he would not confront Ricky. I was afraid that he could not control his hatred for him and do something crazy. If Ricky found out about Johnathan, all hell would break loose. I did not want anyone to get hurt because of me. Once again, I had put myself into a dilemma. Ricky finished his assignment in Germany and came home. I was not living in my own place before he left. It was his first time seeing where I had moved while he was away. It only took a few days before Johnathan rode by my house to check on me. I could tell every time he came by because he had a loud muffler on his car, and he would race the engine several times as he passed. Soon, Ricky noticed that his car kept coming by and got curious about it. I told him it was one of my neighbors from down the street going in and out of the park. Johnathan was putting me in danger by trying to keep me safe. When I got a chance, I made a quick call to Paulette, when I was able to escape the watchful eye of Ricky. I asked her to please call Jonathan and tell him to stop riding by my house. Ricky was starting to accuse me of cheating on him while he was away, which was not unusual, but I was guilty this time; I had put lives at stake, including my own. I knew Johnathan didn't want me to be with Ricky, but this was how things were at the moment; it was unavoidable. I hoped that Paulette's call would be enough to get him to stop making my situation worse.

Later, Ricky informed me that he had been ordered to go to Tacoma, Washington, and he wanted me to go with him. That gave me an unexpected problem. I was uncertain about what I was going to do about it. Before he returned home, I thought I would spend some time with Ricky, and then he would be leaving again. If I tried to stay, he would get suspicious as to why. If I went with him, it would break Johnathan's heart. I had another choice to make, again. I had to choose between being with Ricky or being with Johnathan. The last time I had to make a decision like this, I regretted the choice I made. Reluctantly, I decided that it would be best if I went with Ricky for all concerned. If he found out about Johnathan, I would get beat up, and if Johnathan found out that Ricky had beat me up, there was no telling what he would do. It broke my heart to make this kind of determination twice, but I created this problem. I rued once again for pulling someone else into my dysfunctional life; I was a married woman. I especially did not want to hurt Johnathan. Unfortunately, I did not get the chance to explain myself to him before I left. He did not know that I had chosen Ricky over him. It would have been too dangerous for us to meet somewhere. Ricky didn't leave me alone long enough to see him and talk to him to explain myself.

Ricky had a few weeks of leave, which gave us time to arrange to get all my household goods packed up and shipped, plus the travel time we would need to get to Washington. He spent time with his family, and I quit my job. I told my dad that I would be moving to Washington for 18 months with Ricky. I believe he was afraid because he remembered what happened when I left home to be with Ricky before, but he accepted that he was my husband. I knew my dad was always praying for me, and I was grateful for his prayers. I had to say goodbye to my dear friend Paulette, but she understood that I was trying to rebuild my marriage. I would miss her so very much. Every time life gave me an out from the disastrous life I was living with Ricky, I turned it down, thinking that I was doing the right thing. Doing the right thing always made me regret my decision. I had opportunities to remove myself from my messy marriage, but I couldn't bring myself to do it. I was in such an addictive relationship that I frequently talked myself out of making a break for it. I felt guilty for hurting Johnathan, but I felt the need to be loyal, in a sense, to Ricky. No matter what happened between us, he would always be who I chose. Not because he was a terrific man but because I carried his last name, and that was it.

It's Time to Just Stop

I considered all the things I had been doing and how carelessly I had been living my life. I concluded that it was time to stop. It was against my faith, which I had long ignored, and I believe it all started to weigh heavy on my soul. My dual life was hurting too many people. I knew right from wrong because my parents had taught me. I was heartsick over what I had to do to Johnathan; it was not fair to him. I didn't expect the unforeseen circumstance that was happening to our relationship. I could have stayed with him and dealt with the fallout of my decision, but I cared for both of them, and I was married to one of them. After I crushed Johnathan with my reckless behavior, I wanted to make a new start, hoping that it would benefit the choice I had made. Besides that, I was just so very tired of my life imitating a soap opera. I was at a turning point. I had wrecked Johnathan's life, and I did not want to do that to anyone else. I promised God and myself that I would no longer have extramarital affairs. I wanted to be the kind of wife I should have been, no matter what Ricky was doing—being vengeful and the lack of integrity and faithfulness added to the destruction of my marriage. From the beginning, the things I was doing did not agree with the narrative I had written in my heart for my life. I always dreamed of getting married to a wonderful and loving man and having a beautiful family with him. That dream did not seem to be working out so well. Perhaps the man I was married to could not promote my dream the way I had dreamt it. You can plan out your life all you want, but life happens, ignoring your plans. We deceive ourselves if we believe anything other than that.

From East Coast to West Coast

We started on our long drive to Washington State. We planned to go south and then go northwest towards the coast to avoid the winter weather. We took our time and enjoyed the trip, stopping for food, gas, bathroom breaks, and stretching our legs along the way. When we reached California, it was during rush hour. I had not experienced such terrible traffic, and it was uncomfortably warm, too, but we finally got through it and headed for Oregon. We didn't know how far we were from Tacoma, Washington; it was late at night, and we were tired. So, we stopped and checked into a hotel for the night to get some sleep so we could start fresh the next day. We got up the following morning, showered, had breakfast, got back on the highway, and reached Ft. Lewis in just about an hour. Had we known that we were that close, we would have continued on the night before. We stayed on post until we could find a place to live. It only took a few days to find an apartment. We moved into a second-story apartment right next to the main highway. The Base was not very far away. The movers brought our things to the apartment, and I started unpacking. Tacoma was a beautiful, lush green, and misty place. I could look out my front window and see Mt. St. Helen. There was snow at its peak. It was so beautiful that it looked like it was a painting. I liked where we were, although it rained a lot during the spring and summer, and in the winter months, it snowed often. I was used to North Carolina weather, but the change was something different for me to experience.

We settled into our new life together so far from home. Whenever Ricky was off, we would go to the pier and fish. He was used to fishing; he went pretty often with his friends back home before he joined the Army. I don't remember ever going fishing as a child. I found it boring, and I got tired of it quickly.

The view from the pier was gorgeous, though. I would sit while Ricky fished and watch the ships coming and going. I wondered what it was like to be out in that beautiful blue water. I had never been out on the water before, so I was intrigued by the boats and ships as they sailed by. Ricky decided to teach me how to fish. At first, he started out baiting my hook for me, and I would throw it into the water. I was afraid of the worms and did not want to touch them. He talked me into baiting my hook one day; he showed me how. After a while, I got the hang of it and started doing it myself. That's when it became more interesting, but I felt sorry for the worm. When we caught a fish, it would always be a flounder. He cleaned them when we got home, and I would fry them for dinner. Sometimes, in our spare time, we took rides to places we had not seen. Seattle wasn't very far from Tacoma. I think we took a ride there maybe once while we were in Washington. We went up into the mountains one day and came across a cute little village. As we toured the village, I noticed that there were no people who looked like us, if you know what I mean. We felt it was in our best interest to spend as little time there as possible and headed back down the mountain. I made dinner, we ate, and sat on the couch to watch some TV. It was getting late, and Ricky had to go to work the next day. He turned off the TV, and we got ready for bed. It was not hard to fall asleep because we had a very active day. The next thing I knew, I was screaming because I had been punched in the mouth while I was asleep. Ricky said he was having a nightmare about fighting someone, and he hit me by accident. He calmed me down as best he could. I couldn't understand how he managed to hit me right smack in the mouth if he was asleep. My lips were swollen for days. He may have been dreaming about hitting me, or maybe he was fighting his alter ego. I knew for sure two different people were living in one body. I was in love with one of them and feared the other.

He Did It Again

Every once in a while, Ricky went to field training for two weeks in Spokane, and I would spend that time alone. I didn't have a job, and I did not know anyone where I lived. I kept busy, though, taking care of our home and different things around the apartment. I spent time reading, listening to music, and watching TV. Right before he was due to return, I gathered all the dirty laundry together so I could take it to the laundromat in the apartment complex to wash it. I wanted to get the laundry done because I knew he would be coming back home with more. Ricky kept his dirty clothes in one of his duffle bags. I started pulling out his laundry when a letter from Germany fell out of the bag; does that sound familiar? My heart sank into my stomach. I had been down this road before. I knew this would not be a good thing because Ricky had promised me that it was over between him and Edith. Like a fool, I trusted and believed him. I picked up the opened letter. As I touched it, I realized there was more inside than a letter. I pulled it out, and there was a picture with the letter. It was a picture of Ricky, Edith, and their baby son. Looking at it, I knew that the child was his because he looked exactly like him. My mouth fell open, and I dropped the letter and picture on the floor and then backed away from it. I could still see the picture in my head as I gasped for air with my hand on my chest because it started to tighten. It appeared they were in an apartment. Ricky was holding the baby while sitting at the kitchen table in his underwear, and she was standing by the stove, seemingly preparing breakfast. I couldn't believe what I was seeing. The whole time that he was in Germany, he had been lying to me about what he was doing. He had been living off post, playing house with Edith, and had even started a family as though he was married to her. I can't even explain the pain that went through my entire body. I had never known the kind of heartbreak that made me feel like I was physically being ripped apart. He gave her what was supposed to be mine, his child. I cried uncontrollably as I fell to the floor on my knees. I felt that I was going to lose my mind from his betrayal. Then, it occurred to me that I had been set up to find this on my own. He knew I was going to do his laundry at some point. Being the coward he was, he left it in his bag for me to find so he would not have to tell me himself. Then, I had another revelation. I was also manipulated in the same way when we were in Texas. I guess he decided that since it worked before, why not do it again? He never left that letter in his pocket by accident; he planned it that way. That was his insane, evil plan from the beginning. He knew he was shamefully wrong and wouldn't be there when I found the letter. He did it to protect himself from the fallout he would get from me. Maybe it was his way of getting rid of me again, but to what end? It was obvious that he couldn't make up his mind about who he wanted to be with. He could have told me he wanted to be with Edith, and we could have gotten a divorce. He was a greedy, arrogant invertebrate and wanted to have it both ways. He never took into consideration what he was doing to me. I was so unspeakably brokenhearted. What I could not understand was why he kept making me think that our relationship was good when, the whole time, he had a serious relationship with another woman and had even started a family with her. Why did he keep stringing me along? He only had to say that he wanted to be with someone else. That would have been kinder than to continue to put me through all the lies and the terrible deceptions. I could have stayed home and started a new life with Johnathan; he had one, but I guess I was his contingency plan just in case his new relationship didn't work out. It does not feel good when you know that you have been taken advantage of and manipulated unnecessarily. Telling me the truth could have prevented all of the pain I was feeling. How much more suffering Ricky could be capable of inflicting on me was the question that was pulverizing my brain.

I pulled myself together just long enough to get into my car and drive on post to the liquor store. I was in such agony that I needed something to numb the pain; it was tearing my heart apart. I went in and purchased a fifth of Southern Comfort. Normally, I would get something to mix with it, but this was not a normal situation. I wanted to forget what I had just witnessed. I returned home, got a drinking glass from the cabinet, sat down at the kitchen table, poured myself a drink, and cried. Then I poured another drink and cried, then another, and sobbed some more until I was so drunk, I could scarcely stand. I believe I drank almost that entire bottle. I could not walk, so I had to crawl to the bathroom to throw up. I rested my back against the wall as I sat on the floor by the commode with my head hanging in despair, unable to move. I must have passed out because the next thing I remember was Ricky picking me up off the floor and carrying me to the couch. When I came to my senses and remembered what had transpired the night before, I began to weep again. Ricky tried to console me, but I didn't want him to even touch me. I screamed, "Get your hands off me," and cried because I couldn't describe how badly he had broken my heart and how badly he had broken me. Of course, he said he was so sorry for what he had done. I didn't care anymore. I told him not to touch me; I did not want him to handle me with the same hands he had been using to touch Edith. I just wanted to be left alone. He left me alone and allowed me to grieve the loss I felt in my heart. What he had done to me, our marriage, was despicable. Why did these terrible things keep happening to me? I knew I was not a saint, but he could have had the decency to tell me himself.

I walked around in a fog for days. I don't remember how I made it through each day. All I remember is that I was hurt in a way like never before. Weeks went by, and I still couldn't get it together. Ultimately, I had to let go of the pain because I was starting to lose myself in depression. Feeling sorry for myself would not change a thing. I had to pick myself up and escape the dark, depressing place I had retreated to, or I may never find my way out. I had to discover a way to accept the truth of never getting the chance to have his first child. That right was given away to his side piece. Saying it now, I don't know how I managed to make it through that life-changing event. But I am here to tell you that I did. Somehow, someway, I gathered enough strength to press forward. Ricky did all he could to explain, but there was no explaining this away. The photo was proof positive that what he had done could not be undone. You know how sometimes the more a person hurts you, the more you love them? That was me. My mental health was depleted so much that I forgave him for everything. I believe I gave up on having my dreams come true. There is no way this man could ever live up to my dreams; it was impossible. There was no benefit in fighting it any longer. Perhaps that is why he continued to do whatever he wanted because he knew I would forgive him. Remembering it makes me feel sick, and I feel so stupid for falling for his self-serving antics over and over again.

Life Goes On

I refused to let my predicament keep me down. I was a long way from home, family, and friends. There was absolutely no one to talk to. So, I buried it deep in my mind and kept on living my life as best I could. Every day, I wrestled with holding on to my sanity. It was a constant daily struggle. As if I hadn't already been through enough pain, more was about to invade my life. I started having some lower abdominal pain. I just thought that it was terrible pre-menstrual cramps. As the days passed, it began to get worse. I was in so much pain that I could hardly stand up straight. Before he left for work one morning, Ricky advised me that if I was in such terrible pain, I should see a doctor. I went to the hospital emergency room on post. I was examined and given all kinds of tests, but they could not figure out what was wrong with me. I was in excruciating pain. I was told not to take pain meds until they could discover what was wrong with me because the meds would disguise what it was, and then I was sent home. Every day, I would return to the hospital complaining that my severe pain was advancing to a higher degree. This went on for a week. I couldn't sit, I couldn't stand, I couldn't rest; I was so miserable and afraid of what may be going on inside my body. When I went back to the hospital to get help for the unbearable pain I was experiencing, miraculously, a genius ordered an ultrasound and bingo, they knew exactly what was wrong. It was a test that should have been done the first day I went to the hospital. I did not expect to hear what they were about to tell me. It took them a week to figure out that I had an ectopic pregnancy and my fallopian tube was about to rupture. I was rushed into surgery so fast that I signed the papers on my way there. I have no recollection of how long I was in surgery, but when I woke up, Ricky was there, sitting by my bed. I was still groggy, but I remember Ricky crying and telling me that while I was in surgery, my heart stopped. I died on the operating table that day, but God was with me. Once I came to myself, I remembered what had happened. I put my hand on my stomach, and it felt hard as a brick. I wondered to myself, "Why now?" It seemed cruel for me to be pregnant after finding out that Ricky had impregnated another woman and their child was alive and healthy, but our child did not survive. After I left recovery, I was put in this massive room with other women patients. As I lay in my hospital bed, I wondered why it happened this way. It was my right to be the mother of his child, not Edith. Unfortunately for me, it did not occur that way. I felt as though I was being punished for the wrongdoings of my past.

I have always dreamed of having children, but I destroyed my first chance to become a mother. I made the wrong choice and could not shake the feeling that it may have been my one and only chance. I was very disappointed in the outcome of my pregnancy, but it was over. There was nothing I could have done to prevent the extremity of my pregnancy. This event certainly put a spotlight on the emotional disaster that had turned my life upside down. It seemed that tragedy followed me wherever I went. It appeared to chase me down no matter how much I struggled to escape it; it always caught up with me.

Well, I'm Still a Woman

On another note, no matter what a girl is going through, she must consider how she looks. I asked Ricky to get me some scarves to tie on my head; I was embarrassed by the alopecia I had developed after marrying him.

According to www.MedicalNewsToday.com, Alopecia areata is a common autoimmune disorder that often results in unpredictable hair loss. It affects roughly 6.8 million people in the United States. In the majority of cases, hair falls out in small patches around the size of a quarter. For most people, hair loss is nothing more than a few patches, though in some cases, it can be more extreme.

So, I braided my hair in small bunches and wrapped my head with one of the silk scarves Ricky had bought for me. After seeing the scarves and how beautiful they were, I felt in my gut that Ricky did not pick them out on his own. His taste was not that good. Ladies, you know how your intuition warns you sometimes? Well, I got a ding, ding, ding in my head. I let it go because, at that moment, I needed the scarves and him. I was not well, and I did not feel like trying to investigate the mystery of the scarves. I spent a week in the hospital without being able to eat. I had a tube in my nose going down my neck, draining a puss-like substance into a bag attached to my bed. It was so uncomfortable. I could feel the tube in my throat every time I swallowed. All I could have to eat was ice chips. After a few days, the doctor removed the tube. Then, I was taken to an examination room, and she removed the catheter. That was a harrowing experience: very, very painful. She told me I needed to use the bathroom naturally before I could be released to go home. Ricky visited me a couple of times while I was there. He must have had something more pressing in his life, more important than being with his wife. Who was in the hospital because she had emergency surgery after getting pregnant in her tubes with his child. I was not surprised by it; he often chose other people before me. Putting all that aside, I thought this could be a great chance to make an effort to stop smoking since I had not been able to smoke for a solid week. I told myself that's just what I'm going to do. At least something good could come out of this ordeal. But as soon as I could get my hands on a pack of cigarettes, I went right back to puffing on one. It was going to take more strength than I could summon. I used the excuse that a lot of people often use, "I need a cigarette to help calm my nerves." With what I had just gone through, I was convinced that it helped me.

CHAPTER 9
MOVING ON

I left the hospital with my incision open with a staple on each end. Ricky cleaned it with peroxide and changed the bandage daily until the incision closed independently. That meant no baths or showers. I had to bathe with soap and water from a washbasin. This was not a new thing to me. I was taught as a child how to take a complete bath using just a pan of water, a face cloth, and a bar of soap. I was thankful that my mama had taught me well, though I did need help from Ricky because I was sore from the surgery. I did not allow myself to process what had happened to me and what it meant in my relationship with my husband. Before the pain started, I did not know that I was pregnant. I lost my child because of the chlamydia that Rickey had exposed me too early in our marriage. My reproductive organs had so much scar tissue that the Doctor said that I had a fifty-fifty chance of ever having children. That didn't have much of an impact on Ricky because he had already started his family with someone else. My vision of having a family was even more impossible now. You know, just living that American Dream and having that "happily ever after" life that so many of us search for our entire lives. It did not appear that was the plan God had for my life. I believe everything happens for a reason, but I couldn't figure out why my life was so chaotic and painful. At that time, I didn't turn to Jesus for help. I just kept right on making mistake after mistake, doing whatever I thought was best for me. We always believe that we know what we are doing, even when we have never done it before. I wasn't going to church. Attending one did not cross my mind. I had been living my life without counsel from God or anyone else. I believed I did not need anyone to help me make decisions in my life. However, my track record would beg to differ.

The healing process was slow; I was very sore for weeks. Ricky helped me to get around and to do the things that I could not do for myself. My incision closed up, and I was on the mend and ready to go back to my everyday life. I appreciated his help, but I constantly remembered why I was in that position in the first place. I daydreamed of how things could have been. What if I had made it to term with our child? Would our lives have changed? Would it be wise to bring a child into an already volatile situation? Not giving birth may have been a blessing in disguise. Sometimes, a blessing does not look like one until it completely unfolds. God works in ways we do not understand. Trying to reduce the danger of living with Ricky was horrible enough without the presence of a child. I could not imagine attempting to maintain my safety while taking care of an infant child. It is scary thinking about it, knowing what I would have had to endure. I cannot swear that Ricky's attitude would have changed if we had a child together. People are who they are, no matter the circumstance. But then, it was no longer an issue that I had to concern myself with. My child never had a chance anyway because of the damage to my reproductive organs.

Moving On | 147

Unforgettable Holiday

The 4th of July was coming up, and I wanted to get out of the apartment and do something fun. On that day, Ricky told me about a park not too far from where we lived, with a beautiful lake and paddle boats that people could rent. I thought it was a great suggestion. We went to the park, and I sat down at a picnic table, enjoying the view. I remember thinking how cool the temperature was for the July Holiday. I was happy that I had brought a sweater with me, just in case. Ricky walked over to me and said that he needed to pick up someone else and bring them to the park. I said okay because I thought that it was probably some guys from his unit who didn't have transportation of their own, and he was doing a good deed by helping them out. I thought it was very nice of him to do. I sat there and waited for him, threw my sweater around my shoulders, occasionally looking at the entrance to the park. There were a lot of people at the park that day. Children were enjoying themselves running and playing; couples were picnicking on blankets. I watched them for a while, and then I looked up and saw our car coming through the gate.

As the car approached, I could see that Ricky had a carload of females, not men. I had a puzzled look on my face, wondering why Ricky had gone and picked up a bunch of females to bring to the park. How did he know these women? Remember that ding, ding, ding alarm going off in my head at the hospital? This was the reason why. They were riding in our car as if that was not their first time doing it. I felt humiliated sitting there, seeing my husband with other women in our car. Is this why he did not have time to come visit me in the hospital? After letting them out of the car, he came to where I was sitting and behaved as though everything was normal. And I'm looking at him, waiting for an explanation as to why he just drove up with a carload of women. I asked him, "Who are those women?" His reaction to my question was that they were just some friends. I remembered how the one sitting in the front with him was leaning towards him, resting on the armrest as if she belonged where she was. I felt they knew all about me, but I knew nothing of them. I was enraged. I could not get a satisfactory answer from him. Where did he meet a bunch of women? He indeed did not work with them. I was placed once again in a disgraceful position that I did not like at all.

I knew he was deceiving me, and I had no leverage to do anything about it, and he knew it. Having a wife was not enough to prevent him from doing whatever he wanted. He knew he held all the power. I had no one that I could turn to except him. He did manage to get me to agree to a boat ride on the lake, possibly hoping it would calm me down. It did not dissuade me from feeling immense anger towards him; constantly putting other people ahead of me was atrocious behavior for a husband. Returning to the dock, I got out of the boat and stomped off to sit in our car, waiting to be taken home. He took me home first and then went back to pick up his so-called "friends." I was distraught that he had the brazen audacity to pull this on me. I suspected that he was having an affair with one of those women or maybe more than one; I don't know. That was the only conclusion that I could come up with that made any sense. This was classic Ricky behavior. He had never been the kind of man who was faithful to one woman, even if she was his wife. He acted as though he would miss something if he didn't find out what another woman had to offer. He kept his options open by holding on to me, just in case. You know, I look back and ask myself, "Why did I put up with so much from this man"? I cannot come up with an acceptable answer to my question. It was like he had power over me, from which I could not break away. He kept doing what he wanted, with whom he wanted, and I foolishly continued to forgive him.

Not My Choice

It came time for Ricky to go to his next assignment. He told me that his superiors had given him a choice of being stationed in Hawaii or West Germany. I made it known that I wanted to go to Hawaii, but Ricky wanted to go back to Germany for the third time. I was troubled by his decision, but I had no control over what he decided; even though the choice should have been made by both of us, it was entirely up to him. I told him where I wanted to go, but it did not faze him. I now realize that he probably chose where he wanted to be reassigned at all the other places he had been stationed. The only thing that made me feel better was that I would accompany him this time. In the back of my mind, I knew Ricky wanted to get back to Germany to see his son and Edith. I just suppressed those thoughts and told myself that everything was going to be alright. I mean, how bad could it be after all the things I had already survived? This was a chance to go to another country without having to pay, so I thought, forgetting nothing is free; there is always a price to pay. I would have never visited another country if Ricky was not in the Army. So, I took advantage of that perk. He always talked about how beautiful and different Europe was. I wanted to see for myself, although I would have preferred to go to Hawaii. I had already missed that chance once. It was nice and warm there and unmistakably beautiful. It would have been the ultimate duty station as far as I was concerned, but my opinion didn't mean very much to him.

Homeward Bound

It was late winter when Ricky and I prepared to drive home to North Carolina to spend time with our family and friends before we departed for West Germany. The car that we drove to Washington was a little worn, so we went car shopping. We found a newer model of the car we already had. It was a very nice car, so Ricky bought it. The movers came and packed all our belongings, boxed them up, placed them in wooden crates, and took them to be shipped to Germany. I didn't know what may lie ahead, but I was aware of my circumstance, and I was prepared to deal with it, come what may. I just couldn't give up on my marriage. I wasn't built that way; I was not a quitter, so I continued to fight for it. On a very early cold and snowy morning, we left Tacoma. It was in the middle of the night. We were so anxious and excited about going home that I think we did not realize that we probably should have waited until daylight to have better visibility. I believe that Ricky was confident about driving in the snow because he had done it in Germany and thought this would be a piece of cake. We had to drive through the mountains, and let me tell you, I was scared out of my mind. We couldn't see where the road ended and the shoulder began. There were no railings to keep people from driving off the side of the mountain. It was snowing so hard that we couldn't see two feet ahead of us. I wanted to pull over when we reached an area with space enough to do so, to wait until we could see better, but Ricky wanted to keep going. We passed 18-wheelers by the side of the road that could go no further. Some people stopped to put chains on their tires for better traction. We didn't own chains for our tires. Now, let me stop and say this. I know that it was the hand of God that was with us as we traveled through those mountains. That is the only way we made it out alive.

It was a very hazardous situation. I was terrified, thinking that we could drive off the side of the mountain without even realizing it. I was so nervous I was pressing my imaginary brakes and steering my imaginary car from the passenger seat. There were so many twists and turns traveling through those mountains. The only guidance we had was following the tire tracks from the previous cars that had gone through, which could have ended up being a mistake. Thank God, we made it through that treacherous journey, finally coming down off the mountain and making it to Oregon in the early morning hours. The snowplows had cleared the highway, making the drive less risky. I was thankful and relieved that we were heading towards California, where it was not snowing and much warmer. The pent-up tension slowly left my body.

We took the same route back home that we used to get to Washington. It was winter again, and we surely did not want to run into any more winter weather. It took days, but we were getting closer to home. When we got to the Deep South, we ran into some terrible stormy weather. I don't know if it was a hurricane or a tropical storm, but it was fierce. It was raining so hard that we could barely see the taillights of the car ahead of us. I was holding on to the door handle, all tensed up, hoping and praying that the rain would stop or Ricky would have the sense to pull over at a rest stop or a convenience store and wait until the storm passed. I was so afraid that something awful would happen. The highway had a lot of traffic, but of course, Ricky did not want to stop. Even though neither of us deserved it, the Lord kept us through that too. After the storm, we went through state after state, enjoying the beauty of each one. We finally reached home in the mid-afternoon. It was beautiful weather in North Carolina. There were clear blue skies, and the temperature was in the eighties. I was thrilled to see home and our families again. I didn't discuss losing our baby, hoping no one would ask me about it. It was a private matter, and I did not want to talk about it. I just wanted to put it behind me and move on. Ricky hung out with his family and friends as though nothing had happened. I was not particularly shocked by that because, remember, he already had a child, plus all the other dishonorable things he had done while we were away that no one knew anything about except me. He concealed them without any trace of guilt on his part. Being a man whose ego needed to be stroked, he probably bragged about the son he had in Germany to his family and friends when I was not around. After all, his illegitimate son was part of his family, not mine. I even remember that Edith had sent a beautiful clock encased under a glass dome as a gift for his mother, her son's grandmother, like she was Ricky's wife. I remember someone mentioning where the clock came from, as though they wanted to make sure I knew about it, and my mother-in-law displayed it like she was proud of it. He had to have given her the address to his parent's house. I would not be shocked if they knew about his child before I did. His mother probably had talked to his baby mama on the phone. It would not surprise me. Another kick in the teeth.

A Whole Other Country

We spent about twenty-five days at home. I had to get a passport and get vaccinated with multiple shots to leave the country. It came time to say so long to our families. Ricky asked his father to take care of our car until we returned from Germany. We caught a military flight out of Charleston, South Carolina. I had never seen a plane as large as the one we were about to board. We were shown to our seats, and we waited for the plane to take off. I gripped both armrests in anticipation of our flight leaving the ground. I held on for dear life, trembling, questioning how that gigantic plane would be able to stay in the air. I was not a fan of flying. The flight attendant told us that the flight would take around ten hours to reach West Germany. Finally, we leveled off at 30,000 feet, and we were on our way to Europe. I spent as much time as I could sleeping to keep my mind off of all the water we were flying over to reach Germany. I could not entertain myself by looking out the window because it was nighttime. We landed at Ramstein Air Force Base in Frankfurt, Germany, during the morning hours. Germany was like no other place I had ever seen. I felt as though we had traveled back in time. It was a cold and beautiful place. After leaving the airport, we checked into a lovely Bed and Breakfast in Frankfurt. The bed had a thick goose-down comforter on it, lucky for us because it was freezing out, and it kept us warm and toasty through the night. The following day, we had a breakfast of freshly baked rolls, sliced meat, cheeses, jam, fresh butter, and freshly brewed coffee with cream delivered to our room. The coffee was excellent, and the rolls were too. After eating, we showered, got dressed, packed our things, and checked out.

We then caught a cab to the military base, where Ricky was stationed. I was stunned that almost all of the taxi cabs were Mercedes-Benz's. In America, it was a car that only the rich drove. I had never been in one before, which made the ride to the base extraordinary. On the way, I noticed that there were other vehicles on the road that had American car makers' names on them, but I had never seen one like them in the States. I was like a wide-eyed child, taking it all in, amazed at all I was seeing. When we arrived at the post, they provided a place for us to stay until we found an apartment. We were put on a waiting list for military housing. That was going to take a long time. So, Ricky scouted out some of the villages that surrounded the post and asked around until he found an apartment in a small village not far from his duty station. He took me there to have a look at it.

The village had a massive wall surrounding it with one way in and out. There was a short tunnel entering the village, and the streets were made of cobblestones. All types of artisan shops were aligned on the street. We drove up in front of a two-story building. The apartment we were going to look at was located on the ground floor. The owners of the building lived on the top floor. The walls were made of cement at least a foot thick. There was a stone plaque on the outside of the building that said it was built in the seventeenth century. I truly felt like I was in another time in history. The apartment was ok, but not that great. It was not as modern as the ones that I was used to. It was decorated with dark earth tones, had very little furniture, and what was there was very old. It was close to where Ricky went to work, so we took it. It was an opportunity to live amongst the people of the country we were now living in. The apartment owners were German and could speak very little English, but they had children who could. They translated for us and told us how much the monthly payment would be in Deutsche Marks. We agreed and rented the apartment. We notified shipping where to bring our things. I was excited to move off the post and fascinated to experience living in a foreign country. I wanted to get back to preparing our meals again and sleeping in a bed in our place. Ricky asked other soldiers who lived off post where they had gotten their furniture. He was told we could sign out the items we needed from a warehouse on post. There were no queen or king-size beds available, so we got two twin beds that we pushed together to make it a king-size bed. I placed a folded blanket between the beds to fill in the gap to make it more comfortable.

Our boxes arrived, and I started unpacking. I knew once I had some of my things in our apartment, it would start to feel a little more like home. We got everything unpacked and in its place. But I began to feel uneasy about being surrounded by people that I couldn't communicate with. I don't know what came over me. Perhaps it was knowing I was thousands of miles from home in a foreign country. I thought about how isolated I was from English-speaking people and went into depression. I wouldn't go out while Ricky was working. I felt so all alone; I did not see anyone that looked or spoke like me. The shows on TV were all in German, so Ricky bought a VHS tape player so we could watch video tapes. There were different types of artisan shops in the village that I wanted to go to, but I was afraid. In the mornings, I would look out the window and watch the people go from shop to shop carrying baskets to pick up their food for the day. This was a task that they performed every day. I don't believe they had access to the type of refrigerators we did in the United States. It appeared to be a great way for them to greet their neighbors every morning. I watched them as they stopped along the sidewalks in small groups to chat. I could hear them speaking German, wishing I could understand what they were talking about. It was fascinating watching them every day. I would get up early in the morning to see Ricky off to work, and then I would entertain myself by peeking out the lace curtains of my apartment windows at them. Finally, Ricky taught me enough German to patronize the shops when I was comfortable enough to do so. I got my nerve up and went out on my own one day. First, I went to the bakery to get some freshly baked bread. They had some delicious-looking baked goods I had never seen before. Along with my bread, I chose a sweet bread that looked like a bear claw but wasn't. It had a nutty-flavored filling inside, drizzled with icing. Then I went to the deli and purchased some sliced meats and cheeses for sandwiches. I was so proud of myself walking back to the apartment. From that day forward, I was no longer afraid to venture out. Once I confronted my fear, it disappeared. I regained my confidence and challenged myself to face my next obstacle with bravado.

Sometimes, the things that scare us the most are what we need to face.

No Longer in the USA

When I got to Germany and found out that there were no hairdressers for black women, I had to figure out what I would do. My hair was styled in a Jheri Curl. I had to hypothesize about how to do my hair myself. There may have been some American women living on post that could have done my hair, but I was new there and didn't know any females yet. So, I went to the commissary and bought hair rollers of different sizes, a hairdryer with a cap, and hair products to achieve the results I wanted. After several attempts, I learned how to give myself a Jheri Curl after three months 'worth of new growth. It took me almost a full day to complete the process, but it was worth it. That was something I never thought I would end up doing, but I learned how to make things work for me.

I got more and more comfortable living in Germany. I was accomplishing things that I had no skills in. Ricky met a guy on post that was returning to the States (going back to the World, as they liked to say) and needed to sell his car. We needed transportation, so he bought it. We could now travel to different places. The car was an Audi 5-speed stick shift. Most of the cars in Germany were stick shifts at the time we were there. My problem was I did not know how to drive a stick shift. My dad had tried to teach me in his pick-up truck where the gear shift was located on the column when I was sixteen, but I could not get the hang of it. Ricky took me to some less-traveled roads so he could teach me to drive a stick to get my German driver's license. He stopped by the DMV on post while at work one day and picked up a driver's manual so that I could study it to pass my test. It was not easy because I had to learn and understand

German road signs, but I did it. I studied very hard every day until I felt I was ready. Ricky took me on post to take my driver's test, and I aced it. I was so very proud of myself. It was a challenge that I faced head-on, and I crushed it. I think he got a little jealous that I had done so well, but I did not let that stop me from celebrating my accomplishment. I was now equipped to drive.

Driving was scary at first, but I grabbed hold of my big girl pants, adjusted them, and started going out on my own. One of the first things that I did was go on post to apply for a job. The post-employment office representative told me that they didn't have anything available at that time, but I could work at the commissary for tips only, so I took it. It was hard work, and customers sometimes treated me like I was beneath them, something I never understood. We were all Americans living in a foreign country, trying to make the best of our situation. You would think that we would support each other and not judge people by what they did for a living or the color of their skin, but some of them needed to feel superior. I placed all their groceries on a cart similar to a hand truck, pushed it to their car, and unloaded them. They did not have to tip me if they did not want to. That was the chance I took working there. No matter how heavy the bags were, I had to put them into the car all by myself. There were very few gentlemen who would offer to help. Some would let me do all the work while they stood back with their arms folded and watched me, then got into their car and drove away without a thank you.

I worked with a great group of women who were also dependents and were not afraid of hard work. We talked about our lives in Germany and back home and helped each other out if needed. One day, as I was taking some groceries to a customer's car, I heard a woman screaming and crying that she had locked her keys in her car along with her infant child with the car running. The baby was crying, and she could not get in the car. Someone called the Military Police. It was so frightening to watch. Anything could have happened while she was in the commissary away from her car. I didn't have time to stay and see what happened, but I know she got in trouble for putting her child at risk while going inside the store to pick up a few things. The military was very strict about people doing that kind of thing. I did not understand why she couldn't see the danger of leaving her child alone in a running car beforehand. I'm sure she regretted the consequences of her actions. I can only hope that she never made that mistake again.

The post-employment office called me one day to tell me about a position that was open at the bowling alley. I went into the office and filled out an application. I kept working at the commissary until I got that long-awaited phone call letting me know I had gotten the job. I had never even been to a bowling alley before, so I did not know what to expect. When I reported for work, I met the bowling alley manager. I was very surprised that he was a German. He was a very nice man, which I was happy to know. I was trained to work behind the counter, preparing food, resetting the lanes, cleaning off the tables, and keeping the floor clean. It was a pretty cool job. I got to meet new people from other states back in the world. Most of them were very friendly. My boss would sometimes get a little frisky with me, but I don't think he meant any harm. Some men don't see that they are committing a crime called sexual harassment; they have been doing it for so long that it seems harmless. I never took him seriously. I would laugh it off and go on about my business. Most women have had to deal with it at some point in their lives. As long as I was not being touched, I could let it go.

New Things

One of the ladies who worked with me was crocheting on her break one day. She was the assistant to the manager of the bowling alley. I had always wanted to learn to crochet but didn't know anyone who knew how. I asked her if she would teach me, and she said sure. She regularly brought her crochet to the bowling alley to work on during her breaks and when business was slow. She showed me a few basics, like making a chain, which is the foundation on which all crochet is formed. She brought me some yarn with a crochet needle and told me to practice making chains. Once I mastered that, she showed me how to make a double crochet stitch that I could use to create a scarf; I did, and it turned out great. I was very proud of myself. Once I finished that project, I wanted to learn more and more. She had taught me well, but I craved more. So, I went to the library on post and checked out a book on crocheting and taught myself to crochet and how to read patterns. Then, I went shopping for yarn and a complete set of crochet needles to improve my skills. When I had time on my hands at home, I worked on my crochet to increase my abilities. It was relaxing, and sometimes I used it to take my mind off things; it was a great way to lower my stress. I still have the very first scarf and Afghan I ever made. I also made Ricky a pullover sweater vest using a pattern that I designed in my head. He went out one night with some friends, got into a fight, and it was destroyed. I have learned a lot since then. Using patterns, I have made sweaters, throws, bedspreads, and doilies. I felt great about having accomplished a long-time dream, and I have passed my knowledge on to a friend. I took a chance at gaining knowledge about something I had only dreamed of, and it paid off. With determination and discipline, this proves that you can do anything you set your mind to if only you believe.

The bowling alley was an exciting place to work. There was always music playing over the loudspeaker, people laughing, and having fun bowling. I was enjoying life in a new place. I had a job, I was getting used to being in another country, I had new friends, and the abuse that I had been enduring in the past seemed to have subsided. Ricky and I went out to restaurants for dinner sometimes. I came to know what a schnitzel, Cordon Bleu, and Calamari were, and they were delicious. I didn't like the Calamari so much because of the legs, but it did taste similar to fried liver to me. We went to beer festivals, wine festivals, and even The October Festival. I always made it my business to get some warm candied nuts sold at the fest; I could not seem to get enough of them; they were yummy. It was incredible to learn of some of the customs of the people. We would be driving sometimes and pass a construction site and notice that the men would be drinking beer. I was shocked, but I found out later they did this because the water was undrinkable. I noticed particles that looked like crystals floating in the water in my apartment, which I only used for bathing. Also, another custom was that they ate their heaviest meal at lunchtime and had two hours off work to eat and relax. They ate their lightest meal in the evening—the opposite of what we do here in the USA.

Sometimes we went out to nightclubs with another couple. A friend of Ricky's accompanied us along with his wife to a nightclub called The Cave. I put on my little black dress, black tights, and a pair of black leather heels that I had bought, and we stepped out into the nightlife of Germany. When we walked in, the walls looked like the walls of a natural cave. We sat at a booth for four and ordered drinks. We had such a great time dancing and enjoying cocktails that I barely noticed that Ricky was consuming more than his share of alcohol. I shrugged off my concern, convincing myself that it was nothing to worry about. At the end of our evening, we said goodbye to our friends and headed home. Returning home that night, we ran into a problem approaching our apartment. It was a freezing night out, and the cobblestones in our village had completely frozen over. We could only partially make it down the street because the car kept sliding. Ricky gave up trying to drive the car to our front door. I could not walk home in the heels I was wearing, so he inched his way to our apartment and got a pair of boots for me to change into. I took off my heels and replaced them with my boots, grabbed hold of the car door to lift myself and get my balance. Slowly, I started to make my way down the street. We walked home, or should I say we slid our way home, trying not to fall. It was funny, but not funny because it was dangerous. There was some laughing, some curse words, and a few oops, but we made it safely to our door without falling, considering we had been drinking. We got inside, laughed about how long it took for us to get there, undressed, and crawled into bed.

Acquiring a Souvenir

We went shopping in a town not far from the village where we lived, stopping in different little shops looking for something unique to bring back to the States. I settled on purchasing some lovely crystal wine glasses, champagne glasses, and water glasses. I wanted souvenirs that would remind me of the time we spent in a foreign country. The US dollar could be exchanged at the local bank into Deutsche Marks. At that time, I could get three Marks for one dollar, which was a great deal. Our money went further in the German economy than it would in America. I wanted to buy some furniture to bring back home with us; sadly, we never got around to purchasing any. Many military families often returned home with furniture they bought in Germany. Wall units were a big thing during my time there. If I had gotten the opportunity, I would have purchased some Scandinavian furniture to ship back home when we left. It was made of solid wood with clean lines and lovely light colors; it was beautiful.

War Games

Once a year, Ricky's unit went to Crete, Greece for two weeks to practice firing missiles at targets from the tank they had been training in. I was left to fend for myself while he was away. I had gotten comfortable with my surroundings and felt confident that I could handle being on my own. I had work to keep me busy and friends at the bowling alley, so I was good. When Ricky would go on these trips, he would bring back items that he had purchased in Greece. This time, he brought back two small, beautiful 18-karat gold-trimmed white flower vases decorated with Greek hieroglyphics, a fifth of Ouzo, and a white Flokati rug. Also, one of the soldiers in his squad brought back a large black vase trimmed in eighteen-karat gold and gave it to me. He wanted to show his appreciation for all the times that I had prepared American dishes for him and other members of his squad. I was stunned and appreciative of the gift. It was lovely. I made pancakes for them sometimes on the weekends when Ricky invited them over. During the holidays, I prepared a traditional Thanksgiving or Christmas meal. Jokingly, one of the guys in his squad, the one that gave me the vase, told me if I ever got tired of Ricky to let him know. I did not know if he was joking or if he was serious, especially since he did it when no one was around. He was not of my race, born and raised in Kansas City. I was shocked by his statement, but I kept it to myself so as not to create confusion within Ricky's squad or with him at home. During one of those Christmas holidays, Ricky made the occasion more festive by giving me a 14-carat gold diamond cut wedding band. I was not expecting anything like that from him. When we got married, we couldn't afford to pay the Justice of the Peace. We certainly could not purchase wedding rings. After being married for several years, it finally occurred to him to put a ring on my finger. I must say, it was beautiful, and I loved it. At that moment, I felt like I was his wife; I felt appreciated and special.

Trips

Ricky and I would often take trips to Frankfurt, a big city compared to where we lived. He let me drive sometimes. To get to Frankfurt, we needed to get on the autobahn. There was no speed limit on that highway. I would think that I was driving extremely fast, and a car would pass me like I was standing still. Once, when we were on our way to Frankfurt, we saw a very bad accident. A car had hit a tree, wrapped around it, and climbed to the top of it. I had never witnessed anything like it in my life. When there was an accident on the autobahn, you automatically knew, more than likely, that everyone involved was dead because of the unlimited high speeds people would travel. When I drove, I tried to drive just fast enough to stay out of everyone's way. We started going to Frankfurt a lot, which I had no problem with. I enjoyed the chance to go to a city. There were times that I stayed in the car while Ricky went to visit someone he said was his friend, saying he would be back soon, after which we went home. I didn't give it much thought. I enjoyed seeing the bright lights of a large city. Watching the people, the different nationalities, and how they dressed was fascinating to me. Because of the freezing nights, they wore leather coats with fur and boots. They were very fashionable people. After seeing the latest styles they wore, I planned to purchase a pair of leather boots with a coat to match. Leather was very inexpensive because of the exchange rate of the American dollar.

Returning to Frankfurt so often started to make me curious. I eventually found out why we made so many trips there. Ricky was purchasing drugs. I knew he smoked marijuana back home, but he could not get that in Germany, so someone introduced him to black tar hashish, cocaine, and heroin. I was astonished at his behavior. I tried to convince him that we did not need to go down this road; it could ruin everything. Of course, he did not listen to me. Once, returning home from one of our trips, he brought out a bag of cocaine, poured it onto a hand mirror on the coffee table, positioned it into lines, then used a tightly rolled dollar bill and snorted it into his nostrils. He utilized heroin in the same way. With the hashish, he would take some of the tobacco out of a cigarette, replace it with hashish, and smoke it. I couldn't believe what I was seeing. He was in the military, and he knew that they would not put up with this type of behavior if they knew about it. He was putting his long-time military career in jeopardy. All this time, he had been keeping his drug use a secret. I thought he was taking me to Frankfurt to hang out, have some fun, and see the sites in another City. All the time, he was going there to buy drugs. By the time I found out what was happening, he was addicted. He asked me to try just a little, but I refused. He continued on this road of destruction until I started to see him less and less, now that I was aware of what he was up to. He knew that I disapproved of what he was doing, so he began to associate more with his friends. I'm sure they were getting high, just like him. I went to work and came home to an empty apartment. Now, I knew that Ricky's absence could also mean that he was spending time with Edith. I had no evidence of that, but I knew she and his son were the main reason why he wanted to go back to Germany in the first place. I didn't know what to think; it could have been both.

Being in a foreign country had brought us closer together, so it seemed. I was always hoping that a change in our environment would help our marriage, not realizing that he was the one that needed to change; the environment did not matter. I worried about our relationship so much that I surmised that if we had more in common, our relationship might improve. The next time Ricky tried to get me to snort some heroin with him, I foolishly tried it. I know it was stupid thinking, but I did it anyway. I was desperate to redeem my marriage. I had no clue what I was exposing my body to. I did it a few times with Ricky and concluded that it was not for me. I did not like the way it made me feel. It made me so relaxed that I would fall asleep; addicts call it nodding off. I didn't feel like myself, and I felt out of control of my body, so I quit. I was blessed because I did not get addicted to it, but unfortunately for us, Ricky was already an addict.

The next thing I knew, he had stopped snorting the heroin and was now shooting it into his arm with a hypodermic needle. I was livid. I tried to talk to him, but he just would not listen. I continued to travel with him to Frankfurt to keep my eye on him, hoping to keep him out of trouble. He was allowing this drug to take over his life, and that scared me. Things got really bad. He started to sneak off to Frankfurt and buy drugs when he got off work before coming home to keep me from knowing about it and me from trying to stop him. He kept this up for a while. Until one night, he did not come home at all. I was terrified that something bad had happened to him. Sure enough, I was right. He came home that morning and told me he had gotten arrested while he was in Frankfurt. He said he had to call his first sergeant to bail him out of jail. It took some maneuvering, but his superiors got him out of trouble with the German government. But it also meant that he was no longer in the military and that we had to leave the country. I was devastated by the position he put us in. I was enjoying where we were living, and now we had to leave because of his disastrous addiction to drugs. I was forced to leave a country and life I had grown to love. It was nothing to be traveling down the road and see huge wine vineyards with spectacular bunches of voluptuous grapes hanging from their vines or large cherry trees loaded with ripe red cherries growing wild beside the highway. We once traveled to see this magnificent castle sitting on a hill surrounded by beautiful wildflowers. Some of the landscapes we saw were like beautifully painted artwork. The German people were so friendly. We may not have communicated verbally in the same language, but kindness and good manners have a language all their own. I was going to miss the great food and drinks of the country. Tearfully, I had to give my notice at my job. I met so many wonderful, loving people at the bowling alley, and it was hard to say farewell to them, knowing I would never see them again. On my last day at work, they all got together to give me a going-away party. I was surprised and hurt at the same time. I received a wine bottle with a lovely portrait of the village I lived in hand-painted on the front of it, along with the name of the village, as a gift. Also, I was given a gorgeous crystal bell that I adore. We shared food, well wishes, and solemn goodbyes. By the time I left work, the tears were flowing like a raging river. I often wonder about them and how their lives are going, hoping that they are okay. It was hard leaving friends I had grown to love. I miss them dearly.

Time to Leave

It wasn't long before we were packing up again to move back to the States. We had to call our families to let them know that we would be returning home earlier than we had anticipated. I didn't reveal why we were coming home early. I never wanted my family to find out how Ricky had let himself and me down by getting involved with drugs so deep that it destroyed his military career. I was so hurt and embarrassed that he had put us in such a dire predicament. Our future looked dark and gloomy once again. His being in the military was the only thing that kept us financially able to take care of ourselves. Due to his drug addiction, that was no longer the case. I was scheduled to leave the country first. There were some things that Ricky had to take care of before he could leave, then he would follow. He had to sell our car, pay our bills, and then get processed out of the army. I packed my bags to leave for my trip home. As I was packing, I picked up the "How to Crochet" book that I checked out of the library, skimmed through it, decided that I had not learned enough from it, and put it in my suitcase. Yes, I took the book that I was supposed to return to the library. It was not one of my proudest moments. I wanted to continue learning all I could about how to crochet. I knew that when Ricky was processed out of the Army, he would have to pay for the book; he had to pay all debts before leaving the country. Why shouldn't he pay for it? He was the reason why we had to leave in the first place. At least, that is how I felt about it. Do I sound bitter? That's because I was.

Ricky had initially joined the military because we were both unemployed. There were no jobs at home. We had no choice in the matter; it was over. We had to leave Germany. The night before I left, I slept in Ricky's arms on the only piece of furniture left in the apartment, a very narrow couch, because we had to return all the things we had signed out from the warehouse. I was so not looking forward to leaving the next morning. Ricky drove me to Frankfurt to catch my flight. I was crying because I did not want to leave him behind. He kept reassuring me that everything was going to be alright. I wanted to believe him; I wasn't sure about that because things had changed for us. We would have to deal with what came next together. I was worried about the drug habit Ricky had acquired while we had been away. How were we going to counteract that after getting back home? That was something that could not be wished away. It had destroyed our life in Germany. Would he have sense enough to get help when he returned home? I was plagued by so many uncertainties for our future. I had ten hours to think about them on my flight back to the States. I checked my baggage and proceeded to the gate. We sat down to wait for them to start boarding the plane. I was a little apprehensive about flying back home alone. It was unnerving thinking about how long I would be up in the air before landing at LaGuardia Airport in New York. I asked the Lord to please keep me safe until I reached home, and I promised Him that I would never get on another plane. It was time to go. We hugged and kissed for a long time, saying our goodbyes. As I walked away, I looked back one more time to say goodbye before boarding the plane. Our life in Germany was now officially over; I was on my way back to the United States.

CHAPTER 10
BACK TO THE WORLD

The flight back home seemed to take longer than ten hours. I was so afraid of flying home alone without Ricky. I had so much on my mind I closed my eyes and attempted to sleep. When we hit some turbulence, it woke me up; I was right back worrying about what we would live off of. Finally, we reached New York. I was so very thankful I had made it safely across all that water. I changed flights in New York and headed for the airport in Fayetteville, NC. I was met at the airport by Ricky's brother, driving the car that we had left behind while we were in Germany. He drove us to his home, where he got out, and I took over the car. I thanked him for picking me up from the airport, said goodbye, and proceeded to my dad's house. I was thrilled to see my family, just not under the circumstances that brought me home. I lived with my dad until Ricky returned to the States. It was frustrating communicating with him because he had to use a payphone to call me, and I could not reach him from my end. It crossed my mind that Ricky could be spending his last days in Germany with his illegitimate family, Edith and his son. I don't believe that he made such a deliberate effort to get back to Germany without seeing them while he was there. He was doing so many things behind my back; I have to believe that seeing them was one of them. I will never know for sure whether he did or not. He most certainly would not tell me the truth if I asked.

The first thing on my agenda after getting back home was to get busy finding a job to help take care of us and money to obtain a place for us to live. The only place I could think of to look for a job was Spanco Yarns. My former boss had always supported me when I would return home from traveling with Ricky. I hoped that it would still be the case. I went and applied for a job; they welcomed me back with open arms. I was rehired in the same position as a machine operator on third shift; the same as before I left to go to Tacoma. Now at least one of us had a job. I started working as soon as possible. It felt almost as if I had never left. When I worked, I sometimes ran into the Plant Manager when first shift reported to work. He always greeted me with a smile and a hello. I had often heard other workers complain that he never spoke to them. They said he was prejudiced, but he never made me feel that way. I was so blessed that he looked out for me when I came looking for a job. Upon returning to Spanco, I was anxious to see Johnathan, but he quit his job while I was gone. It would have been awkward seeing him anyway after what I had done to him. I could not blame him if he never forgave me. It was for the best that he was no longer working there. Things might have gotten ugly if I had to explain to him why I chose to leave with Ricky. I had made a mess of things; there was no need to rub his face in it by seeing me again and me still with Ricky.

Life Change

Knowing that I could not trust Ricky to have access to the money I made because of his drug addiction, I started a checking account in my name to use to pay our bills and save money for a place to live. I needed to take precautionary measures in case Ricky would not seek help for his addiction when he returned home. When he got back to the States, the first thing we needed him to do was find a job. I was relieved that he was back home and safe, but we had to start making some money to support ourselves. We moved back in with his parents, but I wanted us to have an apartment. He started to look for a job, but it was tough. He took odd jobs to keep some occasional money coming in. I was still worried about his addiction and troubled about it overtaking him and our lives the way it did in Germany. I suggested that he try and get some professional help for his addiction. He did not want to hear anything I said. When he got back to the States, his attitude had changed. His obsession with drugs and losing his military career made him an angry person. Getting help for his addiction was out of the question. Our relationship had changed from what it was in Germany. He was truly good to me while we were there; it gave me hope. Now that we were back home, that life disappeared. I suspected there was more going on with him than I wanted to know about.

We accumulated enough money to rent a reasonably priced apartment. We found one in great shape, about six or seven miles from his parents. All our things shipped from Germany had arrived and we notified Ft. Bragg where we needed them to be delivered. Unfortunately, we did not own any furniture, so we bought bedroom, dining room, and living room furniture from a popular furniture store with a downpayment and the balance in monthly payments. By the time we got it all together, we had a very nice one-bedroom apartment. Ricky didn't have a regular job but kept working when he could, which made it possible to pay our bills for the time being. When I came home from work in the mornings, Ricky would use our car to get to whatever job he worked that day. It annoyed me when he would barely make it back home at night with the car in time for me to get to my job before 11:00 pm. I had to break the speed limit a lot to get to work on time. We lived a long distance from my job, so every minute counted. Later, the off-and-on jobs Ricky was working weren't bringing in enough money. The financial burden began to fall more and more on my shoulders, which put a tremendous amount of stress on me. Things were so bad that we couldn't afford to have a phone in our apartment. That was a huge inconvenience because if I needed to talk to anyone, I had to drive about a mile out of the community that we lived in to use the phone booth located next to the main road. I knew in my heart that Ricky was using our bill money to support his drug habit, but there was nothing I could do except try to do all I could to make up for it. Trying to talk to him about it was like wandering into a minefield blindfolded, entering at your own risk. He got violent if I said too much about what he was doing. When we were in Germany, Tacoma, and El Paso, Ricky never raised his hand to hit me. I believe the drugs were helping to bring back the old Ricky. I did what I could with the money I made. Unfortunately, we were right back where we started, struggling to make ends meet.

Buying gas to drive back and forth to my job was draining our finances. More to the point of my problem, I was broke. I had to come up with a way to get some quick cash. The only solution I could come up with was to pawn the beautiful wedding band that Ricky had given to me for Christmas while we were in Germany. It was the very last thing I wanted to do, but desperate times called for desperate measures. I went to the nearest pawnshop and pawned my ring. I hated that I had to resort to taking off my wedding band to buy gas to get to work. I only got a few dollars for it, but the money was beneficial when I needed it. I told myself that I would be able to get it back soon, and I kept telling myself that each time I returned to pay the interest every thirty days. After a while, money got so tight that

I could not spare the cash to pay the interest anymore. With a broken heart, I had to let it go. To make matters worse, I found out that Ricky was still shooting up drugs in his arm. Because he could not acquire heroin here in the States as quickly as he could in Germany, he changed to the drug sweeping the country at that time; he was now shooting up crack cocaine. It made him even more violent. He would do anything to get high. I have heard it said that people who do crack only get high the first time they do it. After that, they never reach that pinnacle again, hence the uncontrollable addiction to it.

Criminal Behavior

One day, I went to get the mail, and there was a letter addressed to me from the District Attorney's office in Hoke County. I opened the letter, and it said that I had written a bad check at a convenience store for fifty bucks and that I had a certain amount of time to pay it off before charges would be brought against me. I had not written a bad check at a store; I always used cash. I knew that Ricky had taken one of the checks from my checkbook and forged my name on it to get money for drugs. I became unglued. Wasn't it enough that I had to struggle to keep a roof over our heads and food on our table? I got my checkbook out of my purse and hid it so that he could not do it again. I confronted him about it, and all he could do was lie and say he knew nothing about it. Did he really believe that I was so stupid to think that he was telling me the truth? No one else had access to my checkbook except him. I could have turned him in, but that would mean even more problems, so I took it upon myself to pay it off. His drug habit, his drinking, his anger, lies, and abuse were tearing me into shreds. I could barely keep my head above water. It was no longer the two of us but just me. Days later, I went by the courthouse to pay off the check before the appointed deadline. I was blessed to have the money to pay it off and relieved that it was over. That very night, I heard a knock at my door. When I opened it, a police officer was standing there asking to speak to Patricia. I said, "I'm Patricia." Then he said, "I have a warrant for your arrest for writing a bad check." My mouth fell open; I was speechless. When I was able to speak, I told the officer that I had already paid the amount of the check that day, and I had a receipt to prove it. I went to the bedroom and got the receipt from my purse to show it to him. The whole while this was unfolding, my heart was beating so fast and my hands were shaking, thinking that I could get arrested for something that I didn't even do. He inspected it and said that he had not been notified that it had been taken care of by the deadline. He apologized to me, said goodnight, and left. I was still shaking even as I closed the door behind me. I could not believe how close I came to going to jail because of some stupid thing Ricky had done to support his drug habit. Tears started rolling down my cheeks. This was getting to be too much for me to handle. I wondered to myself and asked, "Lord, what is going to happen next? I don't know how much more I can take." Ricky got back home that night just in time for me to go to work. I didn't even stop to discuss what had transpired that night with him. I needed to get to work on time to hold on to my job. Someone needed to be responsible.

Night Terror

I would always get nervous when I woke up at night to get ready for work when Ricky wasn't back home yet. I would pray for him to get there soon because we could not afford for me to lose my job. He was no longer contributing to our finances; he continued to take away from them. I was the only adult living in our home. He just flat-out didn't care about anything except getting high. One night, he didn't show up on time, and he knew that I was scheduled to work. I went ahead, got dressed, and sat down on the sofa to wait for him. By 10:15 pm, I knew I needed to call my job to talk to my supervisor. The only way I could do that was to walk to the phone booth in the pitch-black dark of night all by myself to call him. If I did not call in, I would get a written warning put in my file. If I got three of them, I would get fired. I surely did not need for that to happen. I grabbed some change, my keys, locked the door, and started walking to the phone booth. I'm not ashamed to say that I was frightened. I didn't know what I would encounter at that time of night, being a female all alone. I asked the Lord to please be with me and keep me safe.

As I walked, my eyes started to adjust to the darkness, and I was able to see a little better. About halfway there, I heard a dog start to bark in the distance. That really put fear in my heart. I loved animals and wasn't afraid of them, but I didn't want to be bitten by one, either. I continued on, looking around as I walked. The sound of the barking dog got closer and closer. Soon, I could see the image of the dog running towards me. I was shaking like a leaf in a tree, but I knew better than to run. I would not be able to outrun a dog anyway. I just stopped walking and stood still, waiting for the dog to approach me. When he got close enough for me to see him clearly, I almost fainted because he was the biggest German Shepherd I had ever seen. I started to talk to him, hoping that the tone of my voice would calm him down. The next thing I knew, he was wagging his tail vigorously, wanting me to pet him. So I did, and he jumped up on me, putting his paws on my shoulders, enjoying me stroking his head. When he stood up on his hind legs, he was taller than me. I played with him for a few moments, feeling so relieved that he was just a big baby. I continued to the phone booth, made my call, and walked back home. I went back to bed because I would not be going to work that night. I felt bad that I would be minus a night's pay in my next paycheck. I don't know what time Ricky got home. He didn't wake me to avoid talking to me because he knew he had made me miss work. Whatever he was doing was more important to him than ensuring I had transportation to the job that fed him and kept a roof over his head. I woke up the following day feeling guilty about missing work because it had put a strain on my boss and coworkers, who had to make up for my absence. I asked Ricky what was so important to him that prevented him from returning home so that I could go to work. He gave me some lame excuses that I was not in the mood to hear. The next thing I knew, he was out the door and gone again. That was getting to be the norm. I was left alone a lot because I disapproved of what he was up to. He ignored me as much as he could. I just tried to make it through, one day at a time. I had no one to turn to with my problems. His family was around, but sometimes people use the excuse, "that's between husband and wife," to avoid getting involved in troublesome situations. Sometimes, they are in denial about what is happening right before their very eyes, not wanting to get involved.

Stressed Out

The stress of being responsible for everything, along with Ricky's drug habit, was taking its toll on me. Each morning after work, I took a relaxing bath to help reduce the tension I was under. Afterward, I applied lotion to my skin and noticed some spots I had not seen before. I didn't know what they were, so I was not alarmed. I was so stressed out sometimes that I could physically feel it inside my body, but I drew no connection between the two. The more I felt this way, the more I broke out. It started on my legs and gradually spread to the rest of my body. The spots started small, and as time went on, they grew more extensive, and my skin would get so dry that it would flake and turn red around the edge of the spots. I got concerned about what was going on with my skin as it progressed over most of my body. So, I found a dermatologist in the phone book with an office close by. I called and made an appointment with him to get some answers. When I went to see him, he asked how long it had been since the spots first appeared, and I told him. He said he wasn't sure what it was and that he needed to do a skin biopsy and send it to the lab to be identified. It would take two weeks before he would have my test results. After he removed a plug of skin from my scalp, he scheduled another appointment to come back to get my diagnosis of what was happening to me. The spots continued to spread as I waited. I now had them over most of my body and scalp. I was already dealing with the alopecia that had developed, and now this, too. After two weeks, I went back to find out what was going on. The Doctor told me that, at first, he thought that I had Lupus. That is why he wanted to be sure of his diagnosis by doing a skin biopsy before he told me.

According to Google Search: facty.com, Lupus erythematosus disease (SLE) or lupus is a chronic autoimmune condition. In people with lupus, the immune system loses its ability to distinguish between viruses and other invaders and healthy human tissue.

This condition often leads to complications if left untreated. Some people require anti-inflammatory drugs and chemotherapeutic agents to help treat the disease.

The symptoms of lupus are variable, and the condition generally affects each person differently.

He informed me that he was glad to be able to tell me that I did not have Lupus, but then he said, "But you do have Psoriasis." I had not heard of that skin disease. He said that he was shocked I had it because black people don't usually get psoriasis.

According to Google Search: www.mayoclinic.org, Psoriasis is a skin disease that causes red, itchy, scaly patches, most commonly on the knees, elbows, trunk, and scalp. Psoriasis is a common, long-term (chronic) disease with no cure. It tends to go through cycles, flaring for a few weeks or months, then subsiding for a while, or going into remission.

He prescribed a steroid cream that was supposed to help, but the scaly plaques seemed immovable. I was so discouraged by all the physical and mental problems that had manifested themselves in my life. I felt so ashamed of my skin that I attempted to hide it by wearing shirts with long sleeves and long pants, no matter the weather, whenever I went out of the house or to work. I couldn't hide my hands or my face, and when people would see it, they would stare. One night at work, one of my coworkers came up to me and asked me if I was contagious. I couldn't believe that she did not already discern how embarrassed I was and what I must be going through with my skin looking the way it did and that asking me that question would hurt me. I answered her and let her know that I was not contagious; obviously, I would not be allowed to work if I was. At that moment, I wanted to leave and never come back, but that was not an option available to me. I had to endure the questions, looks, and whispers behind my back because I had to make a living no matter what. I faced up to all the obstacles in my life as bravely as I could, even though the stress from it all was growing enormously. Ricky's behavior surely did not help matters at all. There were additional nights that I was either late for work or couldn't get there at all. It was by the Grace of God I was able to hold on to my job.

Life was beating me up, and I was unable to talk to anyone about it. My family lived too far away. Even if they didn't, I probably wouldn't have discussed it with them. My coworkers were more interested in talking about me than talking to me. I did not have a best friend that I could confide in; Ricky made sure of that. I didn't let any of those things stop me from doing what I had to do. Giving up was not a solution. My dad instilled in his children to work hard and never let our circumstances stop us. So that's what I did. I pressed through everything that I was struggling with in my life. There was always something added to my plate, even though it was already overflowing. Ricky kept me stressed by keeping me in suspense about whether or not I was going to have a way to work. He came in late again one night; I was past being upset. I grabbed my things and headed out the door, praying that I would get to work on time. On my way, I approached a four-way stoplight just a few miles from my home as it turned green. I was glad about that because it would shorten the time I needed to get to work. When I was almost at the intersection, I noticed the traffic coming from my left. It didn't look as though the car in the lead was slowing down enough to stop at the red light. Taking into consideration the speed of that vehicle, I realized it was not going to stop. My first thoughts were to put both hands on the steering wheel, my foot on the brake, and brace myself because I was about to be in an accident. Somehow, I don't know how, but somehow, I managed not to panic and tried to stop. I could tell this was going to happen no matter what I did. Before I knew anything, my car collided with the other vehicle so hard it felt like I had hit a brick wall; it was over. I was shaken up but not hurt. A man from the convenience store across the street ran up to my car door to see if I was alright. I told him that I didn't believe that I was hurt. Someone called the police and an ambulance. I got out, and I looked at my car and then the car I had hit. Had I not slowed down enough, that car would have hit the driver's side of my vehicle. I believe that I would have been seriously injured or worse. I was amazed that I was OK, but I was concerned about the people in the other car, too. I found out from one of the persons who witnessed the accident that it was an older lady who had just left the laundromat doing her laundry. She said she didn't see the red light. She was transported to Cape Fear Valley Memorial Hospital for her injuries, and I also went to get checked out, just in case. After the doctor checked me out, I called Ricky's parents to tell them that I had been in an accident on my way to work. I told them that I was okay, but I needed someone to please come pick me up from the hospital. Then I called my supervisor and told him what happened, that I would not be able to come to work, and that I would probably be out of work for a while. My father-in-law picked me up and took me home. Ricky was very shocked to see me back at the apartment. I told him that I had been in a car accident. He seemed concerned if I was alright, but I can't say if his concern was for me or the car. The car was a total wreck. There was no way it could be repaired. He needed the car to be able to feed his drug habit. The next day, we called the insurance company to report the accident and request a rental car. After inspecting our car at the body shop, the insurance adjuster declared it a total loss. We were approved for a rental car, which made Ricky very happy. Later, we finalized our business with the insurance company, and we were given a check for the loss of our car and proceeded to look for another vehicle. After searching numerous dealers, we found one at a used car lot that was in great condition. It was a smaller car compared to the one we had, and it was a five-speed. Fortunately for me, I had learned to drive a stick shift while I was in Germany. The loan was approved, and we had transportation. I enjoyed driving a stick shift again. It brought back fond memories of driving through the countryside in Germany, seeing the beautiful villas littering the spacious farmland. It was a sight to behold. I did not expect to fall in love with Germany. My preference was for Ricky to be stationed in Hawaii. It was just something about Germany that consumed me. The time I spent there, barring the drugs and the baby-momma drama, I hold them dearly in my heart.

CHAPTER 11
OUT OF CONTROL

I went back to work after about a week. Our dwindling financial situation was catching up with us. I was no longer able to afford to pay our bills and make a car payment, too. Ricky still did not have a regular job, so we had to decide to find a cheaper place to live to cut down on our expenses. We looked for a place closer to my job and found a mobile home for rent that would reduce my commute time in half and reduce the amount we were paying for rent. We moved as quickly as we could to avoid paying for two places simultaneously. We settled into another home. It was an old mobile home, but we couldn't be choosy. Our position didn't change very much, though. I still needed monetary help. The stress that I was experiencing caused my psoriasis to spread like wildfire. I had it from head to toe, even in the intimate areas of my body. Psoriasis and the alopecia were taking out my hair. I had to let go of my Jheri Curl hairstyle. My scalp was in terrible shape, forcing me to wear a wig. I wore the wig to avoid being scrutinized by people. I was so uneasy and felt awful about dealing with this disease and all the other problems I had to contend with. Eventually, Ricky got a job driving a truck delivering fresh produce to fast food restaurants. It didn't pay that much, but it helped. He was doing okay for a little while until he won't. He took most of the money he earned to buy drugs. When he no longer had money to get what he wanted, he would come to me. My concern was paying bills, buying food, keeping a roof over our heads, and having money to buy fuel to get back and forth to work. All he cared about was feeding his drug addiction. He'd force me to give him money for his habit. If I didn't, I would get beat up, and he would take the money anyway. He had transformed into a person I did not know and wished I didn't.

I was in the kitchen one evening preparing dinner when he walked in demanding that I give him money to buy crack. I refused, and he grabbed the food I was cooking from the stove, slammed it to the floor, pushed me down, and started to choke me. I couldn't breathe as I fought to get him to stop. He finally came to his senses and released me. Visibly and emotionally upset and defeated, I gave him what he wanted. The turmoil that he constantly put me through was pure insanity. What was most disturbing to me was that he had no regret for his actions. He treated me as though I was not a human being, that I had no rights, and that I belonged to him to do whatever he wanted. He behaved like there was not one person on earth that could stop him. It was starting to look the same way to me, too. I wasn't doing a good job at stopping him. I had to put up with this madness repeatedly. No one was coming to save me. If I wanted out, I would have to get out on my own. I could not see a way for me to do what seemed to be impossible. I felt like a captured animal in a cage with no hope of escape.

My life was a vicious cycle of pain, stress, and mental and physical abuse. It rattled me so much that I started to act out. I cursed him out with every word that I could think of. I never heard words like the ones I said to him growing up, but he had taught me well. It helped to give me some resemblance of release, but in my heart, I wanted to cause him physical harm.

Fortunately for him, I didn't have it in me to do such a thing. At times, I got so angry that I picked up items and flung them against the wall to help satisfy the bitterness that was dwelling inside me. I was no longer myself; I was destroying things that belonged to me. I turned into someone that I didn't know or like. There are no words that can truly communicate the harsh reality I was living with. My day-to-day life was a miserable existence that I could not circumvent. I had to suppress it deep down inside of me to keep moving forward. I had no advocate pleading my case. It was only me feeling my way through the darkness, hoping to find the door that would open and release me from the hell that was my life.

Helping My Daddy

Moving located us closer to my dad, and I was able to see him more. He was beginning to have more debilitating health issues. The doctor told my family that he could not be left alone and should not be driving anymore. Medicare provided him with in-home care, but it was only for a few hours a day. Olivia worked the first shift on her job, and I worked the third on mine, so I stayed with him after I got off work at 7:00 am until the home care nurse came at 1:00 pm. Then Olivia would take over when she got off work at 4:00 pm. I enjoyed the mornings I spent with him. We talked while I made his breakfast. Sometimes, I got very sleepy from working all night. After I washed his breakfast dishes, I would lie down on the couch for a nap. I saw the time I worked and the time I spent helping my dad as a way of getting a well-deserved vacation from my chaotic home life. My problems did not cease to exist, but I was glad for the short-lived peace that I gleaned from the time I spent away from Ricky.

The crack had such a tight grip on Ricky that I would come home from work and find that he had taken things from our home to sell for drugs. I couldn't keep a TV or a VCR in our home. There just seemed to be no way to express to him what he was doing to us. He would not listen to anything I had to say. The lure of crack cocaine blinded him to the destruction of our marriage and our lives. I came home from caring for my dad one afternoon and noticed that the two beautiful vases that he had bought for me while he was in Greece and the one that the guy in his squad had given to me were gone. He had taken them to his drug dealer and sold them all for drugs. I was so heartbroken because those items could never be replaced. They represented a moment in time that we would never get to relive again. It made me cry seeing how out of control Ricky was, and there was nothing I could do about it except try and hold on to my sanity, praying that a change would come. I was starting to realize my only help was the Lord. I didn't understand how I had gotten so lost that I forgot Jesus. I knew how the Bible says that He will never leave me alone, but I was so delusional, believing that I could figure things out, that I did not seek His light. It was always there, but I kept thinking that I could find a way to fix things. I had been trying for years to repair my situation with no success. What I was doing was not working. I desired a different result. I needed to change my approach, but I concluded that it was all out of my hands. I could not fix this; only Jesus could fix this.

Ricky took the car one afternoon and went to who knows where. If I had to guess, I would say that he was probably hunting down crack. Drug addiction is a demon that will not let go of its grasp on its victim voluntarily. Especially a person that is not interested in letting go. I woke up that night to get ready for work, and Ricky had not returned home. Here we go again with the making me late for work thing or missing it altogether. I heard a car pull up in my driveway. Then I heard a door close, and the car started to leave. I went to the door to see who it was and ran into Ricky. I looked in our driveway, and our car was missing. I asked him where our vehicle was. He told me that he had gotten in an accident, and it had been towed to a body shop. Somehow, he had managed to hit another car in the rear and damaged our vehicle so badly that it could not be driven. The same problem of not having transportation kept happening. I could not seem to hold on to a car to save my life. I walked to the store just a short distance up the street to ask the owner if I could use his phone to call my work supervisor. I let him know that I would not be coming to work and why. A day or two later, the insurance company provided us with a rental. Now, I could get to work and continue helping take care of my dad when I got off work. Our economic dilemma had gotten so bad that we were three months behind on our car payments. When the financiers of our car found out that it had been involved in an accident and where it was, they went to the body shop and repossessed it before the body shop started work on it. Our insurance company sent us the check to pay for the repairs on the car we no longer had, making it possible for us to purchase another one. We had heard about a man who sold cars at his home that he purchased from auctions. We went to see if we could buy one with the money we had received for the repairs on our wrecked vehicle. Fortunately, he had a small car that we could pay cash for. I was delighted because it eliminated the car payment from our budget, which was a huge blessing. Things were looking a little better as far as transportation was concerned; the rental was returned. I don't know all the details of the accident Ricky was in, but he failed to tell me he got a ticket for the accident, plus he was driving under the influence of alcohol. When he went to court, they took his license. That meant he could no longer drive the truck for his job. He was able to hold on to his job for a little while because the lady who owned the company came by our home and picked him up so he could help her deliver the produce. Do you know how you can sometimes sense things? I think Ricky had more than a working relationship with his boss. Just seeing them together, I just knew it. They spent an awful lot of time together, and she was always grinning in his face. Ladies, you know what grin I'm talking about. I trust my instinct, and I know the body language of people who have an intimate relationship. Anyway, I don't remember what happened with that job, or maybe something happened in the relationship, but it didn't last very long after he lost his license. Maybe she got tired of having to come to pick him up. I'm not saying I was okay with him cheating on me; I was so exhausted contending with all the problems I had that I did not have the energy to fight another battle. Besides, you can't stop someone from doing what they are bound and determined to do. That was a hard lesson for me to learn, but I did. I don't believe my suspicions would have made a difference to him anyway. Ricky's main concern was getting high, and mine was trying to hold everything together. We were going in two different directions. The constant see-saw effect on our lives was enough to drive me to drink, but becoming a drunk would have magnified the problems I already had.

I got the idea that maybe I could find a part-time job to supplement our income. I stopped by the convenience store up the road one day, coming home from helping my dad, and I asked the owner if he needed some part-time help. It was a bustling little convenience store because they also prepared food there. I had enjoyed some of it myself. The owner said that he could use some help. So, I started working there as soon as I could. I only worked a few hours a week, but that money helped to provide food for us. Being the head of the household is no joke, especially if you are a woman taking care of an able-bodied man who refuses to do it himself.

My spare time was spent trying to make up for what Ricky was not doing. To make matters worse, a few weeks later, Ricky came home without the car that we had just bought. I couldn't believe it; he sold our car to the drug dealer for crack. I was so through. I thought, "What in the world is wrong with this foolish man?" I almost lost my mind. Living with a full-blown crackhead was one of the hardest things I have ever had to endure. It just seemed like I couldn't catch a break from this horror story that he had created. When I told my dad that I no longer had transportation, he was generous enough to loan me his car so I could have a way to work and continue helping him.

My dad loaning his car to me was a blessing, and I was very thankful for it. While I was with him one morning, he talked about Ricky and me moving two houses down the road from him. He had heard that the house, a short distance from him, was for rent. I did not desire to move that close to my dad. I was afraid he would find out how difficult my life had become with Ricky. I didn't want my problems to become his problems. As I remember that time now, I am convinced that I underestimated my dad. I believe he knew all about the issues of my life. Maybe he thought that if he could get me closer to him, he could rescue me from Ricky. Perhaps he could possibly stop him from hurting me, knowing that my family was close by. I know my daddy wanted the best for me, and he always kept me in his prayers because they are still being answered today. He was a true believer in Jesus. The example he and my mama lived before their children laid the solid foundation on which I build my life now.

I worked full-time at my regular job, a few hours at my part-time job, and Ricky chased after crack. It had become a regular occurrence to come home from work and find things missing because Ricky took anything of value and traded it for crack. I can't explain why I kept being surprised by his despicable behavior. I didn't want to believe that he couldn't or wouldn't stop taking our belongings and selling them. I hoped and prayed daily for deliverance from being an unwilling participant in feeding his addiction. I was about to have a nervous breakdown from all the stress heaped on me. I still had to finish paying for the things that Ricky had taken from our home and sold, although I no longer had them. All I could do was keep holding on to a thread. It was a frazzled one that was about to reach its breaking point.

More Problems

Sometime later, my dad informed me that he was going to need his car back because he wanted to drive it again. I don't know how I managed it, but after mentioning my need for transportation in the break room at work, one of my coworkers who owned a used car lot overheard my conversation and told me to come by, and he would help me out with getting some transportation. I went to his car lot and found a stick shift that he let me purchase on the agreement to make weekly payments. I knew that was unusual, but I had to get some new transportation. After making a deal with him, Ricky and I took my dad's car back to him. I thanked him for the help and support he had given me when I needed it. We were okay for the moment, but I knew from experience that it would not be long before something else would happen.

I was now Ricky's ride to the drug dealer's house. I was forced into it or else. I suspect that I knew where every drug dealer lived for miles around. I waited in the car while he went into the house to buy crack. I was always looking around, hoping and praying that the police would not roll up on us while we were there. I could have gone to jail for being in the wrong place at the wrong time. I was so sick of having to do things that I hated. I was stuck between a rock and a hard place. I fantasized about how my life could be without Ricky in it, but I could not see how I would ever be able to reclaim my freedom. Ricky needed me, and he wasn't about to let me go. Time after time, the same scenario played out. I felt like I was a puppet being controlled by some kind of mad evil puppet master in front of an uncaring audience that had no empathy for the pain the puppet was going through, which was me. I was in this all alone without a glimmer of hope, so I thought.

My dad noticed how badly psoriasis had taken over my body. He said to me one day, " I will be so glad when your skin heals." He could not be any happier than me. He knew how I was suffering and wanted me to get better. My psoriasis was bad, and I could not see any remission in sight. I was genuinely struggling with this disease. It not only affected me physically, but it also took a toll on my mental health. The more stress, the more psoriasis. It was becoming increasingly challenging to remain diligent in camouflaging the reality of what psoriasis was forcing me to go through in front of my dad and others. There is no cure for this skin disease. The best I could hope for was that it would go into remission.

During one of my visits with my dad, he discussed with me that when he leaves this world, he will not have anything to leave me. He told me that the only way I could get anything from him after he was gone was for me to purchase a life insurance policy on him. I was shocked and very uncomfortable talking about it. I told him that I was not looking to gain from his death and didn't want to talk about it; he said okay and changed the subject. I couldn't possibly afford to buy insurance; I was barely able to keep food on my table. Then, he informed me that he felt better and wanted to visit some of his fellow church members and friends. That was why he wanted his car back. When he attended church on Sunday mornings, he recorded the Pastor's sermon on a small portable tape recorder and shared it with the sick, shut-ins, and friends he wanted to visit. He was a great man of God. He served as a Deacon in our Church as far back as I can remember. He took his faith and his responsibilities as a believer in the teachings of Jesus Christ very seriously. My older sisters and brothers told me that he used to sing in a quartet group, going from church to church. I don't remember those times; I was very young. I only recently found out that he was also a Scout Master from one of the members of his troop long ago, which, in my eyes, made him even more of a good man.

My Dad's Day Out

When I arrived that morning to do my usual duties, he was getting dressed to go out and visit some people. He had it all planned out what he was going to do that day. I don't know if his doctor had permitted him to drive or if he had just made up his mind what he wanted to do. I made his breakfast and cleaned up the kitchen. By the time I finished, he was ready to go, so we both left around the same time. I said goodbye to him and went home. I got home early that day and had a chance to do some housework before I laid down to sleep. As I did my chores, I wondered how my dad's big day was going. He was so excited about being able to get out of the house on his own. He enjoyed talking with people so much. He didn't like not having the freedom to come and go as he pleased. Later that day, there was a knock on my door. I got out of bed and opened the door; it was my daddy's neighbor's daughter. She told me that she had been sent to tell me I needed to come to my dad's house immediately. That's all she would say, and then she left. I was frightened by her not giving me any explanation as to why I needed to go back to my daddy's house. My heart started pumping fast because I knew in my gut that something was wrong. I tried to stay calm while I got dressed and drove back to his house. His car was in the driveway when I arrived, and another vehicle was parked behind it. I got out of my car, walked across the carport up to the door, and I could see through the screen door that my aunt and uncle, my father's brother, and his wife were standing in the kitchen. I thought to myself, "What are they doing here, and where is my daddy?" I opened the door and walked in. When I approached my aunt to find out what was going on, she started telling me what had happened. My dad managed to visit all the places he had planned to go to that day. He returned home, got out of the car, made it to the carport, had a massive heart attack, fell to the floor, and passed away. I started screaming. I don't remember very much after that; grief took over. I slowly calmed down, wiping the tears from my eyes. I knew that when Olivia got home from work, the screaming and crying would start all over again. My daddy always said he wanted to die at home; he got what he wanted. Later on, people were beginning to arrive to give their condolences as the news spread about my dad's death. I got myself together and went back home to tell Ricky what had happened. I was so shaken up I could hardly drive. When I arrived, he was not there, so I waited. He eventually returned home, and I told him about my dad's passing. He said he was sorry, but those words had only been out of his mouth a few seconds when he said he wanted me to take him to buy some crack. I told him I wanted to go back to my daddy's house, but there was no talking to him. When he wanted to get high, he didn't let anything or anyone stand in his way. I had to take him to buy drugs; I sobbed as I drove. I was upset that I had just lost my dad, and all this man could think of was getting high. There seemed to be no compassion in him at all. Drugs and alcohol were the top priorities in his life. Once his goal of scoring some crack was achieved, I had to take him home so he could get high in private, leaving me free to return to my dad's house. When I returned, I called my supervisor to tell him that I would not be coming to work because my dad had passed away. He gave me his condolences and told me not to worry about anything; he had it covered.

Olivia made all of the arrangements for my daddy's funeral. All my sisters, brothers, nieces, and nephews living in other states came home to say goodbye. There was no need to decide on what outfit he would be buried in. He had previously picked out the suit he wanted to be laid to rest in and had told Olivia his wishes; she picked out a casket and flowers to match his outfit. His funeral was held at our home church, Walls Chapel UMC, and he was buried alongside my mother in Clio, South Carolina. It was a somber day. I had to say goodbye to a man I had known all my life, my last living parent. He had done so much for me and my brothers and sisters. He never wavered as a father; he worked and provided for his family and did it with honor and dignity. I feel he was the most incredible dad that ever lived, and he left all his children with a model to follow. Being the baby of the family, I felt very much alone in the world. My sisters and brothers had families with lives of their own, and they would be returning to them soon, and I to mine. Once again, I failed to mention to anyone how my life was going. I felt it was not the appropriate time to burden them with my problems. I was ashamed and embarrassed that I had let a man take control of my life, and I wasn't ready to disclose that information to anyone. Losing my dad was hard enough for my family and me to get past. He and my mother were together now, and I kept that beautiful thought in my heart and spirit to help with my sorrow in the days to come.

CHAPTER 12
NEVER A DULL MOMENT

My daddy and mama had taught me everything I knew. I was an adult, but it was nice knowing that I always had someone to go to for help whenever I needed it. Now, whatever happened, I was truly on my own. Ricky kept insisting that I drive him around so that he could buy his drugs. Never even giving one thought to what his actions were doing to me. I had no choice in what I did. I hated it so much. I kept thinking, "How can I continue to live like this?" Each day, I never knew what would be coming my way. Our finances were on the verge of collapse; that was all I could think about. I had to find a way to make things better. I had to do the very thing I had been trying to avoid doing: help him get a job where I worked. I remembered how crazy Ricky got the last time we worked at the same place. I certainly did not want to repeat that, but I felt a degree of impending disaster headed my way. One morning, I humbled myself, swallowed my pride, and went to the front office at my workplace to talk to the plant manager. I asked him if he would give my husband a job. I told him about my financial situation and how my life was on the threshold of falling apart, and to my amazement and gratitude, he said he would give him a job. I thanked him for being kind enough to help my husband

and me. I went home and told Ricky what I had done, but before he agreed, I had some stipulations that I needed to clarify with him. I sat him down, and I explained to him that I did not want him going to where I worked and humiliating me. This was a place I had worked for years, and almost everyone knew me. Most of all, I asked him to please not disgrace me by sleeping around with any of the women on my job. Ricky had already convinced me that he could not be trusted, so I explained that it would destroy me if he did not respect me as his wife at my workplace. He promised me that he wouldn't do anything he shouldn't, but I still did not believe him; he was morally deprived and always did whatever he wanted. It was a chance I had to take, but I needed to make my concerns known.

He went to the plant and completed all his paperwork to start work as soon as possible. He was assigned a job on first shift. I felt relieved that I would now have a little help keeping a roof over our heads and food on the table. I still had to cope with Ricky's alcohol and drug addiction, but a little help was better than no help. Soon after he started to work, we began to have transportation problems. The house that my dad had told me about, a couple of doors down from his home, was still up for rent. So, I considered taking my dad's suggestion and moving into the house he had told me about. We both would be closer to our jobs, and maybe Ricky could catch a ride to work with someone we knew living in Clay Hill who also worked first shift. We made the decision to move and went to talk to the owner and rented the house. The rent was a little less than what we were paying, so that was a good thing for us. The house was small, with one bedroom, kitchen, dining room, bath, and a small porch built on the side. We packed up and moved into our new home. In retrospect, I had come full circle because I was right back where I had started after graduating high school. I had been to so many places and seen and done so many things since then. I had done things, some good, some bad, but I had learned more about life's ups and downs and about myself, maybe more than I wanted to. The knowledge I had acquired transformed me into a different person than when I first started. I was no longer that shy, naive little girl who had so much hope for a brilliant future. I had promised myself after graduating from high school to "Become the woman of every young girl's dreams." That enthusiasm and hope seemed so far away now. I was unable to fulfill that promise. Somewhere along the way, I got off track. I made many mistakes in my life and yearned to reach for a better one.

I kept the promise I made to God not to be with any man other than my husband. I was attempting to do better and live a life more in line with my faith. I never forgot my faith, but I didn't rely on it or live by it as I should have at the beginning of this journey. Occasionally, I prayed to God and asked Him to please help me with my marriage. I should have been asking God for strength to help me make it through the trials and tribulations of my life. All I could think about was making my marriage work. I tried my best, but I could not do it without Ricky's cooperation; it takes two. My prayers seemed to be going unanswered. I never speculated on what God was teaching me by allowing all kinds of hell to saturate my life. Maybe I was in a relationship that I wasn't supposed to be in. It had been broken for a very long time, and I was the only one trying to put the pieces back together, or maybe the pieces were never meant to fit. I spent countless hours trying to figure out what to do. If I did this, maybe that would happen, or if he did the other, we could make it. I was so determined that I had a one-track mind regarding our relationship. All I did was prolong the inevitable. I was blind to what was right in front of me because I chose not to see it.

Everything appeared to be alright as months went by. Ricky began to get involved more and more with some of the people living in our community. He socialized with them a lot. I did not socialize with a lot of people. I avoided allowing people to peer into my business, fearing being judged and gossiped about. Ricky and I did have some good times along with the bad, but as time went on, there were more bad than good. We quarreled a lot over money, bills, and his staying gone so often. I questioned whether he cared about our relationship anymore or maybe he never did. Numerous times, I had to overlook a lot of the things Ricky did to keep peace in my home. My mission was to live life as best I could under the circumstances. Surviving each day was my top priority. Nothing changed while months turned into a year. My life was miserable while I continued hoping and praying for a change.

I was having problems with the car I had purchased from the used car lot that my friend owned, so I traded it for another car in better shape, and I liked that this one was an automatic. I was getting weary, having to change gears all the time. The agreement was the same as before. I would make weekly payments until it was paid for. I knew that I would have to be responsible for the payments and the maintenance of the car because I couldn't depend on Ricky. As we drove into the yard one day, he asked me to give him money for drugs and take him to buy them; I was so fed up with his habit that I flat-out refused. He got so mad that when he got out of the car, he slammed the door so hard that it shattered the glass in the window. I was so upset because I had just bought the car, and now, I had to pay to get another window put in. I taped some plastic over the door window to keep the weather out until I could get it repaired. The plastic made it almost impossible to check the traffic coming from my right before driving onto the highway, which was very dangerous. I had to get something done soon. So, I asked a friend at work, a mechanic, to fix the window for me, and he agreed to help me. But I still had to go to a junkyard to find and pay for a replacement window. That was additional money that I didn't have, plus I needed to pay him. I had to explain to my landlord that we would be late paying our rent. He was nice enough to extend the time limit to get it paid. I felt as though I had this dark and gloomy cloud always hanging over my life. When was the rain going to stop? Problems just seemed to hunt me down to tackle me.

No Integrity

I noticed a change had come over Ricky. He never spent any time with me unless he needed money, drugs, or a ride to go get them, which was normal. Nevertheless, I got the feeling something had changed. I could feel it in my gut that there was a mystery afoot. Women can usually pick up on subtle changes in their partners (women's intuition). I began to watch him meticulously and investigated his actions. One of my friends on first shift told me that he was spending a lot of time with one particular woman. They would have lunch together daily at a separate table away from everyone else. I watched him and paid more attention to his comings and goings, the times of day he would get missing, and how long he would be away. I concluded that something was going on between him and that woman at work. I confronted him about it, and to my dread, he confessed that he was having an affair with her and was very proud of it. Suspecting that he was cheating again and hearing him admit it were two different things. I couldn't believe that he had done precisely what he promised me he would not do. I was devastated. I cried so much that my eyes were swollen. After all I had put up with, he had the nerve to hurt me in the same manner he had given me his word that he would not do. The woman he was having an affair with lived about three-quarters of a mile from us. As if that wasn't bad enough, she was also married and had children, and on top of all that, I knew her mother-in-law personally. I got so angry I had to sit down on the couch and completely shut down with my head in my hands. I thought about the people at my job who already knew what had been going on and were talking about it behind my back instead of telling me, calling me a fool. I didn't do anything wrong; Ricky had disgraced me, not the other way around, but for some unknown reason, people always talk about the woman as if she were the cause of her husband's infidelity. Now that I knew what had been transpiring for months, I was going to have to face the people at my job who knew my husband was cheating on me the whole time. Even more distressing, I found out that some women I had worked with for years and thought were my friends were throwing themselves at my husband to see if they could, as they say, "Take him away from me." They didn't have a clue who and what they were chasing. Others were enjoying watching the public annihilation of my marriage. Some of them may have been successful in their quest; I don't know.

I was so hurt and embarrassed by it all that I wanted to hurt Ricky and his trollop like they had hurt me; I wanted revenge. She knew he was married to me but developed a relationship with him anyway. I didn't want to face them on my job, and I didn't feel I should have to. So, I called my plant manager and told him what was going on. He asked me how did I know? I told him that my husband admitted it to me. The next thing I knew, they both had been fired. Come to find out, it was against company policy for married employees to have romantic involvements with other employees. If I had done what Ricky did right in his face, he would have been ready to kill someone. I felt so low, aggrieved, and regretted that I had to continue working there, knowing everyone knew my business. I could feel people looking at me. I reported for work, kept my head down, did my job, and went back home. But I soon found out that a woman I knew resented me, for whatever reason, and felt this was an excellent time to get her shot in. Mind you, this was a person I considered to be my friend. I was in the break room after everything had come to light, and one of my coworkers made it her business for me to hear what she said. You can tell when people talk about you, and I knew this statement was meant for my ears. She said, "That just goes to show you everything that glitter is not gold," with hatefulness in her voice. Her words were directed towards my husband cheating on me. People will surprise you in a way you never expected. That may have been her perception of him, but it most certainly was not mine. I purchased what I was getting out of the vending machines and sat down at a table. I never gave her a reaction to what she said. I was sad that she would try to hurt me at one of the lowest points in my life. That is the actions of someone who hates you and enjoys seeing you hurt. She made it clear that she was not a friend, as she had led me to believe. Kicking me in the gut when I was down was pure pleasure for her.

Ricky got mad when he found out that I had called the plant manager and told him what he had done. He forgot that all of this was his fault. He broke his word to me. Who knows, I may have saved someone's life that day. What if I had been so hysterical over my husband's betrayal that I came to the job with a gun, looking to exact some vengeance? What if that trollop's husband had come to the job looking for Ricky? There could have been an unnecessary tragedy that could have caused someone to be hurt or even lose their lives. I blamed myself somewhat for helping Ricky get a job at my workplace, even though we needed the money. I knew he always flagrantly disregarded my well-being; it always came down to what Ricky wanted, and that was that. My needs were always cast aside. He dismissed his responsibility as a married man, which included forsaking all others like it was nothing. Our marriage was disintegrating right before my eyes, but I did not want to accept it.

Ricky could no longer see his girlfriend because her husband found out what she had been up to, and all this after he flaunted his love affair in my face, saying that they were so in love and how great she was. He began to squander even more time and money on getting high and drinking than before. The constant stress and pressure of Ricky's egregious behavior caused my psoriasis to react to my ascending level of stress. I tried unsuccessfully to hide my skin because I was mortified by it, and my life existed on public display. The medicine my Dermatologist prescribed for me wasn't working at all. Wherever I would sit or lie down and then get up, I left dead skin behind. It fell off me like leaves from the trees during fall. I did my best to brush it away before anyone could see it, but sometimes I was ineffective. It was time to look out for my well-being. I had suffered plenty. I had allowed this thing between Ricky and me to go on long enough. My solution to my predicament was to ask Ricky for a divorce. I was so weary of trying to make something out of nothing. It had taken me a long time to acknowledge that our marriage was over and had been for years. Of course, he told me no. He did not want to lose the person taking care of him while he threw away his life, my life, and every cent he could get his hands on to use for drugs and alcohol. He slept with anyone and everyone that stood still long enough with no regard for me. I had reached my breaking point. I didn't know how it would happen, but I made up my mind that I was done, and I wanted out. I believe that when I finally stopped trying so hard to have my way, God stepped in, and things started to go His way. When I let go, I let God be God!

CHAPTER 13
GOD'S DOING A NEW THING

After a few weeks passed, Ricky met a man needing help in construction work, and he gave him a job. His boss picked him and his other workers up each morning, and they traveled to different areas in the community to build homes. Ricky seemed to like his new job, but it gave him no incentive to care for his home and family. He bought drugs with no remorse while I struggled to make ends meet. I was stuck in my situation, like being in quicksand. The more I tried to escape it, the deeper I sank, and I didn't see how God could make a way for me. Why should He, with all the mistakes and bad choices I had made? I stayed when I should have left, thinking I could make a way. He did not owe me anything. Ricky was learning some new skills from his job. He brought some lumber home one day and built a bookshelf. He did a decent job on it, too. Then, he enclosed the porch with a wire screen. It was good to see him take an interest in his home. The owner had no objections because it improved his property. Months passed with no modifications to my life. I wanted a simple, good life more than anything I could think of in this world, better than the one I had been living. I could imagine it, but it seemed to be beyond my grasp. I asked Ricky repeatedly for a divorce, but he always said no. He'd tell me that I was his wife and that he was never going to let me go. But what he didn't know was that I had already changed my mind about continuing to be his wife and putting up with all the crap I dealt with during the years we had been together. In changing my mind, things were set in motion that would eventually set me free. I couldn't comprehend how I had made it through so much. All I knew was that in some way, somehow, I was going to get out of this sham of a marriage. I wanted to be free from being taken for granted, the drugs, the physical abuse that dominated my life, the mental abuse that manifested as a skin disease, and having to take complete responsibility for two adults. I might as well be living alone. At least I could lower my stress level and reduce my cost of living if I didn't have to take care of a grown man like he was my child. From then on, that was all I could think about: escape and redemption! I didn't care anymore. I searched for every opportunity that would aid in my liberation from him.

In the meantime, since I spent most of my time alone, I decided to go out that upcoming Saturday night to this little nightclub in my neighborhood, a place we Southerners call "A hole in the wall." Ricky was always out, doing who knows what, so I wasn't worried about him showing up and finding me gone. I wanted to get out of the house for a while, relax my mind, and listen to some music to reduce the stress that was thriving inside me. Once inside the Club, I stood on the balcony watching the people below dancing. I had not been there long when, all of a sudden, I felt someone tap me on my shoulder. As I turned around, the first thing that caught my attention was a brilliant smile saying hello to me. Not to be rude, as I turned around, I said hello. He introduced himself as Charles, and I introduced myself. As we exchanged pleasantries, I iterated upfront that I was not looking to meet anyone; I was a married woman. I wanted to divulge the truth so as not to be accused of misleading anyone. I was at the club because I sought to be around people and have some fun for a change; that was all I desired. He said that he only wanted to talk for a few minutes. He told me it was his first time there, and he only came to pick up his friend and would leave soon. He told me he was single, but he had a little girl. We chatted for a while. It was nice to have someone to talk to who paid attention to what I was saying for a change, even for a little bit. I was not looking to add to the mountain of problems I already had, but he was pretty cute. I reminded myself that I did not want to break the promise I had made to God, so I said to myself, "Don't even think about it, girl." We danced a couple of times, after which he said that he had to leave. But, before he left, he slipped me his phone number written on a piece of paper and told me to give him a call sometime. I was surprised that I took it, but I said to myself, "I'm not going to use it," but I did not throw it away. A few minutes later, I walked back home. I did not want Ricky to find his number, so I hid it in my car.

I Can't Believe I Did It

My mind was racing a mile a minute. I found myself considering giving him a call. I asked myself, "Girl, what's wrong with you? You know you have a jealous husband." But if I was honest with myself, I hadn't had a real husband in a very long time. We hadn't been husband and wife for years, not in the way it should have been. We both had done things that could not be forgiven and forgotten; we were both equally guilty of infidelity. I asked him frequently for a divorce because I wanted to end our marriage correctly and legally, but he refused me every single time. I remembered what my parents taught me by the example they lived and my belief that when you get married, it is for life, but I didn't believe that it was meant to be like this. With all that my husband had done to me and me trying so hard to make our marriage work, he had destroyed all the love I ever felt for him. There was no going back to the way things used to be. I refused to believe the Lord wanted me to stay in a relationship that had become so toxic that I was afraid for my life. Some men think that when they marry a woman, she belongs to them as if she is a piece of property bought and paid for. I believed it was time to move on if I wanted to live. I know that in God's Word, He says He hates divorce; coupled with my belief that God's Word does not change, I was in between a rock and a hard place. I had made a vow to God never to cheat again. When I made that vow, I meant it from the bottom of my heart. I did not want to go back to my old habits. Honestly, I was in a place where I was (damned if I did, and damned if I didn't) that was presently my mantra.

Days later, I made a decision that changed my life. I thought about it and thought about it until something came over me, and I decided to give Charles a call; yeah, I sure did. Whether my marriage was legally over or not, I took a chance. We talked for a little bit, and he asked me to come by his apartment to see him. Well, I admit that I was captivated, so I said OK. I had to wait until I knew Ricky was not around so I could visit him. He tried to tell me where he lived, but I couldn't follow his directions. We agreed to meet at a shopping center that we both knew, and he would drive us back to his place. When we arrived at his apartment, he invited me in. It was a nice place. We sat on the couch, watched TV, and talked. He told me about his job at a meatpacking plant, which I thought was a long way for him to drive to work, but he said he couldn't find a job close by where he lived. Soon after, I looked at my watch, and I needed to get going because I had to beat Ricky back home to avoid any questions. He would want to know where I had been, and I didn't feel like explaining myself and probably getting beat up for being gone in the first place. I didn't tell Charles about what my life was like for the time being. I didn't know him well enough to do that. He asked if I would come back to see him again. I said to him that I would think about it. I wasn't quite sure what I was doing, but I knew it was something I had never done before. We got into his car, and he drove me back to mine. I got home in time to make dinner and straighten up before Ricky got there. When he got home, things went as usual. He ate dinner and then went to hang out with his friends. I was alone again. I started thinking about what I had done that day, the chance I took. I felt like a different woman. For as long as Ricky and I had been married, I had never spent time with another man while we were physically living together. I know that doesn't seem like much, but to me, it was respecting my husband enough not to do my dirt right in his face. Nothing had happened between Charles and me, but I wasn't sure I did not want to see him again. He was kind, funny, and, let's not forget, he was easy on the eyes. Speaking of eyes, I adored his light brown eyes. I felt guilty for going behind Ricky's back and spending time with someone else, but not enough that I didn't consider seeing him again because of it. I'm not blaming my actions on Ricky, but he is partly responsible for me even thinking about another man. Any choices I made were mine alone, and I would be the only one to answer for them. I had been faithful to him ever since we went to Tacoma, Washington together, and I did everything humanly possible to rebuild our marriage. I could no longer kid myself; it was over, and I knew it. I did not plan any of this; my perception of what my life could be was growing. I did not know what I wanted, per-say, but I knew what I did not want, and that was to continue to live my life in the manner I had been living it. My mind was spinning around with so many thoughts. It was getting late, and it was a work night. I looked at the clock; the time was zooming by. I needed to lie down for a while before going to work.

On the Down-Low

When Ricky got angry with me, he would frequently say hateful things like, "Nobody loves you, not even your family. Besides, who wants to look at that skin of yours?" He did not have a problem hurting my feelings. He didn't know it, but he was encouraging me to look to Charles for comfort, for love, for my future. I daydreamed about being with him. It would be nice to be with someone whose first thought wasn't to hurt and degrade me. I did my best to resist the temptation, but I wanted to be loved. I had been hurt and in pain so much that Charles was looking pretty good right about now. Whenever Ricky went to work, sometimes after I got off work, I visited Charles. A relational bond was starting to form between us. He didn't pay any attention to my psoriasis. He treated me like I was a beautiful woman despite my skin disease. It felt good to feel like a woman again instead of a bank, a ride to the drug dealer's house, someone to be taken advantage of, or a human punching bag. I didn't know where our relationship was going, all I knew was that I was starting to have feelings for Charles. When I visited him, I never wanted to go back home. I felt so safe when I was with him, but I knew I had to leave. Everything was up in the air, and I did not want it to come crashing down on top of me as it would if Ricky found out what I was doing. On the days I could not slip away to spend time with Charles, I would be so depressed that I would stop by a convenience store on my way home from work to buy beer. By the time Ricky got home from work, I would be passed out on the couch. I was so fed up with my life that I used alcohol as a means of escape.

Ricky only worked four and a half days a week because his boss let his employees off work at 11:00 am on Fridays to give them time to take care of their business. I would loan Ricky money and buy and cook food to help him make it through the week until he got paid, with the promise he would give it back to me at the end of the week. At first, he would do just that, then one Friday, he didn't even bother to come home. I was aware that if Ricky had some money, the lure of crack cocaine would overrule his ability to stay true to his word. I just didn't know that he would take all of it and put it in drugs. He showed up late Sunday night without a dime to his name. The money he owed me went into his arm, and I was left to struggle to make it through the next week. I had to go without food sometimes to pay bills and get back and forth to work. I couldn't afford to buy heating oil, so I spent many days and nights without heat. When I could get kerosene, I used a small space heater, but I had to turn it off at night because I was afraid of the house catching on fire or the kerosene would run out and fill the house with carbon monoxide poisoning. During those cold nights, I would not see Ricky. I don't know where he was. I had to put on as many clothes as I could and put all the quilts and blankets I could stand on my bed to stay warm. I don't know why I kept on helping him when he kept doing the very same stuff over and over again. Our bills were behind, and my landlord was demanding payment for the rent. I did not make enough money to take care of me, Ricky, the car, pay all the bills, and buy food. Sometimes, I had to borrow from Peter to pay Paul. Things were out of control. When I could get away, I visited Charles to escape my problems. Things became so complicated that I started confiding in him about my personal life. I had to let it all out before I exploded. I explained what I had been through and what I was currently enduring. He comforted me by holding me in his arms, saying everything was going to be alright. I have to mention I had not felt such a level of peace and comfort as I did after confiding in him for a very long time.

A New Plan

I didn't want to spend my life renting. I eventually wanted to own a home. I needed to develop a strategy to remove myself from the hardship I was in. Ricky persistently forced me to take him to buy drugs. I would lose my mind if I had to continue to live like that. I hated going to the drug dealer's house. I am ashamed to say that I prayed for something to happen to him that would remove him from my life, and not anything good. That was very wrong of me, I know. I was on the verge of a mental breakdown, but I should not have been praying to a loving God to harm another one of His children. It was getting increasingly more and more dangerous for me. I was afraid that Ricky would get so possessed by his uncontrollable anger one day that he would hurt me badly or worse. My fear was pulverizing me. Suddenly, I heard a voice inside me saying, "If you don't leave him, he is going to kill you." I was very startled by it the first time I heard it. I said to myself, "Did I just hear what I thought I heard?" Then, the voice repeated it. That voice kept on repeating the same thing over and over again. Did I imagine what I was hearing? Maybe I was cracking under the pressure of coping with so much. Even so, I felt I needed to believe and listen to the warning I was receiving because that voice would not leave me alone. I believe it was Jesus warning me of what was to come if I didn't do something and do it quickly. It was on my mind all the time. I couldn't escape the feeling of catastrophe that loomed over me. The thought of doom gripped my entire being so aggressively that I knew the voice I kept sensing deep inside me was warning me of potential danger in my immediate future. That voice was warning me that Ricky was my bane.

While at work one night, I heard some ladies talking about a man selling mobile homes set up on a plot of land. They said that he wanted a substantial down payment to secure it. Their conversation piqued my curiosity. I asked them, "Who is this man, and where can I find him?" They told me that he had an office in downtown Raeford, and his name was Mr. Thurston. It sounded like I had stumbled upon the answer to my prayers. I didn't know where I would get the down payment, even though it appeared the Lord was opening a window for me. I could buy my own home, escape Ricky, and stop wasting my money on renting all at the same time. So, I went to see Mr. Thurston to talk to him about his requirements to purchase a home. He told me that if I could not pay the total downpayment in one lump sum, I could make payments to him until I had paid the amount he required, and then I could move in. No credit history was required, which was a plus for me because my credit score was practically non-existent. He had several different properties where he was selling plots of land. He asked me, "Which one do you want me to show you?" I chose a property a few miles outside of Raeford that was not far from my work. He took me to see the only home that was still available in that area. When I saw it, I knew it was the place for me. The yard did not have grass growing or a driveway. The home was right smack dab in the middle of a plowed field. The land had previously been farmland. I did not care. I was so excited to walk through the home to see what it was like. It was a used three-bedroom with one and one-half bath mobile home. It didn't take much to convince me; I loved it and wanted to buy it. It was a better place than where I was currently residing. It was all-electric, which meant I would not have to worry about buying heating oil. He had repaired and decorated it nicely. It had no furniture in it, but that was okay because I had my own. We went back to his office, and we discussed the interest rate, which was high, note the no credit history required. Then we talked about how much my downpayment would be, the monthly payments I would need to make, and how many years it would take to pay it off. I probably should have paid closer attention to the interest rate because it was very high, but I was so over the moon about having my own home that I let go of my financial common sense. I was more concerned about getting away from Ricky and believed I had found my answer; no matter what it cost, my freedom would be worth it. This place was going to be my salvation. We agreed, I signed the papers, and I had a new home that would belong to me one day. I did not tell Ricky anything about what I had done. I had no intention of taking him with me when I moved. I wanted my life back after living in pure misery for over 20 years. It was time to move on without him. I didn't know how I would manage to get away from him. I held on to my faith for dear life because it was my life I was trying to hold on to. I called Charles to tell him what I had done. He was very happy for me and gave me words of encouragement.

New ideas were emerging in my mind on how to make my down payment on my new home. I could pay some of it every time I got paid. It wouldn't be much because I was still responsible for all of the bills where I was currently residing. A coworker told me that I could borrow money from my 401k if I were using it to purchase a home. I went to Human Resources to check that out. I was told that I could. That made me very optimistic. Also, twice a year, my job gave us bonuses at vacation time, on the 4th of July and Christmas, which also helped. It took me months to come up with that down payment. With the help of the Good Lord, I found a way to get enough money to cover the full amount. I felt a sense of exigency because my rent where I was living was getting farther and farther behind. I could not let this opportunity to have my own home pass me by, even if it meant getting behind on my rent. The longer I stayed there, the more money I would owe my landlord. I needed to move as soon as possible. It took some doing, but I finally walked into Mr. Thurston's office, paid my down payment, and received the keys to my new home. After that, I had to get my home inspected by the county to get my electricity turned on. It took a long time to get the county inspector to come out and do his inspection. He had to ensure that the electrical wiring met all the county requirements to get the okay to get my power turned on so I could move into my home. All the while I was getting this done, Ricky was still in the dark about the whole thing. When I signed the papers for my home, his name was not on them. I didn't even tell Mr. Thurston that I had a husband. This was going to be my place and my place only. While talking one night to my supervisor, in our conversation, I mentioned that I had recently purchased a mobile home and that it was taking such a long time for me to get my home inspected so that I could move in. So, he made a phone call or something; after that, it took no time to get my electricity turned on. I was very grateful for his intervention, and I thanked him for it.

Now I needed a way to move all my things to my new home. I could not figure out how to make that possible. I had to break down and do exactly what I didn't want to do. I had to tell Ricky what was going on to get help to move. I thought after I moved, I could convince him to give me a divorce, at least, that is what I told myself. I knew it would be difficult. I could only deal with one problem at a time. I knew deep inside that getting divorced from Ricky was wishful thinking. He would never let me go now because he was under the impression that he owned a home without doing anything to get it. I was trying to do what that voice inside of me kept telling me, and that was to get away from him. That wasn't working out so well. I needed his help to settle in my home, but I also needed to get away from him. I had to remember that the battle was not mine; it belonged to the Lord, and I needed to stop trying to make things happen according to my understanding. I had lived like that over the years, and it was a hard habit to break. I was slowly learning to rely on my faith in God. That was how I was going to make it out of this nightmare.

The night before moving day, Ricky stayed out all night long. I didn't have a clue whether he would show up to help me move or not. I had already rented a truck and acquired some boxes to put all our belongings in. Needless to say, I did not get any sleep that night. I was excited about moving into my own home and worried I would not have anyone to help me do it. The following day, he finally showed up and brought some help with him. It took most of the day, but we moved everything out of the rented house that we had been occupying and placed our things into my new home. After everything had been moved out, I cleaned the house we had been living in to get it ready for the next person to rent. I still owed my landlord rent money, but I told him that I would do my best to pay him all I owed. I didn't know how I would do that, but I hoped I could find a way.

I spent my first night in my new home. It was wonderful knowing that my money would be going towards investment in my future. The next day, we started unpacking all the boxes and putting everything in its place. It was a three-bedroom home, but we only had one bedroom set. I hoped, somewhere down the line, I would be able to afford furniture for the other bedrooms. I had a very tiring day trying to get my home situated. It certainly is true that you don't know how much you have until you have to move it. Ricky seemed pleased about the house, but the whole time, I was thinking about how I was going to manage to remove him from it and from my life. I didn't know how that would happen, but that voice kept repeating to me that he was going to kill me if I didn't get away from him.

I could not afford to put a phone in my house, so the only way for Charles and me to communicate was in person, or I would call him from a phone booth. After I got home from work, I waited long enough to make sure Ricky was at work and went to visit Charles. I missed him very much when I was away from him, but that could not be helped. I took a dangerous chance every time I visited him. Our visits continued to be nonsexual until one day, while I was with him, we went to the next level. I gave in to my fleshly desires. It wasn't planned, and I didn't feel pushed into it. It just seemed like the natural progression of our relationship. I was happy for a brief moment in time. My secret life was more like my real life, which I wanted so much. I didn't know where this would lead, but I was ready to go. On my way back home, I felt guilty for breaking my promise to God. I did not set out to do wrong, but it happened, and I was responsible for it happening. That is why I wanted a divorce. I did not want to cheat on Ricky. I knew what that felt like. I had done it to him when he was not physically present in my life, and he had done it to me when he was away from me and right in my face. I know that is not an excuse for what I did. I just wanted to be free to live my life as I wanted without domestic violence, drugs, and alcohol complicating it. Life by itself was hard enough. I didn't want to hurt anyone; I just needed to get my sanity and my peace back. The only way to do that was to remove what was causing my insanity. I had invested over 20 years into my marriage, and despite the few good moments we had, it was still a total disaster. It was time to let go. It had long been time to let go, but Ricky didn't want it to happen. The way he saw it, I belonged to him no matter how badly I wanted to be released from the hell he put me through. It is amazing how things can change once you change your mind. I changed my mindset, and my life and future proceeded to change. When I think about it now, I am so amazed by the thought that my life seemed like it was falling apart, but in reality, it was falling together. I did not understand what was happening. I only knew that this was the way it had to be. No one can own another person, and Ricky held on to me the way he did as though he owned me. My life was mine. I deserved to be happy in it. God had given me life, not Ricky, and I wanted it back.

I reckoned that I could not wait any longer for Ricky to see the wisdom in our need to be divorced. I went to Raeford and found a lawyer's office and asked to speak to one. I sat down and waited to be called. When I was, I went into his office, introduced myself, and proceeded to tell him my story: how I had been begging my husband for a divorce, how he kept refusing to agree and give me one. I explained how he was physically and mentally abusive to me, and I was afraid it would go too far one day. He told me that he sympathized with my situation and that it would be very costly to get what I wanted. I knew I couldn't come close to the price he was asking, so I asked him, "Can you give me some advice on what I should do?" He said, "I hate to tell you this, but the only thing you can do is wait for him to hit you again and hope that he doesn't hurt you badly. Then go to the Magistrates Office and file for a restraining order on him." That was the only option he could give me. I thanked him for his time and advice and left. I decided right then and there that I would do just that. I had to get away from him if I wanted to continue to stay alive. My decision had absolutely nothing to do with my relationship with Charles. I had been trying to break free from the destructive life I was living way before I even knew Charles existed. I went back home with a plan. I didn't know if I would be okay after Ricky hit me again or how long it would take for it to happen, but I prayed that the Lord would protect me and it would all turn out okay. I went to work daily, never knowing when that life-changing moment would occur. I told Charles what the lawyer had told me to do. He was afraid for me, and he got angry just thinking about Ricky hitting me, but it was a necessary evil to get out of the dangerous situation I was in. I waited patiently for that day. Ricky kept demanding that I give him money for drugs and take him to buy them. He told me one day after I asked him for approximately the one-hundredth time to please give me a divorce, "You might as well get used to me getting high on crack. I will never stop, and the only way you are going to get rid of me is that the police will have to come and take me out of here." I kid you not. Those exact words came out of his mouth, unbelievable, right?

Getting High

After returning home from the drug dealer's house, he went into the bathroom and cooked the crack he had bought in a spoon using a butane lighter. Then he drew it from the spoon through a small cotton ball with a hypodermic needle, wrapped his belt around his arm tightly, and injected the solution into his vein. I watched in disbelief as he did it. I could not understand how he was able to do this to himself. I hated what he was doing, and I hated the smell of it; It made me sick to my stomach. One night, after he got high, he told me if I ever tried to leave him, he would tie me up and set me on fire. I didn't know if he would try to do that to me, but I do know that when someone threatens to do you bodily harm, believe them. So, I took him seriously because he had a history of physically hurting me, and I didn't know how far he would go. I had to look out for myself. I couldn't call for help because I did not have a phone. Even if I had a phone, there was no one to help me. It was a really scary time for me. His anger was escalating, and I knew that it would not be long before he would attack me again, especially if he didn't get his fix when he wanted it.

The Wait Was Over

I visited with some of my girlfriends for a while one evening. After I left them, I took a chance and spent some time with

Charles. When I got back home, I was surprised that Ricky was there, and he met me at the door, asking me where I had been. Of course, I did not tell him the complete truth. I told him I had been at a girlfriend's house just hanging out. One of his friends from down the street had just walked up as we argued over him letting me into the house I was paying for. The next thing I knew, he reached out and pushed me, and I fell down the steps. Thank God his friend was standing at the bottom of the stairs and caught me. It is incredible how God can put people in the right place at the right time to help you. I don't believe in coincidence; I think he was sent there to help me. I got myself together, picked up my purse from the ground, got back into my car, and I left. As I drove away, I knew that he had just given me what I needed to get a restraining order against him, which would lead to getting him out of my life. Thank God I didn't get hurt in the process. I had nowhere to go, so I went back to Charles's place and spent the night with him. There was no going back to my previous life. It was now on the pathway to being over. I thought about how the day before, I was a prisoner of domestic violence, and today, I had been set free, unknowingly, by my captor. It only took 24 hours for my life to change. This was not how I wanted things to play out. I must say I was relieved, though. I knew everything was not entirely over. Ricky would fight to get me back, but I had to do what I needed to break away from him.

My New Roommate

Charles gave me a key to his apartment so that I could come and go as I pleased. I didn't have any clothes because I left my home with what I was wearing, as many abused women are forced to do. Back then, I did not know anything about Domestic Violence Centers like the ones available today. I don't know if there was one in my community. I had to go where I felt safe and where

Ricky could not find me. As soon as I could, I went to the magistrate's office and filed for a restraining order against him. A court date was set for me to appear before a Judge to obtain the restraining order. Ricky was served with papers to appear in court. After I left him, I was offered a job on first shift, and I took it. I could finally sleep during the night instead of getting up to go to work at 11:00 pm. It also made it safer for me to arrive at work and leave in the daylight. I still had to pay close attention to the people approaching me; my life depended on it. Ricky was probably fuming from being served court documents. I know he never dreamed this day would come, but it had, and it was high time that it did.

I started getting phone calls from Ricky at work. I asked him to please leave me alone. I needed to work. He kept on calling until I almost lost my job because of it. I don't know why he finally stopped, but I was so happy he did. More than likely, he recognized that what he was doing was not working, and he needed to devise another plan. In the meantime, I had to be aware of my surroundings and keep watch vigilantly to make sure that wherever I went, he could not sneak up on me. He didn't have a driver's license or any transportation, so that was a plus in my favor. I hoped that no one would be reckless enough to help him with his evil plans. Because I left home with only the clothes on my back, I needed to go back to my house to get some. I was afraid to go alone, so my older sister Samantha offered to go with me. He was still living in my house when we arrived, but he was on his best behavior. He knew that Samantha didn't play. He did not try anything stupid. I took as many of my things as I could, and we left. Eventually, Ricky had to vacate my house and stay with his parents to have transportation to get back and forth to his job, have food to eat, and find someone to help him get to his drug dealer's house. His parents did not know it, but they were about to experience the true Ricky. They were not aware of what I had been dealing with living with him. They would soon find out that he was a drug addict and an alcoholic and that both his habits made him do bad things to feed them. My house was now empty. I didn't dare go back there because he could have someone watching the house to see if I came back home, and they could inform him. It wasn't safe just yet. I had to give it some time and allow things to cool down. His emotions were high and very unpredictable, and I didn't want to end up on the receiving end of his mounting anger. He had lost his control over me, and that made him utterly vicious. His life was falling apart, and he now knew what it felt like to have no control over what was happening to him and his life.

I left Charles's apartment to stay at my dad's home with Olivia and her daughter for a while. I did not want to live with Charles, plus it was more convenient because I was closer to my job. I wanted to get a divorce before my relationship with Charles was public knowledge. It appeared that Ricky had reconciled himself to the fact that we were well on our way to being divorced. I had not heard from or seen him in a good while, which made me very happy. I hoped that he had accepted that I was never coming back to him, that our marriage was over, and that we both needed to get on with living our lives apart. Time moved on, and it was getting close to the time for my family's annual reunion. It was held in Texas that year, and everyone was going except me. I could not afford to go because I needed to keep my bills up to date to hold onto my home. I stayed at Olivia's house alone while she was gone out of town. Ricky knew when our annual reunion was scheduled, and he could easily guess it was highly probable that I would be staying there. There was a good chance that he knew exactly when I would be all by myself. I could have been watched by one of his crack-head friends; I don't know. Olivia and my family were going to be out of town for a week. I prayed that I would be safe while staying at her house alone. I had learned never to underestimate my violent abuser, especially if he refused to let go of what he thought belonged to him. The Lord Jesus had His hand on my life even when I wasn't giving Him a thought. He had been with me all along. I have absolutely no doubt in my mind that He kept me through my entire life and marriage. Once I decided to free myself from the violence, He started making things happen for me. That is the only way I can explain the events that were about to take place in my life.

Obedience

I was alone one evening; I saw no need to cook anything. I decided to go to a convenience store that sold an excellent chicken sandwich. I locked the house up, got in my car, and headed to the store to get my dinner. It was almost dark. I could see the sun setting in the distance, feeling a sense of freedom, a sense of peace as I took my time driving down the lonely country road. When I reached the store, I could smell the fried chicken in the parking lot. It smelled so good it was almost intoxicating. I went in and purchased my food. When I returned to my car, I decided to wait until I got back home before enjoying my sandwich. It was a beautiful summer night, with a gentle breeze blowing through my car window. I let down all the windows to enjoy the wind caressing my face as I listened to my favorite radio station. I thought about Charles, and it brought a smile to my face. He was at work, so I could not call him. It was nice to have someone I could talk to and someone concerned about my well-being for a change. My future was looking better than it had in a very long time. There were multiple obstacles in my path, but I was confident that a way would be made for me. I only had a few miles to go before I would be back at my sister's house. When I reached my turnoff, for some reason, I chose to drive on down to the end of the road a few miles and turn around at the stop sign and come back. I enjoyed the ride so much that I wasn't ready to return to the house. By this time, it had gotten completely dark. When I approached my turnoff again, a voice inside me spoke to me and said, "Don't go back to the house." I was obedient, and I kept going down the road. I was maybe a few hundred yards past my turnoff when I noticed a vehicle barreling down the road at a very high rate of speed for a residential area. When the vehicle passed me, I turned my head to look at it as it passed. I could see that it was Ricky driving his boss's van. He was driving like a bat out of hell. He was so focused on getting to Olivia's house that he didn't notice that he had passed me on the road. The Lord had blocked his view so that he could not see me. I looked in my rearview mirror and saw him take the turnoff to Olivia's house. Suddenly, I realized that Jesus had just saved my life. If I had not listened to Him, I probably would have lost my life that night. All I could say was, "Thank You Jesus." I kept on down the road, afraid and thinking about where I would go now. The only option I had was to go to Charles's apartment. So, I turned onto the main highway and drove to Charles's place. On the way, I stopped to put some gas in my car. When I turned off the highway into the store parking lot, I could see a couple of men running out of the store carrying cases of beer. The store attendant was chasing them. I politely drove back onto the highway. I had enough excitement for one night. I bought some gas farther down the road.

When I arrived at the apartment, I sat in the car for a little while to gather my thoughts and to give God thanks for saving my life. I had dodged a huge bullet that night. I believe that if Ricky had gotten his hands on me, I would not be here right now. Thinking about it frightened me profusely. When all of this was going on between Ricky and me, there had been several women in my hometown whose abusers had recently murdered them. I was so blessed that the Lord spoke to me and kept me safe. I grabbed my food, got out of the car, unlocked the door, and went inside. I was no longer hungry, so I put my sandwich in the refrigerator and went to lie down across the bed to wait for Charles to come home from work. I fell asleep waiting for him because I felt safe. Hours later, Charles got home. He was very surprised and pleased to see me. He knew that I was spending the week alone at my sister's. I told him all about what had transpired that night as I started to feel the warmth of the tears rolling down my face. He put his arms around me and comforted me. He told me I could stay with him for as long as I needed to. I thought, what if I had never met Charles? Where would I be, and where would I go? I would not have had anywhere to go that was safe for me. Ricky did not know about Charles or where he lived. I could relax and feel safe with him. I thought to myself, "What if Ricky shows up on my job?" I hoped that he would be in fear of being arrested because of what was said to him by the plant manager who fired him: do not return to these premises. And that would keep me safe while I was at work, but there was no guarantee of that. I was thinking of all kinds of possibilities and scenarios. My mind was racing with the events of that night until I finally fell asleep again. Charles knew how on edge I was about Ricky. I lived in constant fear that he would somehow find me. Charles took excellent care of me while I was with him. To help cheer me up, one afternoon, I came home from work to his apartment to find a beautiful single red rose in a vase, with a gift box and a card sitting on the coffee table in the den. My mouth fell open. I picked up the card and read it. He expressed his feelings for me; it was lovely. Then I opened the gift box. It was a pair of gold bamboo hoop earrings. They were the first pair of 14K gold earrings I had ever owned. I had never been treated this way in my life. He helped me feel safe and loved. That was something I hadn't felt in a very long time.

Homecoming

When Olivia returned home from her trip, she found her door wide open. Ricky had broken into the house that night he came looking for me and ransacked her home. He knew that my car wasn't in the driveway. I don't know why he kicked in her door like that. I know he was angry that he didn't catch me alone at her house. The door had been open like that for about five days. It was a blessing that no one saw it as a chance to take anything from her house. I was thankful that the house had stayed safe all that time; I felt responsible for it. I could not take a chance and go back there alone. She did tell me that she had left some money lying on her bedroom dresser, and it was gone. I assume that after Ricky had been on his rampage looking for me, he needed some money to get high. I did not want to cause any more trouble for my sister, so I continued to stay with Charles for a few days. When I went back to stay with Olivia, she told me that I could not come back. She needed to keep her young daughter safe. I was sorry that I had brought danger to her home. I did not want to put anyone's life in jeopardy, especially not my niece or my sister. I understood her concern for the safety of her daughter and herself. Ricky was my problem, and I would have to deal with it independently. The only safe place left for me to go was back to stay with Charles. He welcomed me back. I felt he was sent to be a blessing in my time of trouble.

CHAPTER 14
COURT

The day came for me to go to court. I knew I would have to face Ricky, and I was very nervous about seeing him again. My girlfriend Joyce volunteered to go with me. I was very thankful to her for that. I would not have to go through this process by myself. We sat in the courtroom and waited for my case to be called. While I was waiting, Rickey came in, found me, and came and sat down right beside me. My heart started to beat rapidly. He grabbed my hand and tried to hold it. I looked him in the face, snatched my hand away from him, and asked him to please leave me alone. I don't believe that he had a clear understanding as to why he was in court. He kept right on trying to hold my hand, pleading with his eyes. I looked at Joyce and said, "Let's move somewhere else." We moved, and lo and behold, here comes Ricky again, sitting beside me. I guess he was trying to influence me to change my mind. But my mind was made up, and I had no intention of ever going back to him. The court clerk called my name. I got up and took the stand, I was sworn in, and I sat down. The district attorney asked me questions. I testified how Ricky had refused to let me enter my home and pushed me down the stairs. He had been beating me and forcing me to do things that I did not want to do, like giving him money for drugs and having to take him to his drug dealer's house. I also testified that he had threatened my life by telling me that he would tie me up and set me on fire if I ever tried to leave him. When the DA had finished asking me questions, she said, "Your witness." I almost fell out of my seat because Ricky did not have a lawyer. He was representing himself. That meant I had to answer his questions. He started with the night I left him. He asked, "Where did you go that night?" and I answered, "To a girlfriend's house socializing with some friends." Then he asked me, "Did you go anywhere else that night?" My throat seemed to close up on me. I knew I had just sworn to tell the truth and nothing but the truth. Because I feared for my life, I could not tell the truth about that, so I lied and said, "No." I asked God to please forgive me for telling that lie. I also knew that I had just committed perjury, which could get me some jail time. I had no choice; I had to be free of him. When he finished asking me questions, it was his turn to take the stand, and the DA questioned him. Of course, he denied everything. But after he left the stand, the judge made a decision to grant my request for a restraining order and warned Ricky to stay away from me, or he would be arrested. I felt like a weight had been lifted off my shoulders. I now had the full weight of the law on my side. I knew that it was only the beginning of my journey to freedom. I won that battle, but I did not trust Ricky; he knew his life would be forever changed if I was not in it, and I didn't believe he would give up trying to get to me. Joyce and I left the courthouse and went home. When I dropped her off, I thanked her so very much for her support. She had been a real friend that day when I needed one.

The Break-In

I went back to the apartment. I kept looking into my rearview mirror as I drove, ensuring I was not being followed. I felt good that part of my journey was over, but I knew Ricky very well, and he did not see this as the end. More than likely, he felt that if he could get his hands on me while I was alone, he could convince me to come back to him or else. That conversation would lead to violence because the only way he could express himself was by inflicting pain. I relaxed for the rest of the day, waiting for Charles to come home from work later that night. My life was very complicated. I wondered when I would feel safe enough to go back to my home. I made my monthly payments even though I wasn't living in my home at the time. I couldn't lose the investment that had taken me a long time to procure. I went to work every day, hoping that I would not run across Ricky. Weeks went by, and I was starting to feel a little more comfortable. I cooked for Charles when I came home from work. He enjoyed that because he could not cook anything, and he loved to eat. It was my pleasure to prepare a meal for him. I finished cooking dinner and went into the den to watch TV. I skimmed through one of the magazines on the coffee table while listening to a show.

I was feeling right at home when, all of a sudden, I heard a loud noise coming from the front door. I was frozen in my seat. I started to panic because I thought that Ricky had found me and was kicking in the door. It happened so fast that I didn't get the chance to call 911. Suddenly, I heard the door hit the wall, and whoever it was kicking in the door was now in the apartment. As I waited to see who had just broken in, my heart felt like it had stopped beating. Then I saw two guys come around the corner to the den where I was. One was tall, and the other was short. They both had a mask on, and both of them had guns. I took a deep breath and bravely asked them what they wanted, and one of them told me to stay in my seat and shut up! That wasn't a problem; I was paralyzed anyway. I was scared out of my mind. They snatched the TV right out of the wall. Then they grabbed the VCR, too. Sitting there watching them ransack the apartment, I wondered if I would make it out of this alive. It was like watching what happens in a TV show or a movie. One of them went into the bedroom and stole whatever he could find there. I thought that when they finished robbing the place, they could rape or kill me; even though I could not identify them, they could do it just because they felt like it. As I sat there waiting to see what they were going to do to me, I prayed. After they got everything they could get, they took my car keys and the house phone, put everything they had stolen in my vehicle, and used it as their getaway car. Now, who kicks in someone's door to rob them and comes there on foot? Not very intelligent people, that's for sure. That told me that they lived close by and knew Charles and his schedule. How did they plan to carry off their loot? Stupid, right? I waited a few minutes to make sure they were gone. I went out the front door, with my knees and hands shaking, and knocked on the neighbor's door. A lady answered, and I asked if I could please use her phone to call the police; I had just been robbed at gunpoint. She said sure, with a puzzled look on her face, and went and got the phone, handed it to me, and I dialed 911. I was still trembling from being so afraid that I had come so close to almost dying just a few short moments ago. After I talked to the 911 operator, I told the neighbor what had happened, and she said she hadn't heard a thing. I don't see how she did not hear the thieves kicking in the front door; it was deafeningly loud. I sat down on the sidewalk and waited for the police to show up. I told them everything that happened. The officer told me that they would do everything they could to find the people who had broken into the apartment and stolen my car. He walked through the apartment, looking for any clues that could help him find the men that had broken in. Then, the police officer wrote down my statement and left. I had an old car that was valuable only to me. I could not see them going out of their way to find it. I went back to the neighbors and asked if I could please use their phone again to call Charles to let him know about the break-in. As I reflected on what had just happened, I thought about how ironic it was that the tiny thief had a big gun, and the bigger thief had a small one. If I hadn't just been robbed, I probably would have found that quite hilarious.

Charles got off work and came home. I no longer had transportation to get to work. My goodness, how much more was going to happen to me? My mental stability was waning. Mind-blowing event after event was plaguing my life. I thought I had removed myself from danger and stepped right into the thick of it. I would never have imagined being robbed at gunpoint. Wasn't being hunted as though I was prey enough? Life was handing me difficult circumstances to overcome, and I was determined to press my way through whatever was thrown at me. I had made it through 20 years of abuse from Ricky. I wasn't about to give up now. My mind was made up; there was no changing it, no matter what.

Transportation

Charles worked on second shift on his job, and I worked on first shift. I didn't know what I was going to do about getting back and forth to work. I decided to move back to Raeford. A girlfriend and coworker of mine, Susan, offered to let me stay with her. I didn't want to leave, but I needed to get to work to keep my job and continue to take care of my responsibilities. Charles called me every day to check in to see how everything was going. I was still staying vigilant, watching out for Ricky. I could not assume that I was safe because of where I was. Soon after I moved in with Susan, the police found my car parked at an apartment complex. They looked into the glove compartment, and the only phone number they found belonged to Ricky's parents. His mother answered the phone when they called. She told them she did not know where I was. So, she called the only number she had, which was my sister Olivia's number, and asked her to tell me to call her, that she had information about my car. Reluctantly, I called her, and she told me that the police had found my car and that the dealer I had purchased it from had come and picked it up and took it back to his car lot. She said that she didn't even know that my car had been stolen. She wanted to know what had happened. I didn't want to, but I had to lie about how my car had been stolen. I told her that I was at the mall and when I came out someone had taken my car. I was not about to tell her where I was when it was stolen. What if she told Ricky about it? I could not take that chance. Ricky's mother was a very kind and sweet woman; I didn't want to involve her in my situation. I don't think she told Ricky about the conversation we had about my car. I guess she did not want to tempt him into breaking the restraining order I had against him. She knew he acted on impulse and would probably do something unwise.

I went to the car lot where my car was and talked to my coworker about getting it back. He was okay with it after I explained what had happened. My only problem was that there were no keys for it; the thieves kept them. So, my friend put in a new ignition switch so that I could drive it again. I left there very delighted and blessed that I had my transportation back. It was an old car, and I was happy that the thieves didn't feel the need to do any damage to it. What a Godsend that was. I continued to stay with Susan because it saved me money and time. When I got the chance, I went to visit Charles. He had to get his front door repaired and the locks changed because the thieves had taken my keys, and his apartment key was on my key ring. That day, Charles and I were lying across the bed talking when he looked me in the eyes and asked me to marry him. Without hesitation, I just said, "Of course I will." He made me a happy woman that day. I knew I was still married to Ricky, but as I said, my relationship with him was over, legally or not. Charles was offering me a new life. I didn't think about the obstructions in our way. I only knew I wanted to be his wife. But there were some things from my past that I needed for him to know. I had to warn him that I could not guarantee us having children. I explained what happened to me in my past that could prevent us from reproducing. He told me that it was okay. He already had a child, and besides, he only wanted me. I put that out there to eliminate any confusion before making any plans. Other than the issues I was having with Ricky, I wanted him to know what he was getting into. I kept our engagement to myself. There would be people against it, and I just wanted to keep it between us for the moment. I had many problems without solutions, and worrying about what people thought of our relationship was the last thing I needed to be concerned about. To be honest, I did not have the time to worry myself with people. I had some huge hurdles to cross that were more important.

Unsettled

Being on first shift was a little strange to me because out of all the years I had worked at Spanco Yarns, I had primarily worked third shift and some time on second shift. I was starting to get used to it and appreciated sleeping at night. I made some new friends and enjoyed working during the daylight hours. Management was always walking around evaluating what the employees were doing. That never happened on second and third shifts, but if you did your job, there was no need to feel intimidated. Whenever we would get off work, Susan and I had lots of fun hanging out, getting take-out, or cooking a meal. I spent a lot of time on the phone talking to Charles. We'd talk about our plans, and he would tell me how much he loved me and missed me. I really missed him too. It felt as though we had known each other for a long time. I was so comfortable with him in a way that I had never been with Ricky. He seemed to know what to say and when I needed him to say it. Weeks went by, and everything appeared to have calmed down. At lunch one day, I was getting my food along with some other ladies when something was said that I didn't like very much. Maybe the person I felt offended by did not think before she spoke. Some people say things without thinking them through. She may not have been aware that she had upset me; I don't know. When I got off work that day, I went to Susan's house, packed my things, and went back to stay with Charles. I felt safer and more comfortable being with him. Susan asked me why I had left her home the next day at work. To avoid awkwardness, I just said I missed Charles and decided to go back and stay with him. I thanked her for her hospitality and for letting me stay with her. I was in a state of unrest. I could have overreacted about what had happened at work. The slightest thing would set me off. But the only place I could find some peace was with Charles.

Officially Engaged

Charles and I went out together one morning to take care of his household responsibilities. We stopped at a fast-food restaurant while we were out to get some lunch before returning home. He asked me what I wanted, and I said a cheeseburger with fries and a drink, please. He went inside to get the food; he returned and handed me what I had ordered. I was taking the food out of the bag when I noticed a little black velvet box in the bottom of the bag. I reached in, pulled it out, and opened it. My eyes got big, and my heart skipped a beat when I saw that it was a beautiful diamond solitaire engagement ring. Charles took it, placed it on my finger, and said, "Will you marry me?" I said, "Yes, yes,

yes." He had guessed my ring size because he wanted to surprise me. Unfortunately, it was too big, and it would need to be sized to fit my finger. I was so overwhelmed and happy by his second proposal. It was a moment that proved to me that Charles was very serious about us getting married, which made me the happiest woman in the world. I wrapped my arms around his neck, hugged and kissed him. Then I joyfully placed the ring back in the box, elated by what had just occurred, and turned my attention back to my food, too excited to eat. My life was changing by leaps and bounds in a way I had never anticipated. After our lunch, we went back home officially engaged. It wasn't the most romantic way to give me an engagement ring, but it was special to me. I know that it sounds crazy; it was like putting the cart before the horse, but it didn't feel that way to me. I was so in love that I did not care about what people would say when they found out. I was bound to be talked about no matter what, and I'm sure it was already happening. People knew that I was going through some problems with Ricky, but they did not know all of the details and to what extent. They gossiped about me, especially knowing I was still legally married to Ricky. I refused to let people talking about me stop me from being ridiculously happy. After I told him my ring size, Charles took the ring back to the jeweler to be sized. It would take a while before I could wear it, and I planned to do just that. I kept our engagement a secret until he could put that ring on my finger to stay.

Promotion

I was always a little uneasy when I left Charles. I didn't know where Ricky was or what he was up to. I had to remain circumspect in watching out for him. Before I got out of my car, I would take a good look around to make sure that I did not see him. It was physically draining living in limbo like that, but if that was what I had to do to be free of the dreadful life that I had been living with him, then I was willing to do whatever it took. No one should have to live in fear for their lives, especially from someone who supposedly loves them. I had enough and wanted out and was willing to do almost anything to make that happen, barring murder, of course. At work, I got a few looks and whispers, but I did not let that bother me. I kept on doing my job and going back home every day. I was working on my machines one morning when my supervisor came to tell me to go to the front office; someone in Human Resources needed to talk to me. I asked the operator working next to me to watch my machines while I went up front to the office. I went in and sat down. I was told about a lead person position in C-Plant that was open on third shift. They wanted me to accept the job. They were under the impression that I was a valid candidate for the position because of the knowledge I had obtained working third shift for years. I would be working with the spoolers and the scragg operators in C-plant. In this position, I would be in charge of making sure that the first-shift doffers had all the spools of nylon they needed to do the machines scheduled to be doffed the following day. I was also the fill-in supervisor whenever the third shift supervisor was scheduled off. It was going to be a challenge. I had only been in a leadership position once before, and I was a little bit hesitant, but I sure could use a raise. They saw qualities in me that I had not yet seen in myself. I had not noticed that in my dysfunctional marriage, I was gaining leadership skills because of all the things I had dealt with: problem-solving, dealing with high stress, communication skills, and innovation. Without noticing it, I was learning how to be a leader. In previous years, the third shift supervisor had tried to put me in a lead-doffer position. I turned it down, but this time, I saw myself in a different light, and I had more confidence in myself, new goals, and higher self-esteem. I did not mind working at night because I could get my rest and still be able to do the things I could only get done in the daytime. I believed that I could do the job, so I accepted the position, and soon, I was told that I would be instructed to go to C- Plant to be trained by the lead person on first shift.

There was a lot to be learned, but I did it and was now going to my new shift. The lead person on first shift did an excellent job training me. She shared all the knowledge she had acquired over the years working in her position. I was thankful for the kindness and patience she had shown me while I trained for my new role with her. When I reported to my new job on third shift, the people were friendly and helped me continue my education by showing me their job and some of the things I would be responsible for because things on third shift were a little different than first shift. I admit that I sometimes felt a little inadequate, but I kept on consuming all the knowledge I could and refused to give up. With time, I would be confident in doing my job.

Time to go Home

Charles was happy for me. He always supported me in everything. It was great sharing the changes in my life with him, and I look forward to more of it in the future. I told him I had thought about it and felt it was time for me to return home. I was going to have to do it at some point. My new job was a pivotal moment in my life. It gave me renewed assurance and revived my self-worth. I had to stop letting my fear control me and get back to living in my own home. He was afraid for me, and rightly so, but he understood and supported my decision. I had not seen my home in months. I did not know what to expect, but I did know that before I could go home, I needed to get phone service installed so that if anything happened, I would be able to call the police. I got in touch with the phone company and set a date for them to install my phone service. I had to be there for this to happen, so I packed up everything and went home the day before the installer was scheduled to come. My home was a mess when I walked in. I got right to work getting it cleaned up. Charles was coming by that night after he got off work to make sure I was okay. He had never been to my home, and he was looking forward to seeing it. My neighbors were shocked to see me return. One who lived across the street knocked on my door, and when I answered, he said hello and mentioned he wanted to ask me if he could come by and visit me sometimes; in other words, he wanted to date me. I was shocked by his interest in me. I wasn't even aware that this man knew anything about me. Evidently, he knew I was no longer with Ricky. I told him no, thank you. I already have someone in my life. So I closed the door and went back to straightening up. A little while later, I had another knock on my door. I was astonished that so many people seemed to know that I had returned home. I opened the door, and to my amazement, it was Wayne. I could not believe it. I asked him how did he know where I lived and how did he know I had come back home. He told me that he had his ways. We chatted for a few minutes, catching up. In case he had come by for the same thing as my neighbor from across the street, I let him know that I was not interested; I have a man in my life. It is remarkable how some people don't know what they have until they lose it and continue to try to retrieve it, with no success. I was blown away by Wayne, thinking he still had a chance with me, mainly because he had a wife and kids at home. Oh yeah, I had heard how he married the girl that got pregnant by him. They did it up big with the white wedding gown, bridesmaids, and groomsmen in a Church. I did not want to be involved in his drama. He made his choice years ago. I don't know what he expected to happen when he came by to see me. Maybe he thought I would agree to be his piece on the side. I was not going back to my past. I had a new future ahead of me, which was all I wanted in my life. I showed him to the door and said goodbye. I got back to my housework so my home would be nice and clean when Charles came by. He arrived around 2:00 am. I gave him a tour of my home, and then we sat on the couch to watch a little TV and talk. I asked him if he would please stay with me because I was nervous about being alone. If my neighbors and someone I hadn't seen in years knew that I was back home, who's to say that one of Ricky's get-high buddies hadn't also been watching my house and alerted him to my return? Ricky wanted to get his hands on me in the worst way. He had already tried at Olivia's house, but that didn't work out too well for him. I had the feeling that he would try again despite the restraining order I had against him. Charles agreed to spend the night to comfort my fears. He got up the next morning and went home. He needed a change of clothes for work later on that day. I had one more day off to rest and take care of my home. My yard had grown out of control and needed mowing. Without my asking, my next-door neighbor offered to cut it for me. I thanked him, and when he was finished, I gave him a little piece of money to show my gratitude. The man from the phone company came by that afternoon and installed a phone in my kitchen and bedroom. I was relieved to have a way to call for help if I needed to do so. At night, I was always on edge. I kept expecting Ricky to show up. I felt a small amount of peace knowing that he did not have a driver's license and did not own a car. When it came to me, Ricky thought he could bully me into doing what he wanted. He just needed to get in my face physically, and he could regain his control over me. I had let him get by with so much; I understood why he felt that way. He had no idea how significant a change had occurred in me, and I was not about to go backward. I had a bright future ahead of me. And come hell or high water, I was determined to have it without him. Whether I had a great life ahead of me or not, I was not going to surrender to his will ever again!

CHAPTER 15
NO RESTRAINT

It was time to return to work. I got up, showered, put my clothes on, and left for work. As soon as I got on the main highway, I passed a police car going in the same direction I had come from. I didn't think very much of it at the time. Then, I started to see them quite often on other nights when I would be on my way to work. I wondered if they were actively staying in the area because of the restraining order I had against Ricky, just in case they needed to get to me quickly. The violent abusers in my community were murdering so many women; it almost looked like an epidemic. I worked my scheduled days, and when I was off, I spent time with Charles. We talked to each other every day, though. He still had not replaced the phone in his apartment that the thieves had stolen. Sometimes, I would leave work at 7:00 am and go and spend the morning with him until it was time for him to go to work.

One day, he told me that he had decided to buy me a gun to protect myself if Ricky chose to break the restraining order. I didn't like guns. I had never held one in my hands before. The thought of having to shoot someone made me nauseous, but I had to protect my life from anyone who sought to take it. We went out that morning to get a license to own a handgun. I was not very comfortable getting it, but Charles insisted that I protect myself because of Ricky's hostility towards me. He was libel to try and hurt me if he got the chance. After looking at a few guns in several stores, he purchased a Rossi 38 caliber handgun. I did not expect a gun to be so heavy. He showed me how to use it, but I was still afraid of it. I knew how dangerous guns were and had no desire to use them. I would be home alone that night, so Charles gave me the gun to take home with me and told me he would be coming by that night whenever he got off work. I went home, did some cooking, and did some housework. Later on, I took a nap on the couch, trying to kill time until Charles came by. I woke up after a few hours and turned on the TV. I put the gun on the bottom shelf of my coffee table and laid a towel over it; I don't know why I did that. Maybe it was because I didn't like looking at it.

The Final Straw

It was around 2:00 a.m. when I saw the lights from a car turning into my driveway. I got up and peeped through the blinds of the window to see who it was. To my dismay, it was Ricky. He drove the car all the way up to the doorsteps. When I realized it was him, I had to make a split-second decision. Did I want to pick up the gun and use it to shoot him or run to my bedroom and dial 911? I thought about what it would do to his mother and the rest of his family if I killed him. I thought about what it would do to me. I didn't want to kill Ricky; I didn't want his death on my conscience. I also asked myself, "What if I shot at him and missed? He could take the gun from me and kill me with it." After a few seconds, I concluded that I should dial 911 and pray that the police would arrive in time to help me. Leaving the gun covered by the towel under my coffee table, I ran to my bedroom, sat on the bed, picked up the phone, and

No Restraint | 239

dialed 911. I told the operator who I was and that I had a restraining order against my estranged husband, and he had just driven into my yard. As we talked, I gave her my address, and then I heard Ricky kick in the door. I told her that he was now in my house. I could hear his footsteps as he got closer to my bedroom door. While listening to him as he was coming down the hallway, cursing me and calling me everything except a child of God, I was praying that I had made the correct decision. When he reached the bedroom, he saw me on the phone. He did not anticipate that. He wasn't aware I had a phone because when he left months ago, I did not. I believe that was one of the reasons that gave him the confidence to come to my home that night. He thought that I could not call for help. He yelled at me to hang up the phone. Scared out of my mind, I did as he asked. The 911 operator called me right back. I picked up the phone and said hello. She asked me if he was in the room with me, and I said yes. She told me that officers had been dispatched to my residence and to stay on the line. Ricky told me to put the phone down. Instead of hanging up the phone this time, I laid it down on the bed. The operator could hear everything he was saying to me. Then he came around the bed, grabbed me, and dragged me down the hallway, out the front door, down the steps, and forced me into the car. I recognized the car; It was his mother's car. I suspected that she probably didn't realize that he had stolen it. He slammed the door and went around to the driver's side to get in. I wept because I knew that this could be my last day on earth. I could end up being one of the statistics of the numerous victims of domestic violence that happen every day and have occurred in my immediate vicinity. While I was in a fetal position on the car's floorboard, he started punching me in my head, telling me that he couldn't believe that he had a whore for a wife. If a woman is a whore, then what is a man that has been with so many women that you can't count them all? The ones that I did know about were enough for me. I am positive that there were many, many more that I wasn't aware of.

He drove a few miles away from my house, pulled alongside the road, and stopped. I figured this was it; he was going to kill me, but instead, he violently tried to convince me to take him back. He wanted me to avert the restraining order and tell the police that we were getting back together. He knew that they were at my house looking for me. I had to think smart, so I told him whatever he wanted to hear, but I had no intentions of getting back together with him. He made me promise that when he took me back home, I would tell the police what he wanted me to say. I told him that I would. I kept myself calm so he would not suspect that I was lying to him. When we reached my house, I could see about five police vehicles in my yard with the lights flashing. I knew exactly what to do before he turned into the driveway. Ricky boldly pulled up in the yard, and as soon as the car stopped moving, I opened the door, jumped out, ran to the police officers, and told them what he had done to me. They grabbed him as he got out of the car, put him in handcuffs, and shoved him in the back seat of one of the police cruisers. While this was going on, Charles drove up. He jumped out of his car and ran to me. He wanted to know if I was okay and what had happened. I explained to him what Ricky had done as he consoled me. I was visibly upset, trembling uncontrollably as the floodwaters forced my tears down my face. He told me, let's go into the house. When Charles and I walked by the Police car Ricky was in, I felt like everything was suddenly in slow motion; with Charles' arm around me, I turned my head and looked in the car window and saw Ricky crying like a baby. His outburst of tears did not produce any compassion in me at all. The decision he made to come to my house had put him in that police car. He should have obeyed the judge when he told him to stay away from me. I slowly turned my head away, feeling no empathy, and went into my home. I was thankful that I was still alive with minor bumps and bruises, mostly physically unscathed, but mentally I was crushed.

One of the police officers came inside with me to ask me some questions. Charles sat down on the couch beside me, with his arm around my shoulders while I answered them. I started from the beginning when Ricky kicked in my door, took me out of my home, and tried to force me to say what he wanted. I told the police officer about the gun, but I decided not to use it. He got very angry with me and said, "Why didn't you shoot him? He could have killed you!" I told him I didn't want to live with his death on my conscience; killing him was not my objective; I just wanted the freedom back he had stolen from me for years. He continued to tell me that I had every right to shoot him; it would have been self-defense because of the restraining order I had filed against him. I knew he was right, but I just could not bring myself to do it. Jesus was with me that night. I believe I made the right choice. Things could have ended up so much worse than they were. I barely had a bruise on me because the Lord protected me, and I know it! The officer informed me that I would need to come to the Police Station the next morning and give my formal statement. Then he left, and I was relieved and safe from Ricky once again. He was behind bars and could no longer hurt me. He refused to let go of me, and it got him in trouble. Sometimes, people can't hear you when you are saying no. They are so determined to get what they want they become deaf to what you want. I had spent twenty-one years trying to rectify a relationship that should never have happened. I got married for the wrong reasons, and I had paid dearly for that, but it was time to end the nightmare; I wanted the suffering to stop. I believed there had to be a better life for me than the one I was living. I had no happiness and joy, just pain, suffering, fear, and worry. I was only blessed with one life, and I had squandered a vast amount of it on bad decisions. It was time to seek something better for myself. I dreamed about having some peace, joy, and love in my next relationship. I saw Charles as the man I wanted to build that kind of relationship with.

The following morning, Charles went with me to make my statement. I had to write down all the events of the night before. When I finished, I had to sign it. The officer told me that when they tried to talk to Ricky, all he would do was cry. They had tried to get him to tell them his name, and he wouldn't say a word. I told them his name and where he lived. When all the questions had been asked and answered, the officer said to me that the district attorney would be contacting me to give me an update on my case. I thanked them for being there the night before and for probably saving my life. Charles and I went home. Ricky's mother came by later that day to pick up her car. I didn't speak with her long. I just wanted to get on with my life without Ricky in it. To do that, I had to let go of his family and friends. I did not want to give him any hope that he would ever be with me again, so I made a clean break from everyone. I loved his family, but I had to let go of them because I loved myself, too. I found it unbelievably ironic that Ricky had prophesied out of his own mouth his future. It happened exactly as he had said. The police did have to come and get him to get him out of my life. Ricky was locked up, and I must say I felt so much better. I did not know if his bail had been set or how much it was, but I was hoping it was so high that no one would be able to afford to get him out of jail. The district attorney called me to let me know that Ricky was being charged with breaking and entering, burglary, kidnapping, and breaking a judge-ordered restraining order. She said that he could get up to 30 years in prison. I guess the judge must have set his bail after he was arraigned because Mr. Thurston called me and told me that Ricky had tried to use my home as collateral for bail to get out of jail. He told the bail bondsman that he had no record of Ricky buying a home from him. Besides, I had only been living there for a few months. I knew he wanted to believe that he owned a home when he knew he had nothing to do with purchasing it. The gall of this man was unbelievable. Ricky could not get out of jail for the time being. That was okay with me. If he had acted like a grown man with some sense, he would not be in jail in the first place.

Weeks went by. Life was starting to get back to a normal that I had not seen in years. Charles finally got my engagement ring back and placed it on my finger. I was happy to be acknowledged as his fiancé. When I went to work that night, people started to notice the ring on my finger. One of the ladies commented, "Look at you. You don't even have a divorce yet, and you already have a diamond ring on your finger." I just smiled and kept my mouth shut. They had already been gossiping about me like they knew my story. I refused to add anything to what they thought they knew. When I got off work that day, I amassed all of Ricky's things, put them in large black garbage bags, and sat them on my front porch for someone in his family to come by and pick them up. One of his brothers came by. With tears in his eyes, he asked me to please take off the papers that I had on Ricky. I told him that I did not have any papers on him. Ricky had defied a judge's order, and that I was only a witness for the State that he had broken it. I couldn't stop this even if I wanted to, and I surely did not want to. Everyone was so worried about him, and it appeared that no one cared if I was okay. It was almost as if they thought I should let Ricky do what he wanted to me, as if his life mattered and mine did not. He decided to break that restraining order, not me. I was not responsible for his actions. I begged him to leave me alone because we were over, but he would not listen to me. Now, he was going to have to suffer the consequences of his actions.

What's Next?

Charles continued to live at his apartment. On the nights I was scheduled off work, he would call me from his job and talk for a while before he got off work. To contact me after work, he had to walk to a phone booth a short distance from his apartment because he still did not have a phone. One night, while he was walking to the phone booth, a car pulled up beside him, and some guys commenced talking to him. The next thing he knew, one of them pulled a shotgun on him. When he saw the gun, he ran as fast as he could, but they still managed to shoot him in the thigh. I did not find this out until the next day because he was in the hospital. I told him, "That's it. You are coming to live with me. The area that you live in is too dangerous." When he was released from the hospital, he informed his landlord that he would be moving out of his apartment. A few weeks later, he rented a truck and moved everything out of his apartment. To store what we could not move into my home, he rented a storage building. I helped him to clean up so that he could get his security deposit back. We were now living together. I could not sit by, knowing that his life had been threatened and do nothing. When I needed a safe place to stay, he provided one for me. So, I returned the kindness he had shown me. He was now much closer to his job, making it easier for him to get to work within a reasonable time.

Months went by when, all of a sudden, Ricky started writing letters to me from jail. He still hadn't given up. He tried to use Scriptures from the Bible and my faith in God against me to convince me to get back together with him. I could not believe he would use Jesus to lure me back to the hell he had put me through. He had never cared about Jesus or the Bible before. Whenever I did get the chance to attend Church service, he did not go with me. He knew that I was a believer, and he tried to use it to manipulate me. That just showed me how low he would go to regain control over me. What he had done to me was not about love; it was about control, and he didn't care what he had to use to get it back. Needless to say, I did not fall for it. I was done with him, and no one could make me change my mind about that. I held onto the letters just in case I needed them when I went to court.

CHAPTER 16
THE BEGINNING OF THE END

It felt so good knowing where Ricky was. I no longer had a reason to fear for my life. It had been a long time since I felt such serenity and peace. The district attorney called and asked if Ricky had damaged my home the night he kicked in my door. That was a yes because he broke my door, forcing it open. She informed me that he would be paying for that. I did not have to go to court to testify because Ricky pleaded guilty and got a deal. He was sentenced to time served and five years probation. He could not come anywhere near me for that length of time. If he broke his probation, he would go to prison for a very long time. I think he got off too easy because he did not have a criminal record, and his years of service in the military probably aided in the judge's decision. Any way you slice it, I was one relieved and guardedly optimistic woman. I hoped that after five years, he would forget me and move on with his life. I was no longer a part of it. Knowing Ricky's persistence, I still did not let my guard down. He was now out of jail, and he could try to get at me again. When I was at home, I kept my thirty-eight handgun wherever I was. I even gave it a name, "Sally Sue." I confess that I took a massive leap of faith when I decided not to shoot him. The police officer was absolutely right and highly upset that I didn't. He told me that I would have been totally justified if I had. I was not gonna risk my life like that again. I may have escaped with little to no physical damage that time, but I bore the brunt of some severe mental impairment. I had PTSD (Post Traumatic Stress Disorder.) Every noise, every creek, every knock on my door shook my very being. I was always afraid that Ricky would try to get to me. The threat of going to prison could not be enough to prevent him from trying to hurt or kill me. In the past, I had seen him so out of his mind with anger that it reminded me of a junkyard dog. There was always the possibility that he could give up on life and kill me, then himself, too. It was taking a tremendous amount of time for me to feel completely safe from him. My imagination was in overdrive. I thought about all sorts of things that could happen to Charles or me. He had access to either of us, and he could show up without warning. These are some of the things that crossed my mind. It was hard, but I had to try not to let my negative thoughts consume me. They could steal the joy I had anticipated for Charles and me. That would mean Ricky was still in control. I did not want to live victimized anymore. This individual had controlled me for two decades; that was enough to last me for the rest of my life. I was afraid, but I refused to let that fear prevent me from pushing forward and being happy.

Perplexed Again

Charles started having trouble with his car. Some days, when he got in it to go to work, it would not start. When that happened, I would drop him off at work, and he would pay someone to bring him home because I was working when he got off work. He was so determined to get to his job that, on occasion, he would walk to work, which was a long distance to be on foot. One day, when I was able, I dropped him off in front of the plant. As he was getting out of the car, I noticed someone staring at us. Lo and behold, it was Ricky. He had gotten a job at the same place Charles worked and was on his way inside the plant. It was probably a condition of his probation to get and keep a job. I warned Charles to stay away from him. He did not want to see us together. Hopefully, the threat of going to prison for 30 years would keep him in check, but I would not bet my life on that. I kissed him goodbye, turned my car around, and went back home. I thought that Ricky was out of my life for good. Unfortunately, that was no longer true. Charles had to work; I just hated that he now had to work in the same place as Ricky. That was going to be a problem. Charles was very protective of me and was ready to defend me if he needed to. He was able to get his car repaired after a few days. It was inconvenient for me to drop him off at work because I would normally be sleeping when he needed to be on his way to work, and when I'd drop him off, I had to take into consideration what Ricky might try to do when he saw us together. Charles could now drive to work and use the parking lot across the street from the plant to park his car. He was walking from the parking lot to get inside the plant when he ran into Ricky and exchanged words. One thing led to another; insults were made, and they started fighting. His friend pulled Charles off of him and jokingly told him to stop fighting; they would be late for work as if nothing had happened. Charles got up, straightened up his clothes, clocked in, and reported to his job. Soon after, his supervisor came and told him to go to the Front Office. Ricky reported Charles because he was embarrassed that he had gotten his butt whipped in the parking lot. He thought that doing this would get Charles fired. Well, he was right, but they fired both of them. Charles came back home and told me all that happened. He was out of a job, and jobs were scarce. I knew when I saw Ricky that he was going to cause problems for us. I was able to keep us going for a while with what I was making. I did not include Charle's salary in my budget when I purchased my home, so we were not in dire need yet, but I wanted him to carry his weight. I had been caring for a man for years and did not want to relive that experience again. It was not his fault that he lost his job. He was doing what he felt was right by defending himself and me. He did what he could to help out around the house. He washed dishes, cleaned up, and rearranged my cabinets, but he could not prepare a meal. He had no skills in that area. Charles loved to eat, though. He was enjoying having someone cooking for him. So much so that he gained quite a few pounds while he was unemployed. It didn't look bad on him, but he was beginning to add a little pouch to his stomach. It was time to get a job. He had been trying everywhere he could think of to no avail.

I was talking to Olivia on the phone one day about how hard Charles had been looking for a job. She suggested he come to the plant where she worked and submit an application. So, I told him what she said to do, and he did it, but the day he was there, the open position was given to someone else. We believe it was because Olivia was not working that day. So, Charles asked the human resource representative if he could call her weekly to check on job openings, and she said yes. That's what he did until he finally procured a position. He worked in the towel factory building in the manufacturing complex. This was no easy job, but I had faith in him and motivated him every chance I got to keep him going. He had to learn how to lay in a towel pattern, thread by thread, as quickly as possible. It worried him so much because he wanted to learn his new job to provide for himself and me. That was one of the things that he was so adamant about. They put him with a coworker to train him, and sometimes, the guy wasn't so nice to him, which bothered him. I kept encouraging him by telling him that he could do this. I had faith in him, and I believed that, eventually, he would be okay. Finally, he caught on and was able to do his job very well, so well that he started working overtime hours. Anytime they needed someone to work, he was always willing. Charles would volunteer because he was saving the extra money he made. He worked a twelve-hour shift for three days one week and a twelve-hour shift for four days the following week. Sometimes, he worked a shift on his days off. He had an incredible work ethic; when he saw an opportunity to increase his income, he took it. I never had to worry about him going to work. That was in him before we met. I was happy that we were getting our financial footing, and I was exceptionally proud of him. He was the exact opposite of Ricky. Ricky always put himself first without any hesitancy. It was a nice change not to have to worry about money. I spent so many years being the only one in the relationship concerned about paying our bills. I embraced that change with optimism and a grateful heart.

Charles and I looked forward to finally moving on with our lives. There was a wedding in our future, but there had to be a divorce first. When only one person in a marriage wants a divorce, North Carolina law requires that a couple be separated for one year before filing for divorce. That year was expiring, but it gave us time to learn more about each other's little quirks and faults; everyone has them. I was not finding anything about him that would change my love for him. He was the man I had needed in my life, all my life. We got to know more about each other's families, which gave me more insight into him. He joined me at all my frequent family functions. I did not want it to be like it was with Ricky. My family did not get acquainted with him before we got married. I needed this time to be different. I met his mother, sisters, nieces, and nephews. I did not get to meet his little daughter. He was having a lot of baby-mama drama; it was okay; she was a small child, and I could meet her later. His family was small compared to mine. He was not aware of how vast my family was, but in time he would find out. I introduced him to everyone who lived close by. I wanted no more hiding and no more secrets. I did not care that he might not be accepted because of some of my family's religious beliefs. I knew that Jesus knew all about us because you can not hide anything from Him. I was not seeking anyone's approval. I did it for my peace of mind and how I wanted to live my life. I wanted to be upfront and honest about our relationship. This man had saved my life. I don't know what would have happened to me if it had not been for the Lord on my side and for him helping to keep me safe. Some people sit back and judge others as though they have never sinned. I knew what God had done in my life, and I was not concerned about what others had to say about it. He did not let my sins get in the way of blessing me. He blesses the just and the unjust because of His unconditional love for all of his children. He was the one who brought me out of my situation by placing people in my life to get me where I needed to be. I was not ashamed of how God worked things out for my good. I am thankful to Him for saving my life, and I owe Him everything.

Our Wedding

As a little girl, I dreamed of having a large church wedding. Unfortunately for us, our finances would not allow us to have anything lavish. That was okay with me; it was only a dream, and dreams don't always come true. I would be okay so long as I got to walk down the aisle and marry the man I was in love with. After the one-year separation was up, I found a lawyer and filed for divorce. This day had been put into motion for years and had finally come. When I got to the courthouse a few weeks later, I was one of many women seeking to do the same thing as I was. They called my name, and my lawyer read my petition to the judge. There was no one there to contest my divorce because Ricky could not come near me. So, I was granted my divorce

The Beginning of the End | 253

decree, and I requested my maiden name back, and it was granted. I was finally free at last, free at last, thank God I was finally free at last. I went home and celebrated my emancipation from Ricky. Afterward, I started planning for my wedding. I was not a big fan of a man and a woman living together without being married, even though I had done it in my time of need and rebellion; my values had changed. I had no choice but to wait a year to get a divorce, but now we felt that it was time to make our relationship legal. I knew that some people did not approve of my getting married again. I wasn't positively sure about it myself, but who is positive about the decisions we make; we all step out on faith. I did know that I loved Charles. Everyone takes a chance when they decide to get married. Charles was so good to me that I felt that our chances of failure were minimal. I know no one can predict the future, but I believed everything would work out for us.

We asked the Pastor of my Church to officiate the wedding ceremony, and he agreed. He came by our home one afternoon to counsel us before we got married. He warned us about all the difficulties that married couples face and how we needed to be sure that this was what we wanted to do. He told us that we should love each other no matter what is going on. To never go to bed angry and always listen to one another. To never let money come between us, and never forget to live life while trying to make a life. We were very thankful and accepting of all of his advice. Charles had never been married before, but I had, and I experienced what not to do in marriage; I had a master's degree. We set a date for our wedding, December 24, 1995. We picked that date because, more than likely, we would always be off work on our Anniversary so we could celebrate; plus, I loved Christmas. We would have a beautiful wedding during the season of giving and love. Everyone enjoys the Spirit of Christmas with happy hearts, and it would be a perfect time and atmosphere to join together and become one. It just so happened that Christmas Eve was on a Sunday, which made it perfect to have our ceremony right after the morning worship service. Most of our guests would already be there. Those that were not there would have time to arrive. Don't forget that I am a plain and simple country girl. I was thrilled with the arrangements; I did not need it to be fancy. To share this day with my family and friends was special. The time of sneaking around was over. I put my relationship with Charles out there for all to see. I was blessed and not ashamed of how it had come to be. We all do things that are not always as clean as a freshly fallen blanket of snow. Life is not perfect because we are not perfect; we were not created to be. We fall, but we get back up and try it again. Shutting myself off from living because my first marriage was not an overwhelming success would have been a disaster and a waste of my life. How could the Lord use me if I did not continue to live? He had saved my life for that purpose. God does not use perfect people for His Glory, and I indeed fit that description. In the past, my mindset was not on what the Lord was doing, only on what I was doing, but there was a larger plan at play that I could not yet see.

Preparations

Charles needed to purchase a new suit; he had been living on a meager salary and could not afford to buy one, and I needed to find the perfect wedding dress. We went to the local mall in search of what we needed. I did not want to wear a gown, so I bought a Semi-formal, off-white strapless lace dress with a lace jacket to match. I also purchased a blue garter belt for Charles to throw at our reception. I was blessed that my psoriasis was in remission; I had a few plaques, but nothing serious. All the stress that was fueling the breakouts was gone. That made it possible for me to choose the type of dress I wanted to wear without worrying about hiding my skin. To make Charles look more like he was wearing a tuxedo, he purchased a bow tie and a white shirt with the black suit he bought. I asked my talented sister Ellen to make my wedding bouquet using red and off-white colors. She did a beautiful job. It was just gorgeous. She also made an alternate bouquet to throw at my reception. She could not attend our wedding, so she boxed them up carefully and placed the box in the mail. We were all set and went on to pick out the wedding bands. We did not plan a honeymoon, but we decided to spend our wedding night in a hotel. Charles's mother offered to do our wedding reception as a wedding gift from her. We rented the County Civic Center as our venue.

I did not want to make our marriage more about the wedding day than about the marriage itself. Our celebration was only one day out of many to come. If I had learned anything from being married before, it is that the things that happen in daily life are what make a good marriage. How you treat each other and what you do to each other matters. Once you allow unkind words to pass through your lips, they can not be unsaid; the damage has been done. I planned to do my best to use that knowledge in my marriage to Charles. In a few months, I would be getting married to the man that I loved, the man who loved me. We were about to embark on a new and uncertain journey, but we were going to do it together.

We went to the courthouse to apply for a marriage license to get prepared for our special day. The path that we were about to embark on led us to new and undiscovered possibilities. I had suffered for so long that I had almost given up hope, and now look at how much my life had changed. I was hoping for the wrong thing; trying to force my marriage to work was a mistake. Now, I had joy, happiness, and hope for the future; I was blessed! I invited my friends from work to our wedding. They were around when I was going through hell, so I thought it was only fitting that they witness the joy after the pain. I was surprised one night at work by them. They had put together a bridal shower for me. All of my friends who worked in A, B, and C plants made food and brought gifts. I was caught off guard because I did not anticipate what they did for me. I was all smiles, a few tears, and my heart filled with joy that they thought enough of me to help make my wedding day special. I was gifted a bottle of perfume that I wore on the day of my wedding. I received household gifts that I still have right now and lingerie for my wedding night. I ate some delicious food and had so much fun. When it was over, I thanked everyone for sharing in my joy and for helping me celebrate my new life with my fiancé. I had so much loot I needed help carrying it to my car. When I got home, Charles was as surprised as I was when I walked into the break room. He was happy that my coworkers and friends helped to make our wedding day a special event. We got everything out of the car, put them away, and started preparing for our special day; it was approaching quickly.

A Second Chance

Wiping the sleep from my eyes, I could hear a phone ringing in the background. Then I heard my fiancé speaking to his mother. She wanted him to come and show her where the Civic Center was located; she had gotten lost. She needed to get started decorating to get everything prepared for our reception. After the sleep fog lifted from my brain, suddenly, it dawned on me what day it was. It was December 24th; it was Christmas Eve, my wedding day! My heart started pounding. I was about to say, "I do," to another man. If anyone had asked me three years ago if I would get married a second time, I definitely would have said no. But there I was, preparing to do it again. Charles left to help his mother with the promise that he would be back in time to get dressed for our wedding. I showered, took my time putting on my makeup, styled my hair, put on my jewelry, and finally, put on my wedding dress. After I was fully dressed, Charles walked into the room. His mouth hit the floor. I know that it is not traditional for the groom to see the bride before the wedding, but since we lived together, that was unavoidable. He told me that I looked beautiful, which put a big smile on my face. He showered and put on his black suit with a white shirt and bow tie. I must say, he looked pretty dapper. I grabbed my two bouquets, black coat, and an off-white clutch bag, and we headed for the Church, excited, happy, and terrified all at the same time.

Because I did not want to be seen before our ceremony, when we arrived, I got out of the car to wait in the Pastor's Study while he concluded the Morning Worship Service by giving the benediction to the congregation. Charles waited in the car until directed by Olivia to take his place at the altar. Olivia came to the study to let me know that it was time. I walked back around to the front doors of the Church, fully aware of what I was about to do, but that did not mean I wasn't a nervous wreck. The ushers opened both doors; everyone stood to their feet as I walked to meet my husband to be at the altar. I was trembling something fierce, and hoped it was not visible. When I reached the altar, we faced the Pastor, and he began the ceremony. Olivia served as my maid of honor, and I handed her my bouquet. Charles and I were the very first couple the Pastor had married since he had become a Minister; this day was significant to him, too, which made our ceremony more memorable. It wasn't very long, but it sure felt like it. I was sweating like it was a steamy, hot day in July. We repeated our vows to each other, exchanged rings, and the Pastor closed the ceremony with a prayer. Then he pronounced us husband and wife and told Charles he could now kiss his bride. The kiss was a little awkward because we were both so nervous that the congregation laughed. Then he introduced us to them as Mr. And Mrs. We walked to the door and greeted our guests as they left the church, and we informed them that we would be seeing them soon at the reception. We had some legal business to take care of first. We went to the Pastor's study to sign the marriage certificate and to have our witnesses, which all of them were my cousins, sign also.

It was official; we were now officially husband and wife. We left the Church to meet our guests at the Civic Center to celebrate our nuptials. Charles's mother had transformed it into a beautiful place. She did a fabulous job. I could not have asked for anything better. We mingled with our guests and enjoyed the delicious buffet my new mother-in-law had prepared; after removing the top layer of our wedding cake to be saved to celebrate our first anniversary, we cut our beautiful red and white cake. We fed each other a small piece. When it was almost time for us to leave, I was given a chair to sit in as Charles pulled off my garter and threw it to all the single men. Then, I threw an alternate bouquet to all the single women because I wanted to keep the original as a keepsake of our special day. We had a wonderful time celebrating with our family and friends, but it was time to check into our hotel. We thanked everyone for coming to share this momentous occasion with us. Charles opened the passenger door of the car; I got in. Then he walked around and got in himself. We waved goodbye to everyone as we drove away. It was over; we had jumped the broom into a new life together. Our future was a mystery. But we went into it with love, trust, faith, and open hearts. Together, we were ready to face whatever came our way.

We had a wonderful one-night honeymoon. It was Christmas morning, and we needed to get back home. We had a lovely Christmas tree decorated with new ornaments and twinkling colorful lights that we had bought. I was sad that I no longer had all the beautiful collectible ornaments I had purchased from

Avon over the years. I had to leave the past in the past and start new traditions with Charles. There were presents of all sizes under the tree waiting to be opened. We were expected at Olivia's house to join her, her daughter, and other family members for Christmas dinner. We hurriedly opened our gifts, thanking each other with a kiss between each one being opened.

Christmas day was the perfect day to start our new life together. It was a new beginning for both of us. It was the day we celebrated the birth of our Lord and Savior, Jesus Christ, sent by God the Father to save the world. He came so that we could have life and have it more abundantly. I was looking forward to having a better life with Charles. I am happy to say that I got that life, but no life is without its trials and tribulations.

CHAPTER 17
BETTER DAYS

Being with Charles was one of the greatest joys in my life. If we were not working, we were always together. We went shopping together to find new items that reflected both our personalities for our home. Surprisingly, our tastes were similar. When we decided to purchase anything, we made sure the other was pleased because it would be enjoyed by both of us. We went to movies, on trips to visit family, and out to dinner occasionally. Life was so wonderful and stress-free. I can't express the level of peace that had settled in my life. If you saw one of us, you saw both of us. Charles and I never argued over anything, which was one thing that I did not miss from my previous marriage. In our first few months of being husband and wife, we talked about making changes to the home we were living in. We decided to use the money he had been putting away for a down payment on a new home, but we needed to add more to what we had. The home we were living in had a lot of unpleasant memories associated with it. Charles wanted us to live in a home Ricky had no connection to. I agreed that it was time to make a change.

Charles put in as many hours at work as he could. We hoped that by the following year, we would have enough money saved to make a down payment on a double-wide mobile home. We did not want the burden of a thirty-year mortgage by purchasing a house; we wanted to see it paid for in our lifetime. Plus, I already had the land and everything we needed to place a new mobile home. But first, we needed to speak to Mr. Thurston about our plans because the house I had bought from him came with the land it was sitting on. To put a new home on the land, we needed to sell our current house back to him and only purchase the land. After discussing what we wanted to do with Mr. Thurston, he agreed to our proposal. He drew up a new contract that only covered the land. I signed it, and we were all set for when we found the right home for us. He agreed to move the house we were living in onto another property he owned when it was time.

We started looking for our new home. We visited numerous lots before we found what we were looking for. It was a three-bedroom home. The master bedroom had a full bath, including a garden tub and a separate shower. There was also a full bath between the other two bedrooms on the other side of the house. I fell in love with the floor plan. If at any time we would have guests, they would have privacy, and so would we. We looked around some more to make sure we had found the one for us. We discussed it and decided that we were going to purchase it. I got in touch with Mr. Thurston to let him know that our new house would be brought out to be set up around the second week of September. I was so excited about getting our new home. We would celebrate numerous holidays, birthdays, anniversaries, and memorable moments in our new home. It was going to be a complete departure from both our past. It solidified our commitment to each other and our future together.

Hurricane Fran

I continued to work on third shift as the lead person in C-plant. It was the height of hurricane season. I stayed abreast of the weather because I was in a leadership position, and if required, I would have to go to work no matter the weather unless advised by the plant manager not to come. The news was warning North Carolina that Hurricane Fran would be coming ashore after hitting the coastline. I was scheduled to work that night as the supervisor of A, B, and C-plant because my supervisor was scheduled off for the next two days. The rain was coming down in buckets. I got up that night hoping the plant manager would call me and tell me that he was going to shut the plant down, but he didn't. Against my better judgment, I got dressed, kissed my husband goodbye, and went to work. I was so afraid as I drove down the highway. I could feel the wind hitting up against the car. It was so intense at times that it felt as though it was going to push the car over. I made it to the plant, and when I arrived, wouldn't you know it, the only one there was the plant manager. He told me he had closed the plant and for me to return home. I was happy about that, but I had just risked my life to report to work. Now, I had to risk my life to get back home. I got back into my car and commenced the treacherous nine-mile drive home. The storm was raging worse than before; I could barely see through the drenching rain. I made it out of town safely and took my time driving down the highway cautiously and slowly. I had to be aware of falling trees because the wind was extremely severe. About one-half mile from my turn off of the main highway, a large tree had fallen across the road. I told myself, "Stay calm; you can do this." I managed to drive around it carefully. I turned off the highway at my turn-off and saw another large tree had fallen onto the road. I said, "OK, let me go back and take another turn-off." I didn't usually take that one, which could also lead to my home. So, I took my next option and found another tree across the road. I was starting to think I wasn't going to make it home. I drove back out to the main highway and remembered another route I could use to get home about three miles down the road. I was praying, hoping no fallen trees would block my way. I took a left turn off the highway, driving slowly through heavy rain and wind. As I came around the curve, yeah, you guessed it. There was another tree lying across the road. It was unbelievable that every road I tried to take was blocked. I could not believe this was happening. By that time, I was in tears. I had nowhere else to go to take shelter from the storm. I stopped a few feet from the tree, assessing if I should take a chance, trying to drive around it. I thought about it and concluded that I had no choice because I needed to get out of the storm. I slowly inched my way around the tree, holding on to my faith, doing my best to avoid running into the ditch or getting stuck in the mud. To my amazement, praise the Lord, I made it. I continued down the road, thanking God for His blessing. By the Grace of God, no more barriers were keeping me from reaching my home.

I got to my driveway, and my house looked like it was sitting in the middle of a river. So much rain had fallen that my yard was underneath approximately twenty inches of water. I drove the car off the highway, got out, and waded through the water down my driveway to get to my front porch. I unlocked my door and went inside, grateful I was finally out of the storm. As I removed my rain-soaked shoes and clothes, I looked for Charles to tell him about my hazardous drive home. I walked to the bedroom, peeked in, and he was in bed fast asleep. He was oblivious that Hurricane Fran was making her track through our community at that very moment. I screamed at him to get out of bed in case we had to evacuate our home. I couldn't believe that he could sleep during that awful storm, but Charles could sleep through anything. He was not pleased with me for waking him up, but I thought it was essential for us to be ready to get out of the house if need be. I was awake the entire night listening to the wind and rain bashing against our home. I gathered all the candles I could find in case the electricity went out. The water in my yard was increasing. If it got high enough to come into our home, we would have to. I am not ashamed to say I was so afraid that we would not survive that terrible storm. Before morning, our whole neighborhood had no power.

When dawn arrived, Fran had moved on; as the sun rose, I could finally witness the damage she had caused. There was so much water and debris in our yard in all our neighbor's yards no one could drive anywhere. All day, we kept hoping that the electric company would get our power lines repaired. That didn't happen. There was so much widespread damage that it took days before we had any power. We had to wait our turn. They always repair the electrical lines within the city limits first. We lived out in the countryside.

According to Google Search, Hurricane Fran caused extensive damage in the United States in early September 1996. The sixth named storm, fifth hurricane, and third major hurricane of the 1996 Atlantic hurricane season, Fran developed from a tropical wave near Cape Verde on August 23. Per Wikipedia:

Total fatalities: 27

Highest wind speed: 121 mph

Date: August 23, 1996 – September 8, 1996

Category: Category 3 Hurricane (SSHWS)

Damage: $5 billion (1996 USD)

Lowest pressure: 946 mbar (hPa); 27.94 inHg

Affected areas: North Carolina, South Carolina, Virginia, Maryland

The water had receded enough that we could see the road. Charles put on his knee-high rubber boots to get to the car. I had parked the car close to the highway because it was the highest point of our yard. Thanks be to God, no water had gotten inside it. We were hoping we could find a store open to buy some ice to try and save our food in the refrigerator. Every store he went to was out of ice or closed. We did not open the door to the refrigerator, hoping that it would stay cold inside, preserving our food until we could find some ice. After the second day without power or ice, we lost all the contents of our refrigerator, including the top layer from the wedding cake we had saved for our first anniversary. I was so disappointed. It was challenging to live without electrical power. Charles made daily trips in search of food and water. We needed both drinking water and enough water to flush the commode. No TV or radio. Luckily, we had an old phone that we held onto for such a time as this. We plugged it into the phone socket and communicated with the family. The electricity came back on about two and a half weeks later.

The company we purchased our new home from was constantly calling us to make arrangements to bring it to our property. We kept telling them that would not be possible at the moment because our yard was flooded. I was concerned that when they brought it, it would get stuck in the mud and cause a huge problem. The water in our yard had only receded a little when we heard a large truck out in front of our house. I looked out the window, and they had brought out our house without our approval. After they witnessed the flooding we had warned them about for themselves, they took our home back to the lot and waited a few more days for the water to recede. We could not have predicted the storm would hinder getting our new home set up. Later, they brought it back and parked it right in front of our single-wide and left. When the soil had soaked up the water and the ground became sturdier, Mr. Thurston had our home moved to my backyard so our new home could be set up. A crew from the dealer came to put it together, had it inspected, and after a few days, our house was ready to move into.

Charles asked a couple of his friends to help us move our things out of our house into the new place. When we were finished, I let Mr. Thurston know, and he sent a crew to move our previous home to another lot he owned. We settled into our new home with great expectations. Charles and I made plans to have a housewarming party and invite our family and friends to come to celebrate with us and tour our new home. I invited my Pastor, who presided over our wedding, to come to bless our new home. Our guests blessed us with gifts, well wishes for our future, and joy by coming to help us commemorate the beginning of a new chapter in our lives. We enjoyed Thanksgiving and were looking forward to celebrating our first anniversary and enjoying our first Christmas in our new home. To celebrate, Charles put on a suit, and I put on the fanciest dress I owned, and we went out on a date to the club where we first met. It was nice to return to where it had all begun. We had a lovely evening out.

After the holidays were over, we went back to work. We had so many ideas about improving our home. The first thing Charles wanted to do was take down the manufacturers' underpinning and have it replaced with bricks. Also, he wanted to build a front porch and a back porch with bricks. He worked hard to save money to have these improvements made. He wanted to pay with cash, whenever possible, for the work we wanted to be done. Charles was not afraid of hard work. He made up his mind what he wanted and did what he needed to do to make it happen. It was so nice to have a man as head of household. I had a partner who did not need to be told his responsibilities. I gladly relinquished all of them to him. What a big difference compared to the way I was used to living.

Fast Forward

After my divorce from Ricky, I inherited everything he had not managed to sell for crack. He could not legally be in the courtroom, so he could not contest the divorce or ask for any of our household items to be divided amongst us. What was left from all the things he sold out of our home, I felt, belonged to me as far as I was concerned. It wasn't very much, some record albums, a flokati rug, and some reel-to-reel tapes that I did not particularly care about, but it was all I had left that could one day be of some value. Charles stored all of it in one of the bedroom closets. We had been in our home for four years and were enjoying our life together. Early on in our marriage, I was so paranoid about Ricky showing up at our door that I kept my thirty-eight-caliber handgun close by at all times, especially when I was home alone. I still suffered from PTSD because of the horror I endured with Ricky. When I went to bed, I laid the gun on my nightstand. I was blessed the last time when I could have shot Ricky, but I was not about to gamble with my life like that again. Whenever I had days off from work, sometimes I was alone because Charles was working.

One night, on Charles's job, they ran out of work to do, and he came home in the middle of the night without calling me. I heard a noise at my back door that woke me up. I listened and realized someone was in the house. I grabbed my gun, sat straight up in the bed, pointed the gun at my bedroom doorway, and prepared to fire it. The only thing that kept me from shooting Charles was recognizing him as he came to our bedroom door right before I pulled the trigger. To keep the house from being fully dark, we kept the light over the stove on during the night. It gave me enough light to determine who he was before taking the shot. I was relieved to see him but highly upset that I came so close to shooting him. I could have killed my husband that night. I put the gun down quickly because I lost all strength in my body from being so terrified. It upset me greatly, but Charles did all he could to help me feel safe. I kept thinking what a tragedy it would have been to mistakenly take the life of the man who saved my life. That would have been it for me. Thank God that did not happen. If I had had a bottle of liquor in the house, I probably would have taken a long, stiff drink after that incident to calm my nerves. After that episode, he always called before coming home early when he was supposed to be at work or anywhere else.

It took me a while to let go of the fear of Ricky trying to cause harm or cause problems for Charles and me. Years went by, and Ricky's five-year probation was over. I was cautiously confident that he would not be stupid enough to come to my home after that amount of time had passed. Besides, not seeing me for five years should be enough incentive to let go of what was and get on with his life, but no such luck. I was in the living room one day when I heard someone banging on the side of my house. I sprang to my feet because I was irritated that someone would do such a silly thing. I went to my kitchen window and looked to see if I saw anyone in my backyard. I was flabbergasted that it was Ricky. Can you believe the arrogance of this fool? He came to my house not knowing what he would find. He didn't even know if I still lived there or not, or maybe he did. Anyway, I went to the back door, opened it, and said, "What do you want?" He answered me by saying he came to get his albums. Out of the corner of my eye, I could see someone in a car waiting for him. I told him that I did not have anything that belonged to him and to get off my property. In the meantime,

Charles heard the conversation that was going on between Ricky and me and came to the back door to tell Ricky he needed to leave. The next thing I knew, Charles ran to our bedroom to get the gun. When I realized what he was doing, I blocked him with my body to prevent him from getting to the door. I talked to him calmly, trying to convince him that Ricky was not worth shooting; he would spend the rest of his life paying for it. I said it over and over again, trying to appeal to his common sense, while I continued to prevent him from reaching the door. I had never seen Charles as angry as he was that day. While I was convincing him not to do this, I guess Ricky and his friend surmised that it was time to go. His friend was backing out of my driveway without him, and Ricky had to run to get into the car. I don't know how much the guy knew about what the situation was. Ricky could have given him some lame excuse about where he wanted the guy to take him. I do not know why he thought it would be okay to come to my house, considering our volatile history. At that time, Charles and I had been married for four years. Maybe he thought he still had a chance with me. It all seemed so pathologically foolish. I calmed Charles down, thank God. He almost ruined our lives by shooting someone who had already caused enough damage to my life. Thinking about it now, Ricky had dodged a bullet twice. His life was literally in my hands, and I prevented him from being hurt or killed in both instances. I wonder if he knew that. I wonder if it would have made a difference if he did. Ricky was unstable, and what made sense to me did not make sense to him. To blindly take a chance, thinking he could renew his past life with me after five years, was futile and dangerous. I helped put him where he was. Could he believe I was sitting around waiting to reconnect with him when I had done all I could to evict him? It was such an enigma to me that his thinking could be so ludicrous.

I never saw him again after that incident. It is a testament to me that no woman should underestimate the determination of an abuser. I was blessed to make it out alive from the abusive relationship I had been in for over twenty years. Numerous women in my community during the time I fought for my emancipation were not as blessed as me.

I know that God had His hands on my life. He brought me through so many unexplainable things for His purpose. When I didn't see a way, He made a way. I give Him all the glory, praise, and honor for allowing me to be alive to tell my story.

CONCLUSION

Before I decided to write this book, I prayed and asked God for guidance. I wanted to make sure I was not doing something that was not in His will for my life. It took some time before I concluded that I was going in the right direction. Then, I had to decide if I had the skills to write a book. I have no training in this field. But when God has a plan for your life, you don't need training. "Therefore, my dear brothers and sisters, stand firm. Let nothing move you. Always give yourselves fully to the work of the Lord, because you know that your labor in the LORD is not in vain" (1 Corinthians 15:58).

God has all that you need to fulfill His purpose. Amid a pandemic, I seldom went outside my home. To exercise, I would walk back and forth in my house. As I walked, I would think about things, and on this particular day, I was questioning myself about writing this book when I heard a voice inside me say, "You are a writer." I stopped in my tracks, realized and acknowledged that I was a writer because of the things I had done in my past. I had never seen myself in that way until I heard a voice inside me proclaim it. I had been writing small things like pieces for my Facebook page, prayers, and rewriting song lyrics. I said to myself, "You are a writer." Once I believed it to be true, I was able to do it. Then, I had to do some serious thinking. I had to consider if I were strong enough to endure the criticism I would encounter from some Christians, family, and friends for revealing so much of my life. I knew I would have to unveil some things about myself that no one knew. But if I were going to be effective in helping other abused women, I would have to tell the truth. It was hard to admit the sinful life I led as a young woman until I realized that I had been forgiven for all of it by God. Acts 3:18-19 says, "Repent, then, and turn to God, so that your sins may be wiped out, that times of refreshing may come from the Lord." I so desperately needed that refreshing in my life. I was so burdened with guilt, shame, and blaming myself for allowing the abuse. I had to recognize that I was a victim, not the perpetrator. I let go and let God carry my burden. I did not need the forgiveness of anyone else or the world.

"When they kept on questioning him, he straightened up and said to them, 'Let any one of you who is without sin be the first to throw a stone at her'" (John 8:7, NIV). That truth was powerful enough to encourage me to do what I had to do and to do it with my head held high as a daughter of the King.

Early in my life, God sent someone to let me know that His light had me covered. I believe the lady who told me that I had a bright light around me was sent to assure me that God was with me and that no matter what I did, I could not negate His love and His purpose for my life. I don't know why I never saw how God was leading and guiding me through some tempestuous circumstances. To be a witness for the Lord, I had to experience some difficult situations. I could not witness what I had not experienced. Now, as I take a look in my rearview, I can see God all over my life. He never left me alone, nor did He forsake me. I am incredibly sorry that I forgot about the teachings of my parents momentarily. They made sure that all their children knew Jesus. We went to Sunday School every Sunday morning. We attended Worship service every other Sunday morning. They taught us how to pray by having family prayer with us every morning. At night, I watched my parents read their bible and get down on their knees to pray before they got into bed.

"Train up a child in the way he should go: and when he is old, he will not depart from it" (Proverbs 22:6).

I know there will be skeptics who will believe everything except the Lord saved my life by speaking to me in the Spirit. Had I not listened to that still, small voice inside me, I believe that I would not be here telling you how I made it through. It was like all I had to do was stop trying to make something out of nothing and stop trying to fix it myself. Exodus 14:14 says, "The Lord will fight for you; you need only to be still." I did just that, and the Lord came through for me. That is when real change began to happen. When I realized that I had married a dangerous man, I felt like a door had closed behind me, and I had no means of escape. But when I let go, Jesus opened a window for me to break free of my prison. I didn't acknowledge God when I was out there living what I thought was my life. Despite all the things I did wrong, He never left me alone.

I did some really stupid things that put my life in danger. I wrote this book to encourage other abused women to act as soon as possible to remove themselves from a potentially dangerous relationship. Please don't do as I did, i.e., continue believing that things can work out, even though you are being abused in the meantime. Seek help from organizations set up to help the abused.

Don't think that you can change them! Never believe that they love you! When someone loves you, they will not hurt you; if they hurt you, they hurt themselves. Inflicting pain is not how you show someone you love them. You deserve to be loved with gentleness, kindness, tenderness, and strength. Don't settle for anything less than that, my sister. "Love is patient, love is kind. It does not envy, it does not boast, it is not proud. It does not dishonor others, it is not self-seeking, it is not easily angered, it keeps no record of wrongs" (1 Corinthians 13:4-5). Many waters cannot quench love; rivers cannot wash it away (Song of Solomon 8:7).

If you need help, please don't be afraid or too ashamed to ask for it. There are numerous organizations out there that can and will help you. I had to deal with being abused on my own. No one helped me (not even the people who knew I was being abused), only God. They made excuses to convince themselves that it was none of their business, that it was between husband and wife. And those excuses they made to themselves made it acceptable not to get involved.

When someone's life is being threatened, it is everyone's business. My ex-husband kept me isolated from my family by telling me that they did not love me. I had no friends that I could trust enough to confide in. I was too embarrassed by my life to ask for help. I did not want anyone to know that I was being abused by the very person who claimed that he loved me. I was alone and very vulnerable. I allowed him to control me by listening to his lies and being beaten into submission. My self-esteem was at an all-time low. Confronting the fact that I had hereditary alopecia, as so many other women do, was a hard pill to swallow, too. On top of all that, the abuse I had endured for so long caused so much stress that I developed an incurable skin disease that will plague me for the rest of my life. It is a constant reminder of the years I was abused. Thanks to modern medical science, I now take shots to keep my psoriasis under control, but there were many years that I had to suffer because there was nothing that could help me.

Domestic violence is even more prevalent today. When I watch the news and see women murdered by the men they love, I get so angry and upset I could scream. I feel so helpless knowing what they must have gone through before their situation rose to the loss of their lives.

According to WorldPopulationReview.com, in the United States, an estimated 10 million people experience domestic violence every year. According to the National Coalition Against Domestic Violence, about 24 people per minute are physically abused by an intimate partner. About 1 in 4 women and 1 in 9 men experience severe intimate partner physical violence, sexual violence, and/or partner stalking with injury, PTSD, contracting STDs, etc.

If you or someone you know is a victim of domestic violence, several resources are available to help. Call the National Domestic Violence Hotline at 1-800-799-SAFE (7233).

I support the Domestic Violence and Sexual Assault Center located in my community. I urge you to do the same in yours. Ladies, we need to take care of each other. Be a friend to another woman in need. Donate your time and your resources to help save women's lives and possibly save the lives of their children. Working together, we can stop the loss of life to domestic violence. Located on the back cover are the name, logo, and QR Code of the organization I support in my community. I humbly ask you for your assistance by scanning the QR Code with your smartphone or using the link below to donate. You can also contribute to any Domestic Violence and Sexual Assault organization of your choosing. I urge you to do it today. You can make a difference in someone's life. Thank you so much for your support. "We are better together!"

To make contributions to the Hoke County, NC, center, click here or visit https://www.hokeco-dvsa.org/webstore.

MY TESTIMONY

I didn't write this book for people to feel sorry for me or to seek revenge. Thanks be to God, I have forgiven all involved and moved on from my past.

Instead, I wanted to show people that through it all, Jesus was with me. Through it all, Jesus kept me. Through it all, Jesus gave me strength. Through it all, Jesus protected me. Through it all, Jesus blessed me. Through it all, Jesus still loved me. Through it all, Jesus forgave me. Hallelujah! Thank You Jesus! If it had not been for the Lord who was on my side, my circumstances would have swallowed me up. I would not be here to tell you anything.

This book is my evidence and my testimony that Jesus will never leave you, no matter your situation. Deuteronomy 31:8 says, "The LORD Himself goes before you and will be with you; He will never leave you nor forsake you. Do not be afraid: do not be discouraged." Even when you are doing wrong, God is so good that He will still bless you. If I sound like I am testifying, that's because I am. God has been truly good to me, and I want to tell the whole world about it! And I'm here to tell you, "Don't give up!"

Put your faith in Jesus, and He will bring you through." If He can deliver me out of my hot mess, He can deliver you, too. There is no sin so bad that Jesus will not forgive. Remember that you can be born again. You can become a new creature in Christ Jesus. I am a walking, talking, breathing, living witness to what God can do. Amen.

After going through the hell I endured, life was good, but I still was not where I needed to be so God could use me. There was another trial headed my way that would change my perspective on my relationship with my Redeemer. There was more God needed to reveal to me before becoming who I am today. I was about to collide with a trial that made me question God and His plan for my life.

Patricia McRae Donaldson

RESOURCES

Medlineplus.gov/a1c.html

www.cdc.gov

MedicalNewsToday.com

NCADV.org

Google.com/search

Facty.com

www.mayoclinic.org

kingjamesbible.me/Proverbs-22-6

Dailyverses.net

Worldpopulationreview.com

www.ingramcontent.com/pod-product-compliance
Lightning Source LLC
Chambersburg PA
CBHW070050080526
44586CB00013B/996